Xmas 1923 Scotland

To Calum,

Happy Xmas
Bon Voyage
Much love,

Mum & Jim

"who will miss you"

HOW THEY BROKE BRITAIN

Also by James O'Brien

How To Be Right
How Not To Be Wrong

HOW THEY BROKE BRITAIN

JAMES O'BRIEN

WH
ALLEN

WH Allen, an imprint of Ebury Publishing
20 Vauxhall Bridge Road
London SW1V 2SA

WH Allen is part of the Penguin Random House group of companies
whose addresses can be found at global.penguinrandomhouse.com

Penguin
Random House
UK

First published by WH Allen in 2023

www.penguin.co.uk

A CIP catalogue record for this book is available from the British Library

ISBN 9780753560341
Trade Paperback ISBN 9780753560358

Printed and bound in Great Britain by Clays Ltd, Elcograf S.p.A.

The authorised representative in the EEA is Penguin Random House
Ireland, Morrison Chambers, 32 Nassau Street, Dublin D02 YH68.

This book is dedicated to the memory of James 'Jim' O'Brien

Journalist

(1939–2012)

'As long as the general population is passive, apathetic, diverted to consumerism or hatred of the vulnerable, then the powerful can do as they please, and those who survive will be left to contemplate the outcome'

Noam Chomsky

CONTENTS

INTRODUCTION

YOU CAN'T ACTUALLY BOIL a frog to death by popping it into a pot of cold water, placing it on a stove and slowly turning up the temperature. When the heat becomes uncomfortable, the frog will hop out. Thermoregulation, evolution and the fact that frogs are famously good at hopping will see to that. 'Boiling a frog' remains a popular analogy because it conveys, simply and effectively, something that we know to be true: we often don't notice big changes if they happen in gradual stages – sometimes, so gradually that we struggle even to notice the process until it is finished and the corruption complete. We wake up years later, and reflect incredulously upon how things used to be. And then we wonder how such profound and unwelcome changes could have unfolded in plain sight. We know that we would never have accepted the new status quo if it had been offered to us at the outset, clear and complete. For while we recognise that the old status quo was imperfect and often horribly flawed, we still can't quite believe how far we have drifted from it and how measurably better things used to be.

This is a story of slowly boiled water from which an entire country failed to escape. It is a tale of loss and betrayal; of unbridled arrogance and unchallenged ignorance; of personal impunity, warped ideology and political incompetence. It is too early to say where the

1

story will end and impossible to pinpoint precisely where it began. But nevertheless, it is essential to identify the people and organisations which, sometimes by accident and sometimes quite deliberately, set the United Kingdom on a course of unnecessary domestic decline and international diminishment. Almost all of them remained in positions of power and prominence long after the damage they had done became clear to see. Many have since prospered, both professionally and privately, as the problems and tribulations they blithely ushered in took hold. None of them has ever offered the rest of us a single syllable of contrition or apology. It seems unlikely that they ever will. Worse, by the middle of 2023 it was becoming clear that the supporters of 'austerity', Brexit, Boris Johnson, Liz Truss and sundry other disasters were determined to blame the consequences of their own epic errors on precisely the individuals and institutions that had spent years warning and explaining what those consequences would be. This last is a project that could only be contemplated, let alone completed, in a country already in complete thrall to the lies, prejudices and manipulations of what would once have been referred to as the ruling class.

This book, then, is a charge sheet: a compendium of poor behaviour and bad actors. More importantly, it is also an attempt to record and explain the creation of an ecosystem in which dishonesty could flourish and facts wither. Where ordinary people, divorced from but entirely subjugated to the levers of power and influence, were fed an almost unleavened diet of deceit, division and distraction. We will see that what has happened to the UK over the last few decades – notably since 2010, especially since 2016 and quite spectacularly since 2019 – is as unforgivable as it is immense. Yet because those levers of power and influence are controlled by a comparatively tiny number of people, in three easily identifiable and avowedly right-wing sections of public life

– the media, politics and wealth – the sheer abnormality of the national situation is rarely noted. We have become so conditioned by the parameters of the ecosystem we inhabit that we rarely notice how completely ridiculous our political reality – and *our country* – has become.

The proof is everywhere, careering ridiculously from the seemingly silly to the deadly serious. From tomatoes being *rationed* in British supermarkets to government-inflicted economic catastrophe, what was once unthinkable has become almost unremarkable. Senior politicians, their advisers and their cronies, routinely remain in post after being found guilty of egregious behaviour. When they are found to have broken rules, they join forces to attack the rules. Strikes routinely cripple every corner of the public sector, most notably in the NHS where patient satisfaction has plummeted while waiting lists grow exponentially. For the first time in living memory, children are less likely to own property than their parents. From pubs to pharmacies, businesses are closing every day as costs rise and vacancies go unfilled while members of the government exhort us to celebrate the abolition of our own 'freedom of movement'. Water companies, monopolistic beneficiaries of privatisation, deliver bumper bonuses to executives and shareholders while pumping record-breaking amounts of raw sewage into our waterways.

In the first nine months of 2022, 235 Crown Court trials were put off on the day they were due to start because there was no prosecutor available. By the end of the year, the total backlog of serious crime cases breached the 60,000 mark while in magistrates courts the figure was over 340,000. The pain caused to individuals and families seeking justice is immeasurable. The generation of politicians and pundits that promised to 'take back control' of our borders and immolate unspecified 'red tape' has instead delivered epic delays and miles-long tailbacks at our ports, while making trade in goods with our nearest neigh-bours unfeasibly and unprecedentedly complicated. The 'trade deals' announced by the same politicians and cheered by the same pundits as a corrective to this unnecessary damage have instead put our own farmers at a disadvantage against foreign competitors. In April 2023, 700,000 households missed their rent or mortgage payments. And for the people persuaded by decades of racist propaganda, served up by supposedly 'respectable' media, that the country's problems were caused by a surfeit of foreign arrivals, the overall immigration numbers are higher than ever. Yet, confusingly, the European workers who once helped sustain now struggling sectors such as health and hospitality were stopped from coming and started to quit these shores in their droves. Everywhere, the sense of crisis is exacerbated by spiralling food and energy prices, plummeting wages and crumbling public services.

And yet successive Conservative administrations, presiding over all of this, persist in the demonisation of refugees, meaningless 'anti-woke' rhetoric and bogus 'culture wars'. The home secretary, Suella Braverman, told a meeting at her party conference in 2022: 'I would love to have a front page of the *Telegraph* with a plane taking off to Rwanda, that's my dream, it's my obsession.'[1] The passengers on the plane of her dreams would be asylum seekers and refugees with no prospect of return to the UK, even when their applications had been processed and their bona fide refugee status determined.

The destination of her dreams was later described in grim terms by the former head of the British Army. Richard (Lord) Dannatt visited Rwanda as chief of the general staff in 2009 and sits on the all-party parliamentary group (APPG) on war crimes investigating the Rwandan genocide. He said: 'I've been to Rwanda, and the shadow of the geno-cide there in the 1990s hangs over that country. It's ruled with a very firm hand by [current president and former military commander] Paul Kagame. It's got a pretty dark history, and it's not the sort of environment I would put people from Syria and elsewhere in the world into.'[2]

Braverman's dream still burned bright *after* she was made aware of evidence from the United Nations refugee agency, dating from 2018, that a group of Congolese refugees was shot dead by police during protests over cuts to food rations. And yet, according to Braverman, it is the people crossing the Channel in so-called 'small boats' who 'possess values that are at odds with our country'.[3] She is yet to provide any evidence of this claim or clarify precisely what 'values' she and the rest of Rishi Sunak's government feel they themselves represent. It seems unlikely to be the ones upheld by King Charles, who reportedly described the Rwanda plan as 'appalling'.[4]

All of these commercial catastrophes, national tragedies and rhetorical atrocities occur because we live in a country where 'commentators' are now routinely proved spectacularly wrong by political and economic events without suffering any real censure; where politicians frequently say things that turn out to be demonstrably untrue without ever being reminded of their 'errors' by supine or sycophantic journalists; and where 'experts' whose previous analyses were horribly inaccurate continue to pop up in broadcast studios and newspapers with their status undimmed.

The challenge is to stop seeing every example of national self-sabotage and decay in isolation and recognise instead that they are all symptoms of the same lethal malaise. Without many of us properly noticing, the United Kingdom has become a country where, both for editors and commentators gifted influence by their plutocratic patrons, and for the political figures they favour, *there are now no rules*. The formal and informal strictures and traditions that bind society together, and which render stability and decency at least theoretically important, have been almost completely eradicated. There are no consequences for appalling personal or political behaviour. There is no semblance of public morality. There is no longer any consensual threshold for career-ending conduct. Simple truth has become negotiable and proven liars have flourished as never before.

Citing all the evidence has proved a surprisingly tricky business because, bluntly, there is so much of it. It feels at times like a Russian doll of ridiculousness: twist the head off one example of political or media malfeasance that previously would have been unthinkable, but went entirely unpunished after 2019, and another one immediately appears. Think of one shameful episode and a dozen, arguably more pertinent, cases will spring to mind. They crowd each other out, multiply and merge, until you are left staring, stupefied, at the unbelievable catalogue of calumny, corruption and incompetence that has been visited upon the country. So this account can't be exhaustive. There are simply too many contenders for inclusion. And neither can they be ranked. It would be too subjective.

If, for example, you lost a loved one to the appalling handling of care homes at the beginning of the COVID-19 outbreak you will perhaps be most enraged by the fact that 10 Downing Street subsequently became the site of more fines for criminal breaches of the lockdown laws Boris Johnson introduced than any other address in the country. Or by the fact that the health secretary who claimed to have thrown a 'protective ring' around those care homes, Matthew Hancock, shortly afterwards tried to relaunch himself as a 'celebrity' by accepting £320,000 to appear on a TV game show. Or by the memory of Johnson's most senior adviser, self-styled Brexit 'mastermind' Dominic Cummings, looking down the barrel of a television camera and claiming that he had driven his family on a 60-mile round trip to a local beauty spot on his wife's birthday, in obvious breach of lockdown laws, to 'test his eyesight'.

If, however, you lost a loved one to the Hillsborough tragedy in 1989, you may be most disgusted by the decades-long efforts of one of Rupert Murdoch's newspapers to malign the memories of the dead. If you needed help from one of the 'food banks' or 'warm banks' that have proliferated in recent years, then you may be most enraged by politicians who, while mismanaging the economy, have fetishised the UK's 'growth' and ignored the plight of its people. And if you simply want to live in a country where decency is valued and the government provides safety nets and support for the population – where, in other words, there is such a thing as 'society' – you may reserve most concern for the proliferation of secretly funded lobby groups, masquerading as 'think tanks', that have infiltrated every level of public life despite representing the interests of nobody except the anonymous tycoons and vested interests who bankroll them.

I will endeavour, then, to provide the most illustrative and arresting examples from an unapologetically personal perspective. The ones that, for me, most effectively describe the congregation of circumstances that allowed objectively ridiculous things to happen in a previously sensible society. Even dedicated followers of current affairs may well have struggled to keep up with the speed and size of change. Donald Trump's disgraced consigliere Steve Bannon – an exemplar of the far right who, despite overtly racist rhetoric, coopted political power with the connivance of Rupert Murdoch's empire – vowed to 'flood the zone with shit' in order to ensure that every scandal and shameful incident executed by his boss would soon be eclipsed by another.[5] In the United Kingdom, there was no explicit plan to do the same, but such was the sheer volume of harm and damage done in a few years that the effect has been similar. I hope the experience of seeing the evidence assembled under one metaphorical roof will also be cathartic. It is for me. I apologise now for inevitable omissions.

Consider first the abject idiocy of becoming the first population in history to vote to impose economic sanctions on itself. Worse, it was a vote built on promises that the country would somehow become richer as a consequence of leaving the European Union. There followed an inevitable erection of trade barriers between ourselves and our biggest trading partners. Consequently, in January 2023, analysis by Bloomberg Economics found that Brexit was costing the UK £100 billion a year.[6] The former governor of the Bank of England, Mark Carney, stated in an interview that 'the UK is in the most difficult position of the major economies, full stop', and added, 'it's been amplified by the separation from the European Union'.[7] The following month, Jonathan Haskel, a senior Bank of England official, published a study showing that since the 2016 referendum, the UK had suffered a loss of business investment amounting to £29 billion, or £1,000 per household.[8] In March, Richard Hughes, the chairman of the Office for Budget Responsibility (OBR) – an organisation set up in 2010 by the Conservative chancellor, George Osborne, to detach official economic forecasts from government and provide independent advice on whether declared policies are likely to meet official targets – said leaving the EU had made an impact on the economy on the 'magnitude' of the COVID-19 pandemic, and reduced the UK's overall output by 4 per cent compared to where it would have been had the UK remained in the EU.[9]

Of course, these men are not infallible and at least some of these numbers are debatable. But the overall picture is one of genuine economic catastrophe for which the governing party bears obvious responsibility. Yet you would simply not know this from the massive bulk of media coverage where, if it gets reported at all, it is swiftly dismissed as evidence of an international conspiracy to 'punish' the UK. This is as dangerous as it is daft.

For example, the International Monetary Fund (IMF) is often portrayed in British newspapers and by Conservative politicians as some sort of malevolent and mysterious anti-British organisation dedicated to damaging our interests on the world stage. Jacob Rees-Mogg, who was business minister in Liz Truss's disastrous administration, once said that their forecasts 'aren't worth the paper they're written on'.[10] Many readers of some newspapers and possibly even some politicians would be surprised to learn that it is, in fact, a United Nations agency encompassing some 190 countries that is designed to promote international monetary cooperation, international trade, high employment, exchange-rate stability and sustainable economic growth. Regarded as the international lender of last resort, it also loans money to member states in fiscal peril. In 1976, for example, it made a loan available to the UK's Labour government of almost $4 million, at the time the largest ever requested. While no forecaster is infallible (just ask Michael Fish) it is abundantly clear that the IMF's calculations and predictions are both important and evidence-based. People like Rees-Mogg, whose wilfully ignorant position is frequently echoed in the comment pages of right-wing newspapers, either don't understand or don't care that all budgeting depends upon forecasts. Forecasts are literally the tools with which economists and politicians forge policies and while they are, by definition, imperfect, they are also, obviously, essential. Understand the ecosystem in which these people could break Britain and you will understand why they now have little choice but to denigrate any outlet dedicated to describing reality.

In April 2023 the IMF adjusted its forecast for the British economy upwards. In terms of growth in Gross Domestic Product (GDP), it would still be the worst performing in the G7 group of developed nations but not by as big a margin as it had forecast in January. In March, the Organisation for Economic Co-operation and Development (OECD), another intergovernmental organisation founded to stimulate economic progress and international trade, found that the UK would have the second worst performing economy in the whole of the G20. Only Russia, heavily sanctioned and at war in Ukraine, was forecast to perform worse. Frighteningly, the IMF actually had Russia performing *better* than the UK in the same period. Either way, the picture is obviously bleak and the only way to pretend otherwise is to pretend that these organisations are somehow deliberately misrepresenting data to embarrass the United Kingdom. It is remarkable how much credence these paranoid fantasies, and that's being generous, are still given.

The problem, once again, is that we have become so inured to the madness that we have lost much of our ability to recognise it. It would be foolish to imagine that every utterance and calculation from the IMF or the OECD or the OBR was perfect. But it would be much more foolish to believe that all three of them would wilfully mislead. And yet huge swathes of the right-wing media/political establishment, with the active connivance of the secretly funded so-called 'think tanks', would have us do precisely that. Julian Jessop, a 'fellow' of the grand sounding 'Institute of Economic Affairs' (IEA), even spoke to the *Daily Mail* of the OECD's 'usual institutional bias against the UK because of Brexit'.[11] This ludicrous combination of faux patriotism and bogus victimhood is an essential constituent of the ecosystem in which Liz Truss could inflict epic economic damage on the country.

It is also a particularly clear example of how 'think tank', politician and newspaper can combine to apply a patina of plausibility to what is, to all intents and purposes, gibberish. Shortly before Truss's mercifully brief administration collapsed under the weight of economic reality, for example, her business secretary, Rees-Mogg, claimed that 'the IMF likes having a pop at the UK for its own particular reasons'.[12] When, in May and June respectively, the IMF and the OECD *upgraded* their forecasts for the UK economy, the idiocy of these jingoistic positions would be laid bare. Obviously, neither Jessop, Rees-Mogg nor any of their fellow 'free market' fetishists argued that the institutions were now suddenly acting out of irrational affection for the UK.

Truss's disastrous policies, underpinned by her chancellor Kwasi Kwarteng's politically suicidal decision to exclude the OBR completely from his computations, cost the public purse an estimated £30 billion and were widely regarded as coming straight from the self-appointed economic 'experts' at the IEA. Indeed, Truss spoke at more IEA events between 2010 and 2022 than any other politician, and in 2011 set up the Free Enterprise Group of Tory MPs, arguably the parliamentary wing of the IEA. The organisation's 'director general' (grandiose titles are de rigueur at the IEA, where pretty much everybody is 'head of' something or other) Mark Littlewood has described her as being 'generally engaged in the ideas rather than just occasionally turning up to say a few warm words at a Christmas party'.[13]

When she won the Tory leadership in September 2022, a stalwart of the Brexit/'think tank'/Tory media triangle called Tim Montgomerie tweeted: 'A massive moment for [the IEA]. They've been advocating these policies for years. They incubated Truss and Kwarteng during their early years as MPs. Britain is now their laboratory.' Littlewood, apparently delighted with the analysis, responded with a smiling 'sunglasses face' emoji. The very first experiment in that 'laboratory' would crash the markets and see Britain brought to the brink of recession within days. It culminated in Kwarteng being jettisoned less than six weeks into the job and Truss resigning shortly after, having lost the confidence of almost all her MPs. There is, as we shall see, a grim symmetry to the fact that none of these 'experts' suffer any professional setbacks when their ideas are comprehensively discredited. On the contrary, Jessop's opinions were still being widely sought and published in 2023 and Truss even sought to put Littlewood in the House of Lords.

If forecasts from the likes of the OECD, OBR and IMF seek to plot the path ahead, with all the obvious unpredictabilities, then the UK's Office for National Statistics (ONS) is concerned with mapping the road already travelled. Its export figures for October–December 2022 made grisly reading: excluding precious metals, British exports were down 9 per cent on the pre-pandemic average. Not that you would have been reading much about them in organs still clinging desperately to the carcass of Brexit. Ludicrous but widespread claims that the UK's more general plight was somehow a consequence of the pandemic and war in Ukraine fall apart when we learn that, for example, Italy and Japan enjoyed *double figure growth in exports during the same period*. Analyses by the OBR and the Bank of England for the *Financial Times* showed that the UK's exports may be even weaker still, with the OBR predicting that the underperformance will continue for the next two years. Once again, it is Jacob Rees-Mogg who proves that it is possible to publicly and pompously poo-poo such forecasts if you don't like their content. He stated in 2022 that the record of the OBR – the UK fiscal watchdog, remember, set up by a Conservative chancellor with the express aim of providing the most objective and independent advice available – 'hasn't been enormously good', adding that it is not the 'only organisation that is able to give forecasts'.[14]

As with so many of the problems facing the UK in 2023 and beyond, this brand of delusional denialism and Pollyannaish determination to find 'experts' to only say things that politicians and newspaper editors want to hear can be traced back to the Brexit referendum of 2016. The moral and intellectual compromises needed to sustain and disseminate campaign lies during the referendum created a cohort of Conservative politicians that would become increasingly detached from both observable reality and any semblance of public integrity. That they weren't expecting to win is well-documented, but the lasting damage stems not from their victory but from their inability to disown the deceptions that delivered it. The guiltiest men and women here are not, I would argue, the pantomime characters like Rees-Mogg, previously best known for fighting a by-election with his childhood nanny by his side, or the bigots and weirdos who swelled the ranks of the party's European Research Group (ERG), but the ones who were supposedly 'respectable' or 'sensible'.

It was the co-chair of Vote Leave, Michael Gove, who said: 'I think the people in this country have had enough of experts from organisations with acronyms saying that they know what is best and getting it consistently wrong.'[15] After securing victory in the referendum and prompting David Cameron's resignation as prime minister in 2016, Gove backed his Vote Leave co-chair Boris Johnson's bid to become PM before withdrawing his support, saying: 'I came in the last few days, reluctantly and firmly, to the conclusion that while Boris has great attributes he was not capable of uniting that team and leading the party and the country in the way that I would have hoped.'[16]

Johnson pulled out of the contest and Gove launched his own leadership campaign. He was eliminated from the contest after securing 14.6 per cent of the vote in the first ballot of Conservative MPs and 14 per cent in the second. Theresa May triumphed after the withdrawal of her only remaining rival, Andrea Leadsom, but May was then effectively deposed by her former foreign secretary, Boris Johnson, in 2019. At this point, Gove somehow overcame his reservations about Johnson to serve in his government as, variously, chancellor of the Duchy of Lancaster, Cabinet Office minister, secretary of state for levelling up, housing and communities, and minister for intergovernmental relations. He was dismissed by Johnson in July 2022 after telling the soon to resign prime minister to resign.

Gove, Johnson, Jessop, Rees-Mogg, Truss and Littlewood: these are the type of people who flourished most in post-Brexit Britain, even as everything they touched began to crumble. They sustain support – even, in two cases, after leaving Downing Street in disgrace – by constantly denying reality, inventing persecution, shifting blame and trying to rewrite history. I hope that this book will play a small part in preventing them from doing so.

. . .

By the middle of 2023, many key players in this national tragedy had already embarked on the rewriting history element of this process with gusto. The alternative would have been to admit their role in the shaping of events that had, by any measure, gone horribly wrong. It is a simple concept to grasp, but the levels of dishonesty and disingenuousness required to actually pursue it are breathtaking.

In April, former *Daily Telegraph* and *Spectator* editor Charles Moore's byline appeared in the *Telegraph* beneath the headline 'Why is the Left in the driving seat of Tory government after 13 years of Tory rule?' It is hard to imagine a more perfect example of self-exculpatory tribal delusion. And it is hard to imagine a more perfect example of the sort of characters that flourish in the ecosystem under scrutiny here than Moore. Inevitably, there is an opaquely funded 'think tank' on his CV. He is a former chairman of Policy Exchange, judged by Transparify, an initiative that provides a global rating of the financial transparency of major 'think tanks', as one of the three least transparent 'think tanks' in the UK. His cronyism credentials are similarly impeccable: in 2020, he was gifted a seat in the House of Lords by former *Daily Telegraph* columnist and *Spectator* editor Boris Johnson.

In 2010, Moore was fined for not paying his television licence fee in protest against the lewd behaviour of Jonathan Ross and Russell Brand on BBC Radio 2. Ten years later he was reportedly Boris Johnson's first choice for the chairmanship of the same BBC. It was reported that he demanded a £280,000 salary to take the role,[17] three times the pay of the previous incumbent, but he shortly ruled himself out for 'family reasons'[18] after renewed attention was paid to a 1992 *Spectator* article in which he wrote:

> The Korean sets up the grocery store which the black then robs: that is the caricature which modern America recognises. Why has this happened then? One explanation, made endlessly in conversation and hardly ever in print, is that there really is something different about blacks, or at least about black men, or at least about young black men.

This is a remarkable admission of the sort of conversations that occur 'endlessly' in Moore's milieu. Talking about people in the UK and US, he went on to argue that they 'detect in black youths an aggression and defiance and indifference to normal moral and social constraints which frighten them [...] If it is true, as it surely is that some races – the Jews are the obvious example – are highly enterprising and talented, it may also be true that some are the opposite.'

Moore's disgust at 'indifference to normal moral and social constraints' had apparently been somewhat diluted by November 2021 when he hosted a dinner at London's private members club the Garrick. There, guests including Boris Johnson discussed how the career of Moore's close friend, former environment secretary Owen Paterson, might be saved. Paterson was in trouble after a two-year investigation by the parliamentary commissioner for standards, Kathryn Stone, found he had committed an 'egregious' breach of lobbying rules on behalf of two companies that were paying him more than £100,000 per annum. Paterson, a prominent Brexiter who had segued effortlessly from arguing that 'only a madman would actually leave the market' in 2014 to championing a 'no-deal' departure from the EU in 2019, certainly had a protective ring thrown around him.[19] With the vocal support of the leader of the House of Commons, Jacob Rees-Mogg, former cabinet minister Andrea Leadsom introduced an amendment calling not only for Paterson to be spared the 30-day suspension imposed by the commissioner, but also for a new Conservative-dominated committee to draw up an entirely new set of rules regarding parliamentary standards. Having seen one of their own fall foul of the rule book, in other words, they determined to tear it up and write a new one.

It is important to note the levels of entitlement and presumptions of impunity at play here. Brexiters all, Rees-Mogg had recently misled the late Queen about the unlawful prorogation of parliament, Leadsom's ill-fated bid to become prime minister had been derailed partly by questions about her CV and her tax affairs, while Johnson had already weathered at least three storms that could conceivably have ended his premiership. It is hardly surprising, then, that they thought could get away with such an obvious and self-serving assault on parliamentary standards. What followed constitutes a very rare example of the Establishment cabal failing to get their own way. For while the amendment passed thanks to a three-line whip and Johnson's enormous majority, the backlash was so furious that the plan was abandoned within 24 hours and Paterson resigned his seat on 5 November. Rees-Mogg, who had previously implied that the 72 people who died in the Grenfell Tower tragedy in June 2017 perished because they lacked 'common sense',[20] later claimed that his judgement had been clouded by sympathy for Paterson, whose wife Rose had died the previous year. Paterson himself later sought to blame her suicide on stresses brought on by the investigation into his own 'egregious' breaches of parliamentary standards. Moore, a self-appointed arbiter of public morality who quit the Church of England in protest at the ordination of women priests and once wrote regarding gay marriage 'I wonder if the law will eventually be changed to allow one to marry one's dog',[21] had begun the whole sorry process with another *Daily Telegraph* article, headlined: 'The hounding of Owen Paterson sets a dangerous precedent in Parliament'.[22] Despite the scale of this humiliation, none of Paterson's champions suffered the slightest personal or professional setback as a consequence of their conduct.

Many Fleet Street watchers (including this one) wondered whether the *Daily Mail*'s uncharacteristically strong line on the indefensibility of Paterson's position and the shameful Moore/Johnson/Rees-Mogg rescue attempt might have hastened the departure of Geordie Greig from the editor's office of the *Mail*. A quiet opponent of Brexit, Greig had steered the paper past the *Sun* to become the biggest seller in the UK but he was unexpectedly dismissed by the owner Jonathan (Viscount) Harmsworth just 12 days after Paterson's resignation. His replacement was Ted Verity, a protégé of Paul Dacre, the paper's previous editor. With unmistakable echoes of Charles Moore's preferment, Boris Johnson had sought to put Dacre both in the House of Lords and in charge of the broadcasting regulator Ofcom. The *Mail*'s position as an unquestioning cheerleader of Boris Johnson was swiftly restored. Less than a year later, it reported Johnson's removal from office by his own colleagues with the lachrymose front-page headline: 'What Have They Done?'

Meanwhile, that chairmanship of the BBC from which Charles Moore ruled himself out, perhaps to spend more time conversing 'endlessly' about the fundamental differences of 'blacks', went instead to Johnson's next favoured candidate, Richard Sharp. In November 2020, ITV's political editor, Robert Peston, reported that would-be applicants were being told by ministers: 'Don't waste your time applying, the PM has made up his mind it will be Richard Sharp.'[23] A deep-pocketed donor to the Tory party (more than £400,000 over a 20-year period), Sharp is a former director of the Centre for Policy Studies, judged by Transparify to be one of the four least transparent 'think tanks' in the UK and one of 'a handful … that refuse to reveal even the identities of their donors'. Giving evidence to the Digital, Culture, Media and Sport Select Committee (DCMS) of MPs in January 2021, Sharp said that he was 'considered to be a Brexiteer' and accepted that he suffered from 'confirmation bias' on the issue. He was also Rishi Sunak's boss at the merchant bank Goldman Sachs and, for reasons that remain unclear, was working at Downing Street as an unpaid 'adviser' to his former underling during the COVID-19 crisis. It was during this period that he made his interest in the BBC chairmanship known to both Sunak and Johnson, for whom he had also worked as an 'adviser' when Johnson was mayor of London.

A busy man, in September 2020 Sharp dined with a wealthy Canadian businessman called Sam Blyth, a distant cousin of Boris Johnson, who offered to alleviate Johnson's notoriously precarious financial situation. For despite once describing the £250,000 per annum he received for writing a weekly *Daily Telegraph* column as 'chicken feed', by the time Johnson became prime minister an expensive divorce and child support payments for a variety of progeny born both inside and outside his marriages had left him short of ready cash.

By way of example, in April 2021 it emerged that Johnson and his then fiancée, Carrie Symonds, had overseen a redecoration of their Downing Street apartments that had reportedly cost up to £200,000 and featured £840-a-roll wallpaper. This despite the fact that the prime minister receives an annual grant of just £30,000-a-year to spend on his or her home. Dominic Cummings would later claim that his former boss's 'plans to have donors secretly pay for the renovation were unethical, foolish, possibly illegal and almost certainly broke the rules on proper disclosure of political donations if conducted in the way he intended'.[24] And while Johnson was cleared of breaking the ministerial code by his second ethics adviser, Christopher (Lord) Geidt, the Electoral Commission ruled in December 2021 that the Conservative Party had broken electoral laws by using funds gifted by (another) rich party donor, David (Lord) Brownlow, to pay for the redecoration without properly declaring the money.

The following month, it emerged that Johnson, whose defence hinged upon the claim that he had no idea where the money was coming from, had failed to inform Geidt of a WhatsApp exchange with Brownlow in November 2020. A furious Geidt published the conversation in full. It made for remarkable reading.

> I am afraid parts of our flat are still a bit of a tip and am keen to allow Lulu Lytle to get on with it. Can I possibly ask her to get in touch with you for approvals?
>
> Many thanks and all best Boris.
>
> Ps am on the great exhibition plan Will revert.[25]

Lulu Lytle is the high-society interior decorator retained by Symonds. Her clientele includes Mick Jagger, and her presence at the birthday party in June 2020 that led to both Johnson and Sunak being fined for breaking their own lockdown laws rather undermined their defence that it was a 'work event'. The 'great exhibition' refers to a pet project of Brownlow's that would emulate the 1851 cultural and commercial jamboree conceived by Prince Albert. Downing Street insisted that, despite Johnson's promise, Brownlow's plan was not taken forward. Nevertheless, two months after the text exchange the official diary of Johnson's culture secretary, Oliver Dowden, described a meeting 'with Royal Albert Hall and Lord Brownlow to discuss plans for Great Exhibition 2.0'.[26] Brownlow at least seemed pleased, replying:

> Afternoon Prime Minister, I hope you're both well. Sorry for the delay I was out for a walk and didn't have my 'work' phone with me. Of course, get Lulu to call me and we'll get it sorted ASAP! Thanks for thinking about GE2. Best wishes David

Later adding:

I should have said, as the Trust isn't set up yet (will be in January) approval is a doddle as it's only me and I know where the £ will come from. So as soon as Lulu calls we can crack on – David.[27]

Johnson issued a 'humble and sincere apology'[28] to Geidt (who would eventually resign in June 2022 reportedly telling a confidant that he was 'sick of being lied to'[29]) for his failure to disclose the exchange. Johnson claimed to have no memory of it and also that he had been unable to retrieve the messages because he had adopted a new phone number. The second claim is certainly true. He was compelled to abandon his old number after the gossip website Popbitch revealed in April 2021 that it had been on public view for 15 years after being printed at the bottom of a press release from a think tank.

Geidt was unimpressed, replying:

Had I been aware of the Missing Exchange, I would have had further questions and drawn attention to it in my report. More crucially, I doubt whether I would have concluded, without qualification, what is set out in paragraph 33 of my report, that 'at the point when the Prime Minister became aware, he took steps to make the relevant declaration and to seek advice.'[30]

It was in the midst of this episode of unseemly scrounging, disappearing WhatsApps and prime ministerial impecuniousness that Sam Blyth told Richard Sharp he was keen to guarantee a loan for his distant cousin. Some truly first-class journalism from Gabriel Pogrund and Harry Yorke of the *Sunday Times* in January 2023 revealed that Sharp had introduced Blyth to the cabinet secretary, Simon Case, and that the loan arrangement was finalised in December 2020 before the funds were released the following February. It is still not clear where the £800,000 loan came from, only that Blyth acted as guarantor. Sharp, however, neglected to mention any of this during his application to become chairman of the BBC, despite the application rules stating: 'You cannot be considered for a public appointment if you fail to declare any conflict of interest'. Candidates are also required to declare anything that could later undermine confidence in the appointment.

Without the work of Pogrund and Yorke, it is unlikely that any of this would have come to light: Sharp, a crony of both Johnson and Sunak who had the audacity to pronounce on the 'liberal bias'[31] of the Corporation he chaired, would still be in post. Precedent-challenging behaviour such as sitting on the panel that appointed a new chief executive of *BBC News* would presumably have continued. Instead, in April 2023, he announced his resignation after an investigation by the office of the UK commissioner of public appointments concluded he had broken the rules by failing to declare his link to Johnson's loan, creating a 'potential perceived conflict of interest'.[32] Even here, though, the murkiness at the heart of the British Conservative establishment is still not fully understood.

The investigation into Richard Sharp's appointment was originally to have been conducted by the actual commissioner for public appointments, William Shawcross, who was appointed in October 2021. An avowed Brexiter and former journalist, Shawcross is the father of Eleanor Shawcross, who became head of 10 Downing Street's policy unit after donating £20,000 to Rishi Sunak's leadership campaign. He is also a former director of the 'Henry Jackson Society', a neoconservative 'think tank' described by its co-founder, Matthew Jamison, as having become a 'far-right, deeply anti-Muslim propaganda outfit [used to] smear other cultures, religions and ethnic groups'.[33] Between

2012 and 2018, Shawcross was chair of the Charity Commission for England and Wales and oversaw guidance, later withdrawn, that said charities should only campaign in the EU referendum in 'exceptional circumstances'. A week after telling the shadow culture secretary, Lucy Powell, that he would review Sharp's appointment 'to assure myself and the public that the process was run in compliance' with the rules, Shawcross was forced to recuse himself after admitting that he had met Sharp 'on previous occasions'. Perhaps he had forgotten.

The report was compiled instead by Adam Heppinstall KC, and confirmed Peston's scoop that the panel running the 'independent' recruitment process for the job was informed that Sharp was the only candidate that the government would support. That four-person panel, incidentally, included Catherine Baxendale, who was short-listed to be a Tory parliamentary candidate in 2017 and gave £50,000 to the party when David Cameron was prime minister, and Blondel Cluff, whose husband Algy owned the *Spectator* from 1980 until 1985 and remained as chairman until the end of 2004. The five editors he worked with there included Charles Moore and Boris Johnson. The current chairman is the former BBC presenter and Rupert Murdoch editor Andrew Neil.

If you're finding the labyrinthine links, social connections and rampant cronyism hard to follow, spare a thought for the tiny handful of British journalists minded to actually understand what goes on in the corridors of power and influence. You can surely see now what I mean about Russian dolls. What began a few pages ago as a passing reference to delusional denial in one newspaper headline atop one article by Charles Moore led inexorably to half-a-dozen other examples of just how far we've fallen and just who bears responsibility for it. We will examine some of these examples in more detail later but many of the recurring themes and characters are already plain to see. There is racism, albeit of the patrician variety still espoused in the pages of Andrew Neil's *Spectator*. There is exceptionalism, because just as Brexiters couldn't believe that Britain might somehow be denied special treatment by the EU, so they can't understand why one of their own might be expected to abide by the rules that everybody else is required to follow. There is pathetic bogus victimhood, because just as the IMF supposedly punishes the UK for Brexit, so Moore & co. were arguing throughout that Paterson's treatment was somehow a punishment for his Brexit support as opposed to a consequence of his obvious misconduct. There is arrogance, obviously, and there is ignorance aplenty, but what is perhaps most telling about the Paterson episode is the fact that, for an unconscionably long time, it marked pretty much the only occasion when the liars, cheats and incompetents did not emerge triumphant. This was almost certainly down to the fact that the editorship of the *Daily Mail* was, briefly, in the hands of a principled man.

In the same month that Moore's article appeared, an obscure academic called Matthew Goodwin embarked upon an even more ridiculous flight of fancy that somehow filled an entire book. Previously Nigel Farage's amanuensis, Goodwin's laughable thesis is that the real brokers of power in Brexit Britain are not the people in control of government and most of the media but, inter alia, the footballer turned broadcaster Gary Lineker, the broadcaster and entrepreneur Carol Vorderman and, well, me. The chief qualification for inclusion in this 'new elite' seemed to be a rejection of racist rhetoric, a willingness to criticise successive Conservative governments for presiding over a period of unprecedented decline, and the possession of a decent following on Twitter.

Despite his obvious absurdity, Goodwin received an extraordinary amount of coverage in right-wing newspapers. That the editors of the *Sun* and the *Telegraph* would embrace this nonsense is perhaps not very surprising but it seemed a strange fit for *The Times*. Until you remembered that the newish editor, Tony Gallagher, had previously occupied the editor's chair at both the *Sun* and the *Daily Telegraph* as well as enjoying a stint as deputy editor of the *Daily Mail*. People such as Gallagher, who once stated 'My huge admiration for Paul Dacre is well known', seem to believe that it's not people like his past and present bosses Rupert Murdoch, Viscount Rothermere, the Barclay family and Paul Dacre that most effectively use the UK media to wield political influence in this country, it's Gary Lineker, Carol Vorderman and me.

This is about desperation rather than coordination. Moore and Goodwin did not cook up their ludicrous theses together and they are just two among an army of offenders. Allister Heath, the current editor of the *Sunday Telegraph*, deserves some sort of prize. 'This was the best budget I have ever heard a chancellor deliver, by a massive margin,' he wrote on the front page of the *Daily Telegraph* the morning after Kwasi Kwarteng announced his disastrous mini-budget. He was, I suppose, accidentally accurate when he called it a 'moment in history that will radically transform Britain'. Heath had previously insisted that: 'Our declinist-Remainer class has outdone itself, demonising and dismissing Liz Truss, and working itself up into a frenzy of self-righteous rage and indignation at the supposed incompetence of her new Government.'[34] Like the politicians they protect, these people, often occupying previously august positions in the highest echelons of the British newspaper industry, face no consequences for being frequently and spectacularly wrong. On the contrary, they lurch from one unhinged diatribe to the next with no discernible pause for reflection. By the end of April 2023, for example, Heath was explaining that 'Britain is being impoverished by a Remainer Mind Virus',[35] and in August that the 'Fury of the silent majority is driving a global Right-wing counter revolution'.[36]

They are not fringe outliers or amusing contrarians hired for their willingness to challenge mainstream journalism. They *are* the mainstream and they have all now arrived, through opportunism and necessity, at a place where they can just about persuade themselves that the abject failure of the policies and politicians they favoured for years must somehow be the fault of other factors. They blame it instead on a 'new elite' or 'left-wing' Conservative governments or a 'Remainer Mind Virus'. No matter how flimsy the argument or how objectively pathetic the premise, politics and the media remain full of people still similarly unable to accept their role in what has happened. It is literally impossible to exaggerate the depths they will plumb to pass the buck. Consider Elizabeth Truss herself.

Just as this attempt to deflect and deny their own obvious responsibility for countless disasters was being ramped up to ludicrous levels by British newspapers, the politician who perhaps best embodies the whole, sorry mess popped up in America to claim that her catastrophic 49-day tenure as prime minster was somehow the responsibility of everyone, indeed anyone, but her. 'We didn't just face coordinated resistance from inside the Conservative party or even inside the British corporate establishment. We faced it from the IMF and even from President Biden,' she said in a speech to the Heritage Foundation, inevitably another secretly funded, policy-influencing, right-wing 'think tank'. 'The sad truth is what I think we've seen over the past few years is a new kind of economic model taking hold in our countries, one that's focused on redistributionism, on stagnation and on the imbuing of woke culture into our businesses. I call these people the anti-growth movement.'[37]

Again, it is important to pause and absorb the sheer scale of the absurdity being promulgated here. Liz Truss became a minister in 2012 when David Cameron was prime minster. Two years later she replaced Owen Paterson as secretary of state for environment, food and rural affairs. Subsequently, and under a total of three Tory prime ministers, she has served as justice secretary, lord chancellor, chief secretary to the treasury, international trade secretary and foreign secretary. She had been, by any measure, an integral part of the UK government for over a decade, rising to one of the great offices of state before securing the keys to Downing Street itself. But throughout the entirety of her governmental career a 'new kind of economic model' had been taking over the country about which she had never previously said a single word.

. . .

Let me show you even more of what I mean when I talk about this Russian doll of ridiculousness and the suffocating intertwining of right-wing media, politics and 'think tanks'. For if Truss represents an apotheosis of incompetence being over-promoted, there are plenty of other case studies. Consider the post-Brexit careers of two more people to hold one of the four great offices of state at the pinnacle of British government: Foreign Secretary Dominic Raab and Home Secretary Suella Braverman. As with Moore's article or Johnson's loan, you will see how recalling one example of their gross ineptitude or obvious unfitness for office immediately reminds us of another element or architect of our unfolding national tragedy, then another, and then another. And while it is tempting to hope that the complete abandonment of political integrity or competence ushered in by the elevations of Johnson and Truss to prime minister might have ended with their enforced departures, Raab and Braverman also remind us that this remains far too optimistic a position.

So let's twist a Russian doll, in this case Dominic Raab's swift ascent from richly deserved obscurity to foreign secretary and deputy prime minister, and see what we find. Trace this unlikely trajectory back to its beginning and immediately David Davis appears. Davis was Raab's predecessor as 'Secretary of State and Chief Negotiator for Leaving the European Union'. It is worth remembering why. When Theresa May became prime minister after David Cameron's resignation in 2016, she faced what would prove to be an intractable problem: how to steer the country through the imminent negative impacts of the Brexit she had campaigned against but now had to 'deliver', while somehow appeasing the victorious colleagues and newspaper editors who refused to accept that there would be any negative impacts at all. The madness that flowed from this simple and obvious impossibility will also run through this book like 'Blackpool' through a stick of rock. But for now we are concerned with only one of its consequences: she had to appoint people to key positions whose Brexit credentials were impeccable, regardless of competence or calibre. Both Dominic Raab and David Davis prove this point perfectly. Like most self-styled 'staunch Eurosceptics' their grasp of what departure from the European Union would actually entail was at best delusional and at worst downright stupid. In a rare moment of honesty and acuity, Dominic Cummings, the former campaign director of the Vote Leave campaign and another key architect of the UK's self-inflicted decline, described Davis as 'thick as mince, lazy as a toad and vain as Narcissus'.[38] The accuracy of this accusation is hard to dispute but in the ecosystem under scrutiny here, it would prove no obstacle to advancement. Quite the opposite.

In May 2016, one month before the referendum secured 'Brexit', two months before May charged him with 'delivering' it and several years before either of them understood what might actually be possible, he tweeted: 'The first calling point of the UK's negotiator immediately after Brexit will not be Brussels, it will be Berlin, to strike a deal.' The ignorance on display here is considerable – EU member states cannot conduct trade negotiations autonomously – and the notion that having rendered itself a 'third country' the UK would somehow enjoy favoured status is ambitious to say the least. But by May 2016 it didn't matter. Despite being a prominent British politician, a former leadership contender and shadow home secretary, Davis displayed abject ignorance of quite simple but crucial concepts. As a harbinger of the epic absurdity that would follow, he simply stated what the *Daily Mail*, the *Daily Telegraph* and the whole Vote Leave machine wanted to be true without any reproach or consequence. People with a grasp of the facts were dismissed as 'Remoaners' or tribunes of 'Project Fear', and the truth was simply and effectively subjugated.

Most appallingly at this time, by permitting one of the most prominent members of the hard-right media establishment to masquerade as an impartial senior politics presenter, the BBC undermined much of its own ability to provide a sorely needed corrective. In February 2016, Andrew Neil, a former Rupert Murdoch editor and chairman of the pro-Brexit *Spectator* magazine, was presenting an edition of the BBC *Daily Politics* show in which Davis rehearsed his German car industry delusions while former foreign secretary Margaret Beckett looked on incredulously. It is notable for two reasons. First, the way in which Neil treats Beckett's evidence and experience as a mere and equal counterbalance to Davis's ignorance and bluster. Second, the smugness and cosy cronyism of Neil and Davis.

> **Davis:** The day after Brexit happens, the chief executives of Volkswagen, BMW, Audi ...

> **Neil:** You've missed out Mercedes.

> **Davis:** And Mercedes. I know you've got one. Ha. Ha. Ha. [Indicating Neil] You've got to know how to tease him.

As Andrew Neil chuckles delightedly, Davis continues: 'They will all be queueing up saying we've got to have access for our 16 million – sorry, 16 billion – market.'

Margaret Beckett's response is, in retrospect, chillingly prescient. You can see her briefly considering an uncharacteristic departure from basic politeness and she often seems to struggle to find the appropriate words.

> **Beckett:** I think it's pie in the sky, frankly. And I know David was Europe Minister at one time but I have a bit of experience of European negotiations myself.

> **Neil:** As Foreign Secretary ...

> **Beckett:** Over something like ten or eleven years of intense negotiations both on agriculture and on climate change. And I just think ... Don't give me ... I mean, if I can say so with I hope some modesty I do quite pride myself on my negotiating skills and track

record. Don't give me a brief like that. The risks are huge and the certainties are none.'

A year later, in July 2017, his hubristic arrogance was crystallised in photographic form when Davis, having accepted the brief so scathingly described by Beckett, sat down to begin negotiating the UK's withdrawal from the EU. A process likened to removing the eggs from a baked cake apparently presented no problems at all to this former SAS reservist. The now infamous picture shows him and two colleagues sitting opposite the EU's chief negotiator, Michel Barnier, and his team. The latter have piles of documents on the glass table in front of them. Davis, beaming at the camera, has none. Not a single sheet. It's possible that, looking down, he would have seen only his own reflection gurning back at him. Oliver Robbins, the senior civil servant in Davis's box-fresh ministry, has a slim black notebook and a pen before him but it's hard to imagine any image capturing more perfectly the ridiculousness not just of Davis but of the entire UK government.

And a year after that, in July 2018, Davis was gone, resigning his post after achieving nothing and understanding less. The forces of furious denialism that would shortly propel Boris Johnson into Downing Street were by now stirring in opposition to Theresa May's at least pragmatic plan for a 'UK–EU free-trade area' and Davis, he of the noteless negotiations and mythical trips to Berlin to conclude impossible deals, opined that 'It seems to me we're giving too much away, too easily, and that's a dangerous strategy.'[39] Fellow Brexit minister Steve Baker, who would later start referring to himself as the 'hardman of Brexit', also resigned and Jacob Rees-Mogg, chairman of the ERG, wrote in the *Daily Telegraph* (where else?) that he would vote against May's proposal. It seemed unlikely that Davis's successor in the role, whoever that may be, could be less effective. Unlikely but not, it soon transpired, impossible.

A largely unnoticed housing minister with a brief and unspectacular legal career behind him, Dominic Raab's support for leaving the EU in the 2016 referendum was his only obvious qualification for promotion. May's mission to mitigate the inevitable negative impacts of Brexit was doomed by many factors, not least reality, but it was the necessity of appointing people who 'believed' in the impossible that did her most damage. And it did not take Raab long to demonstrate his credentials. As with Davis, it is important to remember that Raab not only campaigned for Brexit but also professed to have a better understanding of the facts than the 'experts' adamant that we would not be able to enjoy the benefits of EU membership after ceasing to be EU members. And as with Davis, it is hard to decide what is most shocking: Raab's failure to understand the most basic precepts of his negotiating position or the absolute absence of consequences this failure had. Consider the following comment, made in November 2018, long after hauliers, couriers, customs agents and countless other professionals with long experience of importing and exporting goods between the UK and the rest of the EU had warned of the problems ahead: 'I hadn't quite understood the full extent of this, but if you look at the UK and look at how we trade in goods, we are particularly reliant on the Dover–Calais crossing.'[40]

This, of course, is akin to a recently appointed football manager revealing that he hadn't previously appreciated the importance of putting the ball over the opposition's goal line. An Institute for Government report had previously described Dover as 'a key artery for UK trade heading to continental Europe'[41] with more than 2.5m heavy goods vehicles passing through the port every year. It also described goods worth £119bn passing through the port in 2015, 'representing around 17% of the UK's entire trade in goods by value'. Yet Raab's incredible ignorance barely gave him pause. The combination of the Conservative Party's Brexit cultishness and the right-wing media's rejection of observable reality meant that Raab could disgrace himself like this on the grandest stage and suffer not one jot. Indeed, a week later and 129 days after taking the job, Raab himself resigned from May's government, insisting that her plans to keep Northern Ireland attached to EU regulations after Brexit posed a 'very real threat to the integrity of the United Kingdom'.[42] Raab later voted for Boris Johnson's supposedly 'oven-ready' deal that kept Northern Ireland attached to EU regulations but not before revealing, in January 2019, that he hadn't actually read the Good Friday Agreement. The treaty brought fragile peace to Northern Ireland by implying that there would be no return to a hard border on the island of Ireland. Had he bothered to read it, he should have realised that the security installations required to operate a post-Brexit hard border would run foul of a key pledge in the GFA to demilitarise. The 1998 GFA, also known as the Belfast Agreement, represented one of the most significant and substantive challenges to any form of Brexit and runs to just 35 pages in length. Yet Raab explained: 'It's not like a novel, [where] you sit down and say "do you know what, over the holidays, this is a cracking read"'.[43]

History does not relate what he was reading but he was indeed on holiday when Kabul fell to the Taliban on 15 August 2021. By now promoted to foreign secretary by Boris Johnson, whose government had already threatened to 'break international law'[44] by attempting to override its own Brexit Withdrawal Agreement, many expected him to return to his desk. He did not. He remained on holiday in Crete with his family as the Afghan government collapsed and instead delegated crucial tasks to other ministers. Appearing before the Foreign Affairs Select Committee the following month, he refused nine times to reveal when his holiday had begun and later rejected reports that he had been paddleboarding as the Taliban seized control, saying: 'The stuff about me paddleboarding is just nonsense. The sea was actually closed, it was a red notice.' Before August was out, the *Independent* quoted Greek meteorologist Theodoros Kolydas as saying: 'We did not have any significant weather phenomenon in the area of Crete between 12–15 Aug. The winds were north, with a maximum of 6 to 7 Beaufort [25–38mph] and the weather was locally cloudy.'[45] Alexandros Roniotis, whose Cretan Beaches website lists information about the island's coastline, added: 'No beaches were closed. Only some gorges during the big fires, but no beaches.'[46]

Raab was out of the Foreign Office the following month and out of favour completely for the duration of Liz Truss's brief but disastrous premiership. But when Rishi Sunak became prime minister on 25 October 2022, he immediately restored Raab to the position of deputy prime minister. He did so despite Raab facing multiple allegations of bullying from colleagues. After eight formal complaints, and at Raab's request, Sunak set up an independent inquiry by a senior lawyer, Adam Tolley KC. Raab pledged to resign his position if the inquiry found him to have engaged in bullying behaviour. The report, delivered to Sunak and Raab on 20 April 2023, found Raab guilty of 'intimidating' and 'aggressive' behaviour that fitted a description of bullying. It is fair to say that Raab, who described the inquiry he had called for as 'flawed', did not depart gracefully. His resignation letter was an exercise in narcissistic self-indulgence:

I am genuinely sorry for any unintended stress or offence that any officials felt, as a result of the pace, standards and challenge that I brought to the Ministry of Justice. That is, however, what the public expect of ministers working on their behalf.

In setting the threshold for bullying so low, this inquiry has set a dangerous precedent. It will encourage spurious complaints against ministers, and have a chilling effect on those driving change on behalf of your government – and ultimately the British people.

He continued in this spectacularly self-pitying vein in an article published by the *Telegraph* before Tolley's report had even been released. It appeared under the frankly remarkable headline, 'The people of Britain will pay for this Kafkaesque saga'.[47] The usual suspects were soon gathered in agreement. The *Daily Mail*'s front page asked, 'Was This The Day Britain Became Ungovernable?'[48] For their star columnist, Richard Littlejohn, it was Raab's *critics* who were 'entitled' and 'self-pitying'. He went on to share his dewy-eyed nostalgia for the days when it was commonplace for a male newspaper editor to tell a female subordinate to 'fuck off' and, tellingly, blamed the absence of an unspecified 'fully-functioning Brexit' on a 'left-leaning broadcast Blob, a self-important legal establishment and an unelected House of Lords'.[49] The same House of Lords, of course, into which the *Daily Mail*'s editor-in-chief, Paul Dacre, seems so desperate to be elevated; what else explains why the paper continued to cheerlead for his sponsor, Boris Johnson, long after he had been chased out of Downing Street by his own cabinet after being found to have lied again, this time about the appointment of a notorious sex pest to a senior government role?

Incredibly, Raab's own elevation to deputy PM had been only the second most depressing appointment to Sunak's first cabinet. For approximately five hours on that October day, the more optimistic observers of British politics hoped we had finally reached rock bottom and the country was turning over a new leaf. On the steps of 10 Downing Street, Sunak spoke of his determination to restore 'integrity, professionalism and accountability' to his government. Many thought that this heralded a deliberate departure from the legacy of Boris Johnson, under whom the obvious incompetence, ignorance and, crucially, impunity of a character like Raab had been free to flourish. By 5pm, however, it had become clear that Sunak either could not or would not wean his administration off the crack pipe of moral corruption that Johnson and his ludicrous coterie of cronies and sycophants had been puffing away on for the best part of three years. And it was not the reappointment of Raab that signalled this most clearly, it was the reappointment of Suella Braverman to the position of home secretary just *six days* after she had been effectively fired by Truss for a blatant breach of the ministerial code.

In the spirit of those Russian dolls, and as further proof of the way that recalling one scandalous episode immediately prompts memories of others, the mere mention of the ministerial code within spitting distance of the phrase 'legacy of Boris Johnson' conjures up the memory of Braverman's predecessor in the Home Office, Priti Patel. In November 2020, after an eight-month inquiry, Johnson's independent adviser on ministerial standards, Sir Alex Allan, found that Patel had bullied Home Office staff. Johnson not only ignored his findings but also texted Tory MPs with an instruction to 'form a square around the Prittster'.[50] Allen promptly resigned in protest and less than two years later so too did Christopher (Lord) Geidt, Johnson's second ethics adviser, who had been so bruised by 'wallpapergate'.

More on this later, but it is important to note this was the backdrop against which Sunak promised 'integrity, accountability and professionalism' before putting ministerial code-breaker Braverman back in to the Home Office and reinstating soon-to-be proven bully Raab as deputy prime minister. Once there, Braverman wasted little time in laying claim to being one of the most deliberately divisive and wilfully unpleasant politicians of the modern era. And that is a crowded field.

In January 2023, an 83-year-old Holocaust survivor called Joan Salter rose to her feet at a constituency meeting in Fareham, Hampshire, and asked her MP, the newly reinstalled home secretary, to moderate the language she routinely uses to describe refugees and asylum seekers. Salter, who received an MBE for her work on Holocaust education, compared Braverman's rhetoric on migrants crossing the English Channel in so-called 'small boats' to language used by the Nazis during the Second World War.

She said: 'In 1943, I was forced to flee my birthplace in Belgium and went across war-torn Europe and dangerous seas until I finally was able to come to the UK in 1947. When I hear you using words against refugees like "swarms" and "invasion", I am reminded of the language used to dehumanise and justify the murder of my family and millions of others. Why do you find the need to use that kind of language?'[51]

Braverman responded: 'There is a huge problem that we have right now when it comes to illegal migration, the scale of which we have not known before. I won't apologise for the language that I have used to demonstrate the scale of the problem. I see my job as being honest with the British people and honest for the British people. I'm not going to shy away from difficult truths nor am I going to conceal what is the reality that we are all watching.'[52] (Braverman, who does not merit a chapter of her own in this book, has not personally used the word 'swarm' in this context but former prime minister David Cameron and former UKIP leader Nigel Farage, who do, have both done so.)

This episode, and the broader context in which it unfolded, is illustrative for three key reasons: it depicts the shameless commoditisation of hate in public life, the traducing of basic accuracy and the culture of impunity in which politicians like Braverman, Raab and almost everyone else in this book have been able to flourish. For while Braverman, like Raab, is more symptom than cause of the corrupted ecosystem, she has repeatedly shown herself willing to go further and faster down the dirtiest of political sewers than any of her colleagues. And besides, successful diagnoses generally begin with an examination of symptoms. By any reasonable measure, she should not have been in the job at all.

Less than three months previously, on 19 October 2022, Braverman had been compelled to resign as home secretary after 43 days in the job when it emerged that she had used a personal email account to forward a government document to a political ally. At least that was the reason she gave at the time, stating: 'Earlier today, I sent an official document from my personal email to a trusted parliamentary colleague as part of policy engagement, and with the aim of garnering support for government policy on migration. This constitutes a technical infringement of the rules.' She continued: 'As soon as I realised my mistake, I rapidly reported this on official channels and informed the cabinet secretary.'[53]

In fact, she had not only sent the document to a political ally, Sir John Hayes, but had also tried to copy in his wife, who works in his office. It later emerged that she had accidentally sent the draft written statement on immigration, with potential implications for market-sensitive growth forecasts from the OBR, to a staff member of another Conservative MP, Andrew Percy. The BBC later established that it was

Percy who first reported this clear breach of the ministerial code to the chief whip, who is responsible for party discipline. The chief whip passed the information on to No. 10 and the Cabinet Office. The BBC further reported that, according to sources, Cabinet Secretary Simon Case had not at this point been approached by Braverman herself. As with Raab, her resignation letter was petulant and self-serving.

She wrote:

> It is obvious to everyone that we are going through a tumultuous time. I have concerns about the direction of this government. Not only have we broken key pledges that were promised to our voters, but I have had serious concerns about this government's commitment to honouring manifesto commitments, such as reducing overall migration numbers and stopping illegal migration, particularly the dangerous small boats crossings.[54]

Seeking asylum is not 'illegal'. Neither, according to international law, is travelling to a country by irregular means to do so. But as with almost all of the politicians who have flourished since Brexit, it is hard to know whether Braverman is being deliberately disingenuous or simply lacks the intelligence to understand the inaccuracy of what she states with such confidence. It may be unfair to wonder whether she is lying, or stupid, or possibly both, but there is evidence for each of these accusations.

In March 2017, she was deputy chair of the ERG and appeared on BBC *Question Time*. Asked about the financial cost of the UK leaving the EU, she stated: 'This figure of 50 billion doesn't have any legal basis whatsoever. It's been manufactured and, um, it doesn't seem, um, likely that there will be such a bill for £50 million. It's part of

Project Fear. Health warning: don't believe it. And, you know, we pay into the European Investment Bank and so actually we're going to get a windfall from leaving so I think that the scaremongering about having to pay to leave is just not true. We have a lot to gain. Our best days lie ahead and we're going to be enjoying the freedoms and enjoying the benefits that we gain from leaving.'[55] As of July 2022, the Treasury's estimate of the actual 'divorce' bill, best understood as the UK's share of obligations agreed to while an EU member, was £35.6 billion. The OBR foresees payments continuing until 2064. Whether Braverman understood this and lied or failed to understand it but nevertheless persisted in her Brexit beliefs is impossible to say.

Similarly, we cannot be sure precisely what she understood the word 'contributor' to mean when she claimed on the website of her barristers' chambers to have fulfilled that role with regard to the 2007 textbook *Gambling for Local Authorities: Licensing, Planning and Regeneration*. The book's author, Philip Kolvin KC, told the *Big Issue* magazine in October 2022 that Braverman 'did not make a written or editorial contribution to the book. However on one occasion I asked her to do some photocopying for the book, which she did.'[56]

These vignettes are important because, as with Raab, Braverman's career highlights not only how utterly inadequate individuals can rise to the highest offices in the land, but also how obvious, outrageous failures to observe even the lowest standards of basic probity and accuracy go completely unpunished. Even as I write, some seven years after the referendum, 'impeccable Brexit credentials', or at least a refusal to acknowledge its disastrous consequences, remain the only requirements for political promotion. People who would once have been nonentities – or, at the very most, eccentric adornments to a more serious political landscape – have been able to flourish. For example, Braverman succeeded 'Brexit hardman' Steve Baker as chair of the ERG and was herself succeeded by Jacob Rees-Mogg. All three would become ministers after their tenure at the head of the deeply bizarre parliamentary group, who later started referring to themselves as 'Spartans', because – and only because – they would not attract unhinged newspaper coverage. Or the rent-a-quote ire of Nigel Farage, the former UKIP and Brexit Party leader who had stalked the Conservative Party for over a decade by promising that, however xenophobic and dishonest they became, he would always be prepared to go further. Crucially, most of the cast from this tragedy of errors is still on the stage. It is hard to see how anything can improve until they quit it.

. . .

I have a very weird day job. Every weekday, I present a phone-in show on national radio in a slot that has, in the years I've been doing it, become the most popular speech-based programme in the United Kingdom among the commercial stations where presenters are permitted to espouse their views. I mention this not (only) to boast. Its success proves that popularity is not dependent upon complicity in the corruption of our country. But if I sometimes wonder whether things can *really* be as bad as I believe them to be, then goodness knows how easy it must be to suffer similar doubts if you don't pay attention to and talk about politics for a living. There are moments on air when, midway through a tirade against the latest example of epic wrongdoing, I catch myself wondering whether I've accidentally libelled someone, whether the facts can really be as outrageous as I am relating or whether I've somehow misremembered. It's as if saying it out loud (or, I'm often told, hearing it said aloud) delivers an urgency that can be lacking from the printed word. I think humans sometimes need the emotional heft of tone, the squeakiness of incredulity, to see the full picture. I can't provide that here. This book is an attempt to collect as much proof as I can, more for my own peace of mind rather than for 'posterity', and to offer an explanation of how it happened.

Obviously, there was no real plan or secret conspiracy to break Britain, and many of the culprits no doubt genuinely believed that their actions would somehow benefit the country. Some of them still do. It has happened because of a unique congregation of coincidences and circumstances that allowed a phalanx of arrogant, petulant and preternaturally self-important individuals to wreak untold havoc. The ones with their names atop each chapter of this book are best viewed as portals through which we must pass in search of greater understanding of how they broke Britain. Most of them are household names. Some of them are not. Most of them sit within the diabolical nexus of media, politics and 'think tank'. Some of them do not. Most of them have exercised power. Some of them have not. But all of them have made monumental contributions to the immense and entirely avoidable denigration of our nation.

First and most foundational, I focus on a print media grown fat on the commoditisation of hatred and othering, but now in existential decline and desperate for relevance. Rupert Murdoch (Chapter 1) and Paul Dacre (Chapter 2), the editor-in-chief of the *Mail* titles, lead this field by an enormous margin. Murdoch because, as is perhaps best demonstrated by recent revelations regarding his Fox News network's role in deliberately amplifying Donald Trump's lies about the 2022 presidential election, truth will always be subjugated to populism in pursuit of profit. His is a cynicism devoid of ideology and it allows him to excuse any violation of basic decency on the grounds of pursuing money or influence. Dacre, by contrast, seems to be a true believer and is therefore in many ways more dangerous. Because when you believe passionately that your own superiority and worldview – which in his case involves an apparent nostalgia for traditional Victorian notions that Britain is a country where a woman's place is in the home, Englishmen have every right to rule the world and ethnic minorities know their place – are under attack from the forces of modernity and diversity, you will do anything to prevail.

Less obviously, perhaps, I turn to Andrew Neil (Chapter 3), the former Murdoch editor who as chairman of the little-read but dispro-portionately influential *Spectator* magazine has presided over the once august organ of high church Conservatism's descent into a sewer where Islamophobes, conspiracy theorists, racists and even Nazi apol-ogists flourish. Neil also highlights the way in which the last bastion of truly impartial journalism in the UK, the BBC, has been cowed and almost captured by avowedly right-wing interests. Crucially, the media landscape created by Murdoch and Dacre monstered anyone at the Corporation with even the slightest hint of 'leftist' loyalties, yet Neil was not only able to work there as a senior political presenter for years without objection but also preside over his various protégés' cross-fertilisation of the Tory party and those secretly funded 'think tanks'. In return, his most vitriolic, bigoted columnists can shroud themselves in bogus respectability and undertake lucrative work for Dacre and Murdoch. A current columnist and commissioning editor is even the wife of Dominic Cummings (Chapter 8), who himself enjoyed a largely unreported stint as online editor of the title. Through Cummings's partner at the helm of Vote Leave, Matthew Elliott (Chapter 4), we will come to understand how – and, crucially, why – British media became infested with people from hard right, secretly funded lobby groups who are routinely treated with undeserved respect, and who often move seamlessly into government roles.

Into the hideous space created by this collective abnegation of the most basic journalistic standards stepped a generation of politicians equipped with whatever skills were necessary to thrive within it. David Cameron (Chapter 6), an apparently affable patrician who seemed to believe that prime minister was the only job of sufficient status to accommodate his myriad attributes and talents. More dangerously, he also seemed to think that, having risen without trace through British society due chiefly to patronage and inherited advantage, he was just the chap to fend off the jingoistic furies of Euroscepticism that had beset his party for decades and seen off at least two of his predecessors as party leader. If Cameron's downfall was his arrogance, his nemesis was Nigel Farage (Chapter 5). An ingratiating and insidious relic of the 1970s far right, Farage managed to avoid the fate of previously prominent fascist-adjacent politicians by eschewing their sinister surliness (most of the time) and instead dressing up as a country squire while cloaking himself in a miasma of beer fumes and cigarette smoke. A generation left bamboozled and betrayed by the swiftness with which the Britain of Bernard Manning and Enoch Powell had been abandoned took him to their hearts because he made their prejudices feel respectable again. The red carpet of racism down which Farage merrily slithered had, of course, been rolled out by the likes of Murdoch, Dacre and Neil. And however hard they tried to pretend otherwise, Cummings and Elliott could not have triumphed in 2016 without him.

Three years later, the only politician who did even more to deliver that victory, Boris Johnson (Chapter 9), was in Downing Street after all of the factors and characters above combined with the pitiful Jeremy Corbyn (Chapter 7) to offer the UK public an electoral choice between the wholly unconscionable and the utterly unelectable. The costs of that cocktail of political crapulence are still being counted today but, perhaps most remarkably of all, the stage was set for the eventual elevation of a politician who will be seen in years to come as the embodiment of everything that broke Britain, Liz Truss (Chapter 10).

I could continue writing this introduction forever. Every rock I look under reveals ten more rocks. Every day something new happens to deepen the awfulness and the absurdity of what these ten people, their allies and their cohorts, have done to our country and to all of us. I was going to close by portentously inviting you to step into their infernal lair but you are, of course, already in it. We all are. This is how it happened.

Chapter 1
RUPERT MURDOCH

I work for a man who wants it all, and doesn't understand anybody telling him he can't have it all.

Former Rupert Murdoch employee Paul V. Carlucci

ON 21 NOVEMBER 2014, Andy Coulson was released from prison after serving barely a quarter of an 18-month sentence for conspiracy to intercept voicemails – or 'phone hacking' as it is colloquially known. Coulson's crimes were committed when he was editor of Rupert Murdoch's first UK newspaper acquisition, the *News of the World*. He resigned from that post in January 2007 shortly before the paper's royal editor, Clive Goodman, became the first of several Murdoch journalists to be jailed for phone hacking. Just six months after that, in July, Coulson became the Conservative Party's director of communications, and when David Cameron became prime minister in May 2010, Coulson became director of communications for the UK government. On the eve of Cameron's Tory conference speech in October 2009, Coulson's former lover, Rebekah Brooks (née Wade) – acquitted co-defendant in the phone-hacking trial, boss at Murdoch's News International, and recently married to an Old Etonian friend of Cameron's – texted the Tory leader: 'I am so rooting for you tomorrow and not just as a personal friend but because professionally we're definitely in this together!'[1]

Coulson resigned from Cameron's government in January 2011 as the phone-hacking scandal gathered pace. It did so almost entirely due to the tireless journalism of the *Guardian*'s Nick Davies and the advocacy of the Labour MPs Tom Watson and Chris Bryant. Unlike the *New York Times*, most of the UK media and the entire Conservative government remained ambivalent, cowed or downright hostile toward the story until Davies reported that the *News of the World* had illegally targeted the missing schoolgirl Milly Dowler and her family, allegedly interfering with police inquiries into her disappearance.

Three days later, the Murdoch family announced the closure of the newspaper after 168 years in print. The day after that, Coulson was arrested. At his trial in 2014, Mr Justice Saunders told the court that the *News of the World*'s initial failure to tell police that their journalists had 'hacked' the voicemail of Milly Dowler – later found to have been murdered – came from a desire to 'take credit for finding her'[2] and sell newspapers. When he described that delay as 'unforgivable', he was being somewhat optimistic. In March 2017, the public relations firm that Coulson set up after leaving prison, Coulson Chappell, was awarded a contract to enhance the reputations of the *Daily Telegraph* and *Sunday Telegraph*. The *Guardian*'s media columnist Roy Greenslade wrote at the time: 'His main brief is thought to be to promote the papers as truthful and authoritative.'[3]

Despite Coulson's disgrace, Conservative prime ministers continued to hire hacks straight from the stable of increasingly right-wing and later Brexit-addled newspapers. On 10 February 2017, the political editor of the *Daily Mail*, James Slack, became Prime Minister Theresa May's official spokesman, a position he retained after Boris

Johnson became prime minister in July 2019. Eighteen months later, he became director of communications after the resignation of Dominic Cummings ally and Vote Leave's former head of broadcast, Lee Cain. Slack, who had written the *Daily Mail*'s ridiculous 'Steel Of The New Iron Lady' front page claiming that Theresa May was ready to walk away from Brexit negotiations with no deal 'and make EU pay',[4] left Downing Street in April 2021 to become deputy editor of Rupert Murdoch's *Sun*. He was replaced by Jack Doyle, a former associate editor (politics) at the *Daily Mail*.

It later emerged that Slack had thrown a leaving party at Downing Street on the eve of the Duke of Edinburgh's funeral that descended into a drunken debauch with reports of a suitcase full of alcohol being wheeled on to the premises. At the time, gatherings of two or more people indoors and six or more people outdoors were prohibited under lockdown rules forged in the very building where Slack and around 45 colleagues celebrated. Records show that the last two members of staff left at 3.11am and 4.20am, shortly before cleaners arrived to start dealing with the wine spillages and pools of vomit. It all struck a stark contrast with a now famous image of the late Queen sitting alone in St George's Chapel at Windsor Castle the same day, as attendees at her husband's funeral studiously observed lockdown regulations with guests from separate households sitting two metres apart.

The full details of Slack's party were published in Sue Gray's report on lockdown-breaking in Downing Street in September 2022. Even though details of the party, including damage to a children's swing and slide set in the Downing Street garden, filled two pages of Gray's report, the *Sun*'s initial reporting omitted all mention of deputy editor Slack's involvement. It is not known whether Slack, Cain or Doyle were among the 83 people fined by the Metropolitan Police over the various illegal gatherings, but Slack remains a Commander of the Most Excellent Order of the British Empire (CBE), a gong given to him by Theresa May.

There is a logic, perhaps even an inevitability, to politicians seeking media advice from media professionals, but the revolving door of cronyism, criminality and cosiness catalogued above is altogether more dangerous. For while previous newspaper proprietors had occasionally been quite open about their intentions – the first newspaper baron, Lord Beaverbrook, told the Royal Commission on the Press in 1948 that he 'ran the [*Express*] purely for the purpose of making propaganda and with no other object ... I look at it as a purely propagandist project' – their influence was almost always exerted from outside government. Even Bernard Ingham, Margaret Thatcher's highly effective chief press secretary, was a career civil servant. And while Alastair Campbell, who would fulfil the same role for Tony Blair, did come into politics direct from Fleet Street, not even his harshest critics would claim that he continued to serve the interests of his former employers. *Today* newspaper, where he was political editor prior to joining the then leader of the opposition's team in 1994, had been bought by Rupert Murdoch in 1987 and published its final issue in 1995.

Coulson's appointment, by contrast, saw a Murdoch man installed at the very heart of government. A man, moreover, whose former boss and lover had stated that David Cameron's Conservative government and Rupert Murdoch's News International were embarked on a joint mission. This was a mission that, by at least one account, was already well under way when Cameron was still in opposition. The words of Gordon Brown, who Cameron replaced as prime minister after the 2010 general election, must of course be viewed through the lens of his loss, but a speech he gave to the House of Commons in July 2011 is nonetheless striking. Coining the phrase 'criminal-media nexus' to describe the relationships to be investigated by the Leveson Inquiry into the culture, practices and ethics of the British press, Brown revealed:

> I have compiled for my own benefit a note of all the big policy matters affecting the media that arose in my time as Prime Minister. That note also demonstrates in detail the strange coincidence of how News International and the then Conservative Opposition came to share almost exactly the same media policy. It was so close that it was often expressed in almost exactly the same words. On the future of the licence fee, on BBC online, on the right of the public to see free of charge the maximum possible number of national sporting events, on the future of the BBC's commercial arm, and on the integrity of Ofcom, we stood up for what we believed to be the public interest, but that was made difficult when the Opposition invariably reclassified the public interest as the News International interest. It is for the commission of inquiry to examine not just the promises of the then Opposition, but the many early decisions of this Government on these matters.[5]

Brown, it should be said, was being at least a tad disingenuous in suggesting that keeping Murdoch sweet had been a uniquely Tory preoccupation. In the same week he delivered this speech, David Cameron was reported to have met with Murdoch executives on 26 separate occasions during his first 15 months in office, but Brown, and his predecessor Blair, had hardly kept their distance. Lance Price, who worked as adviser to Tony Blair between 1997 and 2001, has written that Murdoch 'seemed like the 24th member' of the cabinet, adding 'His presence was always felt.'[6] And when the *Sun* told Brown that they knew his son Fraser had cystic fibrosis, he worked with the newspaper to ensure sensitive coverage. Nor did he mention in his speech reports that his wife, Sarah, had hosted a 'slumber party' at Chequers for Rebekah Brooks, Rupert Murdoch's wife Wendi and his daughter Elizabeth. But it is clear that seeking support from Murdoch's titles, or at least seeking to avoid attack, is different from actively promoting his commercial aims, especially with regard to the BBC, Ofcom and the proliferation of pay-per-view sporting events.

For a brief moment, it looked likely that the Leveson judicial public inquiry might blow the lid off the relationships described by Brown in a speech he knew would not be widely reported, and Brooks in text messages she never expected to be made public. It is important to remember, though, that Cameron only called the Leveson Inquiry after revelations about the hacking of Milly Dowler's phone finally propelled public outrage at his News International cronies to a level he could no longer ignore. Indeed, that gushing 'rooting for you tomorrow' text Brooks had sent to Cameron on the eve of his 2009 conference speech only emerged through the inquiry gaining access to all manner of private communications at the heart of Murdoch's empire. It is worth examining it, and Cameron's later explanation, in full:

But seriously I do understand the issue with the *Times*. Let's discuss over country supper soon. On the party it was because I had asked a number of NI [News International] people to Manchester post endorsement [the *Sun* had recently declared its support for Cameron] and they were disappointed not to see you. But as always Sam [Cameron's wife] was wonderful (and I thought it was OE's [Old Etonians] were charm personified!) I am so rooting for you tomorrow not just as a proud friend but because professionally we're definitely in this together! Speech of your life? Yes he Cam![7]

Under cross examination by Robert Jay QC, the leading counsel in the Leveson Inquiry, Cameron helpfully put this extraordinary message into context:

> The issue with *The Times* was that at the party conference I had not been to *The Times* party. The major newspaper groups tend to have big parties at the party conference and they expect party leaders, cabinet ministers, shadow cabinet ministers to go, um, and that would be the normal thing to do. The *Telegraph, The Times* and others would do this. I hadn't gone and I think, um, err, that was what this was about and I was, I was apologising for that and that explains her disappointment as it were.[8]

The day after Cameron's conference speech, the *Sun* carried a large front-page picture of him and the headline 'Cam can have a go 'cos we think he's hard enough'. Inside the newspaper, a leader column head-line 'Yes, he Cam' echoed Brooks's text precisely. Rather more seriously, less than six months after that excruciating cross-examination when Leveson published his report, it quickly became clear that, for all his flowery regret and acknowledgement of the need for change, Cameron would not be enacting the legislation to fulfil any of Leveson's recom-mendations. Worse, perhaps, the second part of the inquiry, focused on the relationships between journalists and the police, was originally postponed until criminal prosecutions regarding events at the *News of the World* had concluded. In 2017, however, the Conservative election manifesto pledged to drop the inquiry entirely. Six years after Rupert

Murdoch had himself appeared before MPs investigating phone-hacking and declared: 'This is the most humble day of my life,'[9] and five after the investigation concluded he was 'not a fit person to exercise the stewardship of a major international company',[10] the greatest ever threat to his stranglehold on UK politics and media had apparently been seen off.

By the middle of 2023, a plethora of cases alleging all manner of misdeeds were pending against not only Murdoch titles but also Paul Dacre's *Daily Mail* and the *Daily Mirror*, edited for some of the relevant period by Piers Morgan, a Murdoch protégé and former editor of the *News of the World*. It seemed possible that another, potentially even more damning chapter of the scandal was about to be written. A dizzying array of extremely high-profile individuals, including Prince Harry, Elton John, Hugh Grant and Baroness Doreen Lawrence seemed determined to have their day in court, but it is impossible to predict any outcomes with confidence – or without alerting libel lawyers. Let us turn instead to what constitutes the second biggest scandal – and quite possibly the second humblest day – of Murdoch's life.

This is not the place to delve further into the findings and failings of the Leveson Inquiry. At most, it represents a missed opportunity for enacting changes that may have prevented or diluted some of the damage detailed here. It is relevant now only in so far as it demonstrates the breathtaking extent of the collusion between political power and the media institutions that claim to hold political power to account. Historically, the democratic process has always depended upon the ability and determination of journalists to do things that governments do not want them to do, to reveal things that governments do not want revealed, and to provide populations with the knowledge they need to make informed electoral choices. Murdoch's malevolent genius lies in the early realisation that the same engines of influence could persuade people to vote not in their own interests but in pursuit of his.

Unlike other proprietors of the last hundred years, Murdoch's presenters and columnists do not lie, or incite hatred, or flirt with fascistic ideas because their boss is drawn to fascism. They do so because it is good for business. *His* business. There is even an ideology of sorts at the heart of this overweening thirst. In 2009 at the Edinburgh International Television Festival, Rupert Murdoch's son James, News Corporation's chairman and chief executive in Europe and Asia, gave the prestigious MacTaggart Lecture. Entitled, 'The Absence of Trust', he used it to launch blistering attacks on the BBC, the media industry regulator Ofcom, the European Union and the Labour government. It makes an interesting companion piece to Gordon Brown's later claims of Conservative policies and language coinciding completely with the stated aims of the Murdochs. He even articulated the future he would like to see: 'There is an inescapable conclusion that we must reach if we are to have a better society. The only reliable, durable and perpetual guarantor of independence is profit.' Eleven years later, he appeared to have had a change of heart about News Corporation's own decisions in its apparent pursuit of profit over truth. Murdoch *fils* resigned from the family business in July 2020 'due to disagreements over certain editorial content published by the Company's news outlets and certain other strategic decisions'. And while it has long been impossible to exaggerate the extent of his father's cancerous appetite for money and power, it had not previously been possible to prove it beyond all reasonable doubt.

In April 2023, a defamation lawsuit brought by Dominion Voting Systems against Murdoch's Fox News network was about to go to trial. At the eleventh hour, Fox settled the case for $787.5 million. Dominion's suit hinged upon the accusation that various presenters and contributors on the network (widely regarded as a key architect of Donald Trump's political success and packed with sycophantic supporters of the sex-abuser president) had knowingly aired fallacious 'election fraud' theories about Dominion's voting machines in the 2020 election. In other words, Dominion would have to prove that Fox News hosts, employees and confidants of Rupert Murdoch had deliberately and repeatedly lied to their viewers. As with Leveson in the UK, it led to the disclosure of reams of internal text messages and emails sent and received by correspondents unaware that their communications would ever be made public. And as with Leveson, the content highlighted blatant contempt for the notion of speaking truth to power. Those correspondents included key figures in the company, including star presenter Tucker Carlson and Rupert Murdoch himself.

In his deposition to the court, Murdoch told a Dominion lawyer that he had the power to keep election deniers off Fox News but chose not to. Asked why he continued to allow Mike Lindell – the CEO of a pillow company, major advertiser and one of the most prominent disseminators of election fraud lies – to make outlandish claims on Fox News, Murdoch explained that it was a financial not a political decision and agreed that 'it is not red or blue, it is green'.[11] This last is a reference to political allegiances – Republicans are red and Democrats blue – being completely subjugated to the colour, literally, of money.

What these documents and depositions revealed about people on the Murdoch payroll was, in many ways, even more damning. They provide an insight into the workings of a media empire diabolically dedicated to only advancing the interests of the emperor. When viewed in conjunction with what we know about how completely that empire has infiltrated the British political establishment, the scale of the damage done to democracy by one man's megalomania comes into focus. In the UK, America and his native Australia, everything from the weaponisation of climate-change denial to the promotion of vampiric 'free market' economics has long left observers wondering whether Murdoch and his acolytes actually *believe* what they peddle, or whether facts are entirely irrelevant to their output. With Leveson, the way in which Murdoch's people obtained information was disgusting and illegal but the resulting stories were, in the strictest sense, factually true. The details stolen from people's voicemails were actually real. Dominion, by contrast, demonstrated a deliberate detachment from reality by some of the most powerful and well-rewarded voices in the English-speaking world.

The scale of the moral corruption involved is almost incomprehensible but, as shown by Leveson, such is his power and influence that its disclosure seems unlikely to affect Murdoch's claw-like grip on the windpipe of our democracies. This is no grand conspiracy. At its simplest, if you work for him, or aspire to do so, then you simply cannot call out the corruption that hides in plain sight. There are brilliant journalists working for Murdoch, undoubtedly some of the finest in the world, and there are grubby opportunists like Piers Morgan and, until the Dominion settlement, Tucker Carlson. The tragedy is that the former are compelled to stay as silent as the latter, and consequently the utterly abnormal appears completely normal.

The Dominion disclosures, as with Leveson's, will not detain us unduly here. They certainly did not create the ecosystem in which the moral corruption of Boris Johnson or the serial incompetence of Liz Truss could be ushered into power. Rather, they illustrate the nature of the beast that *all* aspiring British prime ministers of the last 50 years, including Tony Blair and Gordon Brown, have felt obliged to woo and indulge. In many ways, the cooperation and even the collusion are not as concerning as the nature of what is being wooed. And while there is plenty of evidence in Britain, as we shall shortly see, it is worth taking a quick look at one way in which the Dominion case laid bare the utter disregard for truth deployed by key Murdoch personnel in the US. Astonishingly, the biggest star on the network that amplified Trump's lies and groomed his supporters with endless xenophobia and immigration scaremongering was someone who actually couldn't stand the man and fully appreciated the awfulness of his presidency. Still, it was good for business.

On 18 February 2017, Donald Trump delivered a speech in which he cited Sweden's purported problems with immigrant-related violence as a justification for his continuing demonisation of immigrants. 'You look at what's happening last night in Sweden,' he said. 'Sweden. Who would believe this? Sweden. They took in large numbers. They're having problems like they never thought possible.' There was just one problem with this race baiting. There had been no 'incident' in Sweden the previous night. *The Local*, an English-language Swedish news website, went as far as to state: 'Nothing spectacular happened in Sweden on Friday.' Reuters reported that Swedes were using the Twitter hashtag #LastNightInSweden to post 'pictures of reindeer, Swedish meatballs and people assembling the country's famous IKEA furniture'.[12] The former Swedish prime minister Carl Bildt wrote on Twitter: 'Sweden? Terror attack? What has he been smoking? Questions abound.' Trump tried to answer those questions the following day when he tweeted: 'My statement as to what's happening in Sweden was in reference to a story that was broadcast on @FoxNews regarding immigrants and Sweden.' Tucker Carlson, whose show Trump had been watching, gave an interview to his own network in which he acknowledged the non-existence of any actual 'incident' but insisted nonetheless that Trump was right to draw attention to problems being caused by immigrants in Sweden, even though Reuters had reported that official statistics showed the crime rate had *fallen* since 2005 as the country took in hundreds of thousands of refugees from war-torn countries such as Syria and Iraq.[13]

Disingenuous doesn't cover it. And this is just one example of the sinister fact-free symbiosis that developed between Trump, Fox News and Carlson in particular. All the more remarkable, then, to discover what Carlson really thought about the man he had arguably done more than anyone to catapult into the White House. 'What he's good at is destroying things,' Carlson texted his producer, Alex Pfeiffer, on 5 November 2020. 'He's the undisputed world champion of that. He could easily destroy us if we play it wrong.'[14] On 4 January 2021, two days before Trump's call to action saw a mob of his supporters attack the US Capitol, Carlson texted Pfeiffer, 'I hate him passionately,' adding on the subject of Trump's presidency, 'We're all pretending we've got a lot to show for it, because admitting what a disaster it's been is too tough to digest. But come on. There really isn't an upside to Trump.'[15]

When Fox unexpectedly dispensed with Carlson's services shortly after the Dominion settlement, a *Daily Telegraph* columnist in the UK, Tim Stanley, opined that it was not the suspicion of racism, the blatant lies or the revelations about the contempt in which he held his own audience that prompted British 'liberals' to 'hate' Tucker Carlson. It was, instead, his 'polish'.[16] As Stanley unintentionally illustrates, the idea that people may be genuinely disgusted by disgusting conduct is something that the right-wing British media has become increasingly keen to rubbish in recent years. The veteran American newscaster Dan Rather captured the fraudulent essence of this early in Ronald Reagan's presidency when he described attempts to 'convince the public that problems are not problems [but] that the people who call attention to them are problems'.[17] A journalist at Andrew Neil's *Spectator* magazine, James Bartholomew, claims to have coined the phrase 'virtue-signalling' in 2015.[18] It quickly became a pithy way for columnists and commentators to denigrate any acts of altruism, particularly when they are undertaken by members of the 'liberal elite'.

The wider process of demeaning decency serves a much darker purpose too. Calling into question the authenticity and integrity of people at least trying to do the right thing conflates them with people who are clearly and categorically doing wrong. It is why the increasingly popular phrase to describe politicians, 'They're all as bad as each other', is so uniquely depressing. It is a large part of the reason why 'false equivalence', where a guest with extensive knowledge and experience is pitted against an equal and opposite guest with none, has wheedled its way into corners of national discourse that were once respectful of expertise and evidence. And it is why Murdoch and *Daily Mail* 'journalism' routinely spawns social media barbecues of any vaguely prominent critic of that 'criminal-media nexus' who demonstrates fallibility.

The fact that many modern readers will see this symbiosis between political and media power as unremarkable is a mark of how pervasive it is and how successful it has been. It is all a very far cry from 1840 when, in a lecture entitled 'On Heroes and Hero Worship', the philosopher Thomas Carlyle cited a godfather of modern conservatism, Edmund Burke: 'Burke said there were Three Estates in Parliament; but, in the Reporters' Gallery yonder, there sat a Fourth Estate more important far than they all.' The importance of a 'fourth estate' of journalism that scrutinises and challenges the other three (in this context the nobility in the House of Lords, the Bishops in the House of Lords, and the House of Commons) is obvious. That it no longer describes much of the British and American media is a consequence, in large part, of Rupert Murdoch's rejection of these traditional expectations in the early 1980s. He explained it himself to a biographer, Thomas Kiernan, in the 1986 book *Citizen Murdoch*, stating: 'The press is sitting around here doing its usual thing, sneering at Reagan and waiting to pounce on him the moment he stumbles ... The whole Reagan package needs much more support by the press.' It signals the abandonment of any pretence at journalistic objectivity and the active demonisation of dissenting, even arguably accurate, voices in the news media. It is here that the echoes of what would happen in Britain 30 years later are loudest.

On 28 June 1984, Murdoch joined Ben Bradlee, the legendary executive editor of the *Washington Post* when Woodward and Bernstein broke the Watergate scandal, on a panel convened by the American Enterprise Institute to ask 'Is There a Political Elite in America?' In his excellent and exhaustively researched 2012 book, *Murdoch's Politics*, David McKnight describes their contributions as a 'dialogue of the deaf' but, whether Bradlee heard them or not, Murdoch said at least two fascinating things. One predictable; one, almost poignantly, anything but. First, presaging the dismal media-fuelled populism that would usher in Brexit, Trump and Boris Johnson, he accused the press of ignoring 'the traditional values of the great masses of this country' and of 'attempting to change the political agenda'. Second, and almost unbelievably from the perspective of 2023, he said: 'The press should be anti-establishment, should keep its distance from authority ... from big business and all vested interests. It's only natural that it should be questioning and sceptical. That leads to being understood very often as having a liberal position when [it really represents] nothing more than a skill.'

I am yet to come across a finer argument in defence of the often vague accusations of a 'liberal bias' in the media. It is poignant because it reminds us that Murdoch was once, in his heart of hearts, a journalist. Born into the business, there is no way he could have achieved such international domination without a deep understanding of and affection for the trade. Consider, though, the gulf between a professed determination to keep 'distance from authority' and the evident cosiness on display between David Cameron, Andy Coulson and Rebekah Brooks in 2009. It is as if two competing and contradictory components of his character, both on full display here, are vying for supremacy: the journalist and the plutocrat.

I am not sure the battle ever ended. It is this dichotomy, coupled with his epic ambition, that explains the unique nature of his increasingly blurred news and opinion empire. It is one of the reasons why he continues to inspire great personal loyalty, even among former employees who may balk at the activities of some of their erstwhile colleagues. I think it also explains how he can simultaneously publish some of the sewerage we shall examine shortly *and* genuinely superb journalism, such as the work of Gabriel Pogrund and Harry Yorke at the *Sunday Times* referred to in the introduction. Did he found Fox News, for example, because he truly believed that the media was dominated by a 'left-wing' elite, a notion that McKnight points out had been 'a distinctive theme of the Right under Nixon'? Or was it simply because he saw an opportunity to secure a ton of money and influence? Or both? David Yelland, the founder of communications company KTP, was editor of the *Sun* from 1998 to 2003 and deputy editor of Murdoch's

New York Post from 1996 to 1998. His perspective on his former boss, his empire and this dissonance between journalist and plutocrat is uniquely insightful and has not been publicly shared before.

'I first got to know Rupert Murdoch in New York in the years before I became editor of the *Sun* in 1998,' he told me. 'I was then business editor and later deputy editor of his *New York Post*, at that time the only US daily that he operated, in a liberal city and in a liberal era with Bill Clinton as president and the then quite benign Rudolph Giuliani as mayor. The Rupert I knew was not the Rupert I see written about. He was great company, utterly inspiring and he suddenly took a huge interest in me. He would stop and talk with me for long periods. He was interested in my story and why I had worn a wig through all my teenage years [David had childhood alopecia] right up to age 31 when I went topless. He said "that took guts".

'He seemed to understand me and I was of course very excited to have his confidence. He was super-smart, he listened, he had liberal social values, he gave the staff time. He was in the early stages of his courtship with Wendi [Deng] and he was very happy. Most of all he was incredibly interested in Tony Blair and Gordon Brown and how they might change the UK following the 1997 election. He was a wonderful boss and very kind to me when my wife, Tania, was diagnosed with breast cancer during her pregnancy with our son Max. Basically he picked me and backed me. He was a wonderful boss and this is something I must always remember and credit him for.

'Fox News was set up when I was working in the building (1211 Ave of Americas, NYC). Roger Ailes used to come up for drinks at the end of the day. We knew him very well. We all thought he was quite mad and would never succeed. How wrong we were. It was Roger who changed Rupert. Fox News became and remains the most profitable news channel in the world and Roger became an untouchable for a long while. He was the person that showed millions could be made from right-wing media, up until then the major US broadcasters and print press were largely liberal. This turning point made the liberal editors in London under their boss Les Hinton look very pink ...

'I think Rupert is very different person than many realise. He is not a "hirer and firer", he is actually incredibly loyal to his people. Even if senior editors are moved aside they are often offered other roles should they choose to stay. People ask me even now why did KRM [Keith Rupert Murdoch] stay so loyal to Rebekah Brooks. The answer is that this is how he is. He values and applauds people who take "shit" for him and she took a great deal of that, whatever you may think of her. He also values courage and the ability to be able to put up with intense pressure.

'So it is actually his loyalty to his people that cost him in some cases. Some on the News Corporation or Fox boards would have fired Roger and Rebekah years earlier, but he simply would not budge. This "esprit de corps" or buccaneering spirit is imbued in the News Corp culture. It really is "us against the world" and this allows the company to take immense risks and move very quickly. It means there are very rarely leaks from within. But I think it is this culture, with its lack of countervailing power such as independent non-executive directors or a chairman – a lack of really robust advisers, a lack of outside counsel – that resulted in the company drifting toward the far right first under Roger and then during Trump's era. Too few internal people spoke out. And there are good people there. Note how James Murdoch spoke out as he left. A very significant moment.

'I look at the company now and see how it conspired to allow untruths to be told to the British people around Brexit and how it helped create that great national disaster and did the same with Trump and around some aspects of Covid and even worse on climate change. At some point the company began to side with the dark side and not the angels and this is a great tragedy for readers and consumers of the news channels and newspapers. How did it happen? Slowly at first and then quickly. It became apparent that the digital revolution could be fought off if you were prepared to exploit that new world by allowing extreme journalism. This is because only extremes thrive in the digital world. Or at least, that has been the case so far ...'

We can now see the three ways Murdoch contributed to creating an ecosystem in which a country like the United Kingdom could be broken on the wheel of corruption and incompetence. First, and most unprecedented, the complete erasure of the line between media and government: the revolving door of personnel moving merrily from newspaper cheerleader *for* a government to prominent roles *in* those governments. And then back again. If the most powerful media interests in the land see themselves as actively working in cooperation with a government towards shared ends then, even if other parts of the empire occasionally do some proper journalism, the public interest is strangled. On 25 February 2016, for example, the City editor of the London *Evening Standard*, Anthony Hilton, wrote: 'I once asked Rupert Murdoch why he was so opposed to the European Union. "That's easy," he replied. "When I go into Downing Street they do what I say; when I go to Brussels they take no notice."' Hilton stood by his story when, desperate for government approval of a deal allowing his 21st Century Fox network to buy the 61 per cent of Sky he did not already own, Murdoch took the unusual step of writing to the *Guardian* in December of the same year to deny that the exchange had ever taken place.[19] Who knows who to believe?

Second, the deliberate denigration of dissenting voices – whether as members of that largely mythical 'liberal elite' or as agents of 'political correctness' and latterly 'wokeness'. When combined with what Dan Rather identified as the determination to cast the people pointing out the problems as the real problems, it heralds an open season on anyone deemed to be difficult. This last is the trickiest to realise, and it has been achieved by allowing a relatively small number of editors, columnists and commentators to disseminate such vicious and undiluted hatred into public discourse that we are no longer shocked by it. On 16 December 2022, *Sun* columnist Jeremy Clarkson wrote of loathing Meghan Markle 'on a cellular level' and 'grinding my teeth and dreaming of the day when she is made to parade naked through the streets of every town in Britain while the crowds chant "Shame!" and throw lumps of excrement at her'. On 15 February 2020, the TV presenter Caroline Flack took her own life days before she was due to face trial for assaulting her boyfriend. The *Sun* had somehow obtained pictures of her bloodied bedroom, a potential crime scene (more potential Leveson 2 territory), following the alleged assault. Her friend and fellow broadcaster Laura Whitmore had little doubt about where at least some of the responsibility for Caroline's anguish lay, using her weekly BBC Radio 5 Live show to state: 'To the press, the newspapers, who create clickbait, who demonise and tear down success, we've had enough. I've seen journalists and Twitter warriors talk of this tragedy and they themselves twisted what the truth is … Your words affect people. To paparazzi and tabloids looking for a cheap sell, to trolls hiding behind a keyboard, enough.'[20]

Four days after Clarkson's Meghan Markle piece appeared, Caroline's mother Christine called Shelagh Fogarty's show on LBC to express her shock that it had been published at all. She went on to compare this article to press coverage received by her daughter, whose death had prompted widespread but ultimately fruitless calls for an end to the misogynistic language routinely directed at women and girls by prominent media figures. 'My daughter was Caroline Flack, and what was printed in the papers, so much of it was untrue,' a clearly emotional Christine said. 'Why write something so bad? We thought when Carry [Caroline] died this thing about being kind, it isn't a joke, it is a real thing. I can see even though Meghan and Harry have got all that money … even they said, if they can't win, how can anyone else win? Someone like Jeremy Clarkson can just say what he wants, but it gets printed, that's the worst thing!'[21]

The previous March, Piers Morgan had been forced to resign from a lucrative slot on breakfast television after refusing to apologise for publicly pouring scorn on Meghan's account of her own suicidal ideation. There is, of course, only one way to prove that somebody accusing you of lying about suicidal thoughts is wrong but Morgan seemed not to care. Neither had this self-appointed interrogator of Meghan Markle's integrity previously demonstrated much concern about his 'old friend' Donald Trump's obvious contempt for the truth, common decency or any woman's right not to be grabbed 'by the pussy'. His departure from *Good Morning Britain* was a rare example of a right-wing media darling facing genuine professional consequences for an egregious breach of the standards by which the rest of society is expected to abide. At least at work. Clarkson retained his various positions in the Murdoch empire after an unconvincing apology but Morgan, whose obsession with the Duchess of Sussex often seems psychotic, refused to do even that. No matter. He was soon back on the Murdoch payroll at the *Sun* and back on screen at Murdoch's TalkTV, albeit with audience figures that often failed to trouble the scorers. As Christine Flack so powerfully illustrated, people like Clarkson, Morgan and, as we shall see, a surprisingly small coterie of other columnists across Murdoch titles, the *Telegraph*, *Mail* and Andrew Neil's *Spectator*, have commoditised cruelty in a way that now appears completely normal to the British public. It is a form of psychological grooming that demeans us all and, again, it is now almost impossible to achieve any success in the British media without being at least somewhat complicit in the practice.

The third and final element of Murdoch's capture of a country's soul is the willingness not just to mould facts to the agendas shared with governments but to abandon facts altogether in pursuit of them. There are countless examples, but this one is particularly pertinent to our purpose here. Bizarrely, given that there are no majority Muslim countries in the European Union, carefully cultivated Islamophobia played a crucial role in the Brexit referendum. Many of the protagonists in this book, including Boris Johnson, Andrew Neil's *Spectator* and Dominic Cummings, contributed to this ugly phenomenon, but none did so as brazenly as Rupert Murdoch's *Sun*. On 13 November 2015, 130 people died in Islamist terrorist attacks in Paris. Ten days later, the *Sun* published the front-page headline '1 in 5 Brit Muslims' sympathy for jihadis'. Accompanied by an image of British ISIS member, Mohammed Emwazi, known as 'Jihadi John', the story purported to report the findings of a survey of British Muslims commissioned by the *Sun* immediately after the Paris attacks. The intention was clear. Inside the paper, one columnist wrote under the headline: 'This shocking poll means we must shut door on young Muslim migrants.' The *Sun*'s 'respectable' stablemate, *The Times*, followed up the story the following day but, 12 days after that, a paragraph appeared in their 'corrections and clarifications' on page 36, admitting that their headline 'One in five British Muslims has sympathy for Isis' was 'misleading'. This was hardly surprising. The day after the *Sun*'s front page appeared the company responsible for the poll issued the following statement:

> Survation do not support or endorse the way in which this poll's findings have been interpreted. Neither the headline nor the body text of articles published were discussed with or approved by Survation prior to publication ... Furthermore, Survation categorically objects to the use of any of our findings by any group, as has happened elsewhere on social networks, to incite racial or religious tensions.[22]

Inciting racial or religious tensions has, of course, been the stock-in-trade of right-wing newspapers for years.

It was four months later, in March of the following year, before the *Sun* admitted its story had been 'significantly misleading'. A four-month delay, even though the 3,000 complaints received by the press watchdog, the Independent Press Standards Organisation (IPSO), dwarfed the 400 received after another *Sun* columnist, Katie Hopkins, described migrants as 'cockroaches' in an article the previous April.[23] An IPSO spokesman said:

> The newspaper had provided various interpretations of the poll result which conflated important distinctions between those travelling to Syria and those already fighting in Syria; between 'sympathy' for these individuals and 'support' for their actions; and between individuals attracted by the ideology of Isis, and the ideology of Isis itself. The Complaints Committee deemed that the newspaper had failed to take appropriate care in its presentation

of the poll results, and as a result the coverage was significantly misleading in breach of Clause 1 (Accuracy).[24]

The *Sun* was required by IPSO to publish its adjudication on page two of the paper.

Nobody knows who first coined the phrase 'A lie is halfway round the world before the truth has got its boots on.' Inevitably, Winston Churchill, Mark Twain and Oscar Wilde have all been erroneously credited with it. But there can be little doubt about how true it remains or about how completely that truth is understood by Rupert Murdoch's editors and columnists. And it is to two very different Murdoch editors we turn now for, first, an example of just how low they are prepared to go and, second, an explanation of the single, long-denied moment in British history that allowed it all to happen.

. . .

The Hillsborough Disaster may feel a long time ago, but its legacy continues to reverberate – not only for the friends and families of those directly affected, but for what it demonstrates about the insidious power of the media and its close links to government power. On 15 April 1989, Liverpool and Nottingham Forest football clubs met to contest an FA Cup semi-final on the neutral ground of Hillsborough Stadium in Sheffield, South Yorkshire. There followed a human tragedy of almost unimaginable proportions, ultimately leaving 97 people dead and 766 injured. It is important to bear in mind throughout what follows that Leveson 2, abandoned by the Conservatives in 2017, was going to investigate clandestine relationships and inappropriate connections between the police and journalists. And it is important to remember that we are concerned here not with rehearsing all the facts of the tragedy itself but with chronicling the slow decline of British journalism that began when Murdoch bought the *News of the World* in 1968 and the *Sun* in 1969. It has certainly never fallen faster or further than it did four days after the disaster when the editor of the *Sun*, Kelvin MacKenzie, embarked upon a course of personal depravity and professional delinquency that would continue to cause pain and anguish to bereaved Hillsborough families for decades to come.

After multiple inquiries and investigations and one of the most tireless pursuits of justice in British history, we now know that the disaster occurred because the police superintendent in charge of the game, David Duckenfield, ordered an exit gate to be opened in the hope of easing overcrowding at the entry turnstiles. The ensuing rush into the Leppings Lane stand caused the overcrowding and subsequent crushing that would take so many lives. It was *almost 26 years* before Duckenfield finally admitted that his claim on the day that 'a gate had been forced and there had been an inrush of Liverpool supporters that had caused casualties', had been a lie.

It is impossible to imagine this lie remaining at the heart of the 'official' version of events for decades without the strenuous support of Murdoch's newspaper and Establishment figures including Margaret Thatcher's press secretary, Bernard Ingham. Ingham, who visited the stadium with Thatcher the day after the tragedy, would become one of the most vociferous defenders of the entirely bogus and deeply offensive account of events propagated by police and, as we shall see, Kelvin MacKenzie. In 1996, Ingham even wrote to a Liverpool fan, Graham Skinner, who had tried to draw his attention to *Hillsborough*, a television drama written by Jimmy McGovern that saw the story told for the first time from the perspective of Hillsborough families. The letter is reproduced in full here because it provides a truly grim illustration of just how much harm can be done to a democracy when political, police and media interests work in conjunction to deny the public access to the truth. In this case, the parties were South Yorkshire Police, prominent Tories like Ingham and the local MP Irvine Patnick (later knighted), and 'sympathetic' journalists. It creates an environment in which all three institutions believe, with considerable justification, that they can do whatever they please without censure from the only powerful potential critics of their conduct – each other. Precisely the problem that Leveson 2 was supposed to interrogate.

Thank you for your letter of December 11. I believe that there would have been no Hillsborough disaster if tanked-up yobs had not turned up in very large numbers to try to force their way into the ground.

I visited Hillsborough the day after the disaster and I know what I learned then. I have never denied that the police may have made mistakes, but I firmly believe that the Lord Chief Justice whitewashed the real culprits and I said so from the moment I read his report.

I have not seen the McGovern film. But I am long enough in the tooth to know that TV films should never be accepted as evidence. But let us suppose there is something in the film – for example, the 'evidence' that the pens were already full when the gates were opened. What, then were all those people doing trying to get into the ground? I have never, of course, said where they came from because I do not know.

I have no intention of apologising for my views which are sincerely held on the basis of what I heard first hand at Hillsborough. I have, however, one suggestion to make: for its own good, Liverpool – with the Heysel disaster in the background – should shut up about Hillsborough.

Nothing can now bring back those who died – innocent people who, by virtue of being in the ground early, had their lives crushed out of them by a mob surging in late.

To go on about it serves only to confirm in many people's minds that Liverpool has a very bad conscience about soccer disasters. I think it a disgrace to the public service that South Yorkshire policemen have won the right to compensation. But it will do Liverpool no good whatsoever in the eyes of the nation if, egged on by ambulance-chasing lawyers, those who saw their relatives killed at Hillsborough now sue for compensation for the 'trauma'. Is the pain of losing a relative to be soothed away by a fat cheque?

Take my advice, Mr Skinner: least said, soonest mended for Liverpool.[25]

On 12 September 2012, the Hillsborough Independent Panel stated definitively that Liverpool fans had been in no way responsible for the disaster, laying the blame instead at the feet of South Yorkshire Police. The panel also found that 164 witness statements had been tampered with, mostly to remove or alter negative comments about South Yorkshire Police. On 26 April 2016, 27 years after the disaster, an inquest jury ruled that the 96 victims had been unlawfully killed (Andrew Devine became the 97th victim in 2021 when he died from irreversible brain damage suffered on the day) and that the fans had not contributed to the tragic events. Incredibly, Ingham, who was knighted by Margaret Thatcher and died in 2023 without expressing a single word of apology or contrition for his role in disseminating the Hillsborough lies, was not the worst offender in this grim saga.

On 19 April 1989, under the front-page headline 'THE TRUTH', Kelvin MacKenzie published a list of falsehoods so eye-wateringly offensive that even three and a half decades later it is hard to believe they ever saw the light of day. We know from the later testimony of the journalist who wrote the original story, Harry Arnold, that MacKenzie was personally responsible for the composition of the front page, which stated unequivocally that 'Some fans picked pockets of victims'; 'Some fans urinated on the brave cops' and 'Some fans beat up PC giving kiss of life'. And we know that MacKenzie arrogantly resisted all pleas to moderate his outrageous copy because Arnold gave an interview to the BBC programme, *Hillsborough: Searching for the Truth*, in 2012, in which he stated that his original story had been 'fair and balanced' and that it made clear that the claims MacKenzie described as 'THE TRUTH' had been 'allegations'.

He explained: 'On the *Sun*, Kelvin MacKenzie was the rather controversial editor at the time. He liked to write his own headlines. He wrote the headline "The Truth", and the reason I know that is I was about to leave the newsroom when I saw him drawing up the front page. When I saw the headline "The Truth" I was aghast, because that wasn't what I'd written. I'd never used the words the truth, "this is the truth about the Hillsborough Disaster" – I'd merely written, I hoped and I still believe, in a balanced and fair way. So I said to Kelvin MacKenzie, "You can't say that." And he said, "Why not?" and I said, "Because we don't know that it's the truth. This is a version of "the truth".' And he brushed it aside and said, "Oh don't worry. I'm going to make it clear that this is what some people are saying." And I walked away thinking, well I'm not happy with the situation. But the fact is reporters don't argue with an editor. And in particular, you don't argue with an editor like Kelvin MacKenzie.'

A year after the disaster, Peter Chippindale and Chris Horrie published their seminal account of the *Sun*'s first 20 years under

Murdoch's ownership, *Stick It Up Your Punter!* In it, they wrote of that infamous front page:

> As MacKenzie's layout was seen by more and more people, a collective shudder ran through the office [but] MacKenzie's dominance was so total there was nobody left in the organisation who could rein him in except Murdoch. [Everyone in the office] seemed paralysed – 'looking like rabbits in the headlights' – as one hack described them. The error staring them in the face was too glaring. It obviously wasn't a silly mistake; nor was it a simple oversight. Nobody really had any comment on it – they just took one look and went away shaking their heads in wonder at the enormity of it. It was a 'classic smear'.

The grossness, evident even to MacKenzie's traditionally unshockable colleagues, was good for business and for years Murdoch's man revelled in the notoriety. There was a pathetic attempt at apology in 2012 when the Hillsborough Independent Panel's report was published, but four years later his continuing contempt for the bereaved families crept into a column he wrote for the *Sun*. Mulling the prospect of a peerage, laughable then but perfectly plausible now that Boris Johnson has so completely debased the honours system, he wrote: 'Lord Kelv of Anfield has a ring to it.'[26] Anfield is, of course, the home of Liverpool Football Club.

Much more remarkable than the characteristic obnoxiousness this displays is the platform on which it was published. For such is Murdoch's patronage of his most favoured puppets, MacKenzie was back on the paper with a column in 2016 and remained there *after* his utter disregard for the truth in his Hillsborough coverage had become public knowledge. Indeed, it was MacKenzie who wrote that Islamophobic column based on the wilfully spurious reading of the Survation poll.

On 14 April 2017, he wrote a column comparing Ross Barkley, the mixed-race Everton footballer, to a gorilla and once again disparaging the people of Liverpool. He was immediately suspended and, shortly afterwards, left the paper for the final time.

It seems almost ironic that racism had become a sackable offence in Murdoch's empire by 2017. In *Stick It Up Your Punter!*, Chippindale and Horrie quote MacKenzie's own description of exactly how he saw his role and his readers in the early 1980s: 'You just don't understand the readers, do you, eh? He's the bloke you see in the pub, a right old fascist, wants to send the wogs back, buy his poxy council house, he's afraid of the unions, afraid of the Russians, hates the queers and the weirdos and drug dealers.'

Despite, or perhaps because of, wearing his bigotries so blatantly on his sleeve, MacKenzie was hired by Paul Dacre to write a column for the *Daily Mail* in 2011. He lasted a year. In 2013, he was signed up by the online edition of the *Daily Telegraph*. He lasted for one column. When it comes to stoking hatred of ethnic minorities and gay people there is, as this career trajectory shows, little distinction between the *Sun* of the 1980s and ostensibly more 'respectable' organs in the twenty-first century. Just as Charles Moore's racist comments about 'young black men' in 1992 proved no obstacle to him becoming editor of the *Sunday Telegraph* and later *Daily Telegraph*, so MacKenzie's long history of performative obnoxiousness barely impinged on his employability.

In his later years he was mostly to be found running unsuccessfully for his local council on a promise to reduce car-parking charges and spewing bile on Twitter and cable television to a negligible number of followers and viewers. But his life's work remains a testament to what can happen in a once proud industry when someone devoid of morality, integrity and honesty is given free rein by an indulgent billionaire newspaper owner.

The late Sir Harold 'Harry' Evans was, to say the least, a rather different beast. He had been editor of the *Sunday Times* for 14 years when Murdoch bought the title in 1981. Bruised no doubt by his departure from the post a year later, Evans, a critic of Margaret Thatcher's ailing premiership, later maintained that Murdoch immediately moved him to the editorship of the daily *Times* in order to weaken his position and make it easier to show him the door soon after.

When archived papers were released by the Margaret Thatcher Trust in 2012, Evans, who had led a failed staff takeover of the *Sunday Times*, saw a 30-year-old suspicion spectacularly vindicated. Despite denials both from Downing Street at the time and later in *The Official History of The Times: The Murdoch Years*, published in 2005, Murdoch *had* met with Margaret Thatcher in 1981 to discuss his desire to add *The Times* and the *Sunday Times* to the *Sun* and the *News of the World* in a deal that would give him control over just shy of 40 per cent of the UK's print media. A note by Bernard Ingham refers to a lunch with Mr Murdoch at Chequers on 4 January 1981, 'to be treated Commercial – In Confidence'.[27] It contains details of Murdoch's plans to buy *The Times* titles from the Thomson family and shows that the meeting was held at Murdoch's request. Despite sending a thank-you note two weeks later, Murdoch claimed to have no recollection of the meeting in his evidence to Leveson in 2012. Something to which Lord Justice Leveson referred pointedly in his final report:

That there was a confidential meeting between the then prime minister and Mr Murdoch, the fact of which did not emerge into the public domain for more than 30 years, is troubling in its lack of transparency. It serves as a reminder of the importance of contemporary practice to make public the fact of such meetings. The perceptions at the time and since of collusive arrangements between the prime minister and the preferred bidder are corrosive of public confidence …

It is perhaps a little surprising that he does not remember a visit to a place as memorable as Chequers, in the context of a bid as important as that which he made for Times Newspapers. However, perhaps that is all I need to say.

At issue at the time was the question of whether Murdoch's mooted purchase would be referred to the Monopolies and Mergers Commission (MMC). It was, to say the least, a delicate matter. The Fair Trading Act 1973 required all newspaper takeovers to be submitted to the MMC unless the secretary of state for trade certified a paper was unprofitable and under threat of closure. Evans insisted to the last that the *Sunday Times* was in a much healthier financial position than its daily stablemate and so should be subject to MMC referral. Murdoch was seemingly less keen on the prospect. Either way, immediately after returning to Downing Street from Chequers, Thatcher summoned her trade secretary, the famously robust John Nott, and told him he was being moved to defence. The rather less robust John Biffen was immediately installed at trade and elected not to refer the deal to the MMC.

Evans, who died in 2020, always insisted that the *Sunday Times* books had been cooked and that Biffen consequently misled the

House of Commons. Biffen, who died in 2007, later wrote in his auto-biography that 'The *Times* deal relied on both the *Times* and *Sunday Times* being loss-making. There was no doubt about the former but the *Sunday Times* was a close-run thing.'[28] On 27 January 1981, barely three weeks after the Chequers meeting that Murdoch presumably still can't recall, his takeover of *The Times* and the *Sunday Times* was approved by the House of Commons. Margaret Thatcher, who would enjoy the full-throated support of Murdoch's titles for the duration of her premiership, imposed a three-line whip on her MPs.

In 2015, Harry Evans updated the preface to his 1983 memoir, *Good Times, Bad Times*, to accommodate subsequent events. Perhaps with Andy Coulson and Kelvin MacKenzie in mind, he wrote:

> All the wretches in the subsequent hacking sagas – the predators in the red-tops, the scavengers and sleaze merchants, the blackmailers and bribers, the liars, the bullies, the cowed politicians and the bent coppers – were but the detritus of a collapse of integrity in British journalism and political life. At the root of the cruelties and extortions exposed in the recent criminal trials at the Old Bailey, was Margaret Thatcher's reckless engorgement of the media power of her guest that January Sunday. The simple genesis of the hacking outrages is that Murdoch's News International came to think it was above the law, because it was.

Any contemplation of Rupert Murdoch's decades-long dominance of British and American media, his capture of governments and his deliberate demolition of journalistic values leaves one burning question: why did he never emulate the corrosive but considerable success of Fox News in the United Kingdom? The answer is sadly simple: on

this side of the Atlantic, the lucrative business of taking the commoditisation of hate, the othering of minorities, the demonisation of racial
or religious difference and the denigration of dissent to a whole new
level had already been almost completely sewn up. By Paul Dacre and
the Viscounts Rothermere's *Daily Mail*.

Chapter 2
PAUL DACRE

Dacre's paper is like the drunken lout at a party who can't get anyone to like him. Suddenly all the girls are sluts and all the men are poofs and he's swinging at the chandelier before being huckled outside to vomit on the lawn.

Andrew O'Hagan, *London Review of Books*, 1 June 2017

ON 4 NOVEMBER 2018, Paul Dacre delivered the keynote speech to the Society of Editors (SoE) Annual Conference. Unchallenged and valedictory, it was the perfect platform for a rare public foray from a man who is terrified of scrutiny and considers accountability to be a dirty word, at least for himself. Having recently glided upstairs to the chairmanship after 26 years as editor of the *Daily Mail*, the tone of self-congratulation in his speech was probably to be expected. Dacre's personal decades-long desperation to see the United Kingdom heading out of the European Union had been recently realised. Theresa May, his preferred successor to the despised David Cameron, was safely installed in Downing Street and Jeremy Corbyn's Labour Party was in a state of such epic disarray that Dacre anticipated her staying there for the foreseeable future.

'In Westminster,' claimed the self-appointed sage of Fleet Street, 'the Echo Chamber has decided that Brexit is doomed and that the terminally incompetent Theresa May is toast, which is why the last rites are gleefully read over her every other day. Earlier this month, she was pronounced so dead that I'm surprised she was able to get up in the morning. She is, of course, still here and will, I predict, take the Tories into the next election.'[1]

May, of course, hung on to the crumbling vestiges of power for just nine months more and would never lead the Tories into another general election. She was undone, inevitably, both by the impossibility of delivering a Brexit both feasible and desirable, and also by the willingness of Boris Johnson to betray anyone and lie to both party and country about what was achievable. The accuracy of Dacre's smug prediction here is of a piece with the entire speech. A masterclass in paranoia, delusion and imagined persecution, it provides an insight into the strange, unpleasant mindset that drives the unprecedented damage that he, through his newspaper, has visited upon us all. Like MacKenzie but unlike Murdoch, Dacre *was* his readership, at least as frightened by progress and by history and by foreigners and working mothers and sexual liberation as he exhorted his readers to be. Also unlike Murdoch, he was always at enormous, endless pains to prove that his worldview was the only one worthy of respect.

The level of subconscious self-doubt that presumably lies behind such an aggressive desire to decry any opposition to his views must be off the scale. But at the heart of his mission lay not just the denigration of dissenting voices but the destruction of disagreement itself. For while Murdoch seeks to bend power to his will and revels in the respectability that his more 'broadsheet' writers deliver (he secreted himself in the room when Michael Gove interviewed the newly elected President Trump for *The Times* in January 2017, although it was not mentioned in the article), Dacre always seemed dedicated to torching anything that might highlight his own ignorance, insecurities and bigotries. Arguably, he used his newspaper to hide from himself so successfully that he ended up gaslighting a country. In his splendid 2017 unauthorised history of the *Daily Mail*, *Mail Men*, Adrian Addison quotes 'Duncan', one of the many journalists eager to pour scorn on their former boss: 'I felt Dacre just saw life – the world – as an awful, threatening place where he wanted to be in his bunker. Firing salvos out, you know – blowing up his enemies. That bunker mentality.' It is as if in addition to his own cosseted existence, he needed to create a public sphere in which he did not feel ridiculous, inadequate and frightened. He needed to turn Britain into a bunker. And in many ways, he succeeded.

Accordingly, nothing was off limits or safe from his vitriol: the independence of the judiciary; academic freedom; even parliamentary democracy itself would come under extraordinary fire. All while claiming that he somehow upheld British or Christian 'values' despite championing serial 'sinners' and routinely trashing the institutions and traditions that would once have provided vital checks and balances for the United Kingdom. Latterly, some of this mission can be explained by base avarice. In November 2021, he returned to the *Mail* as editor-in-chief of the paper's parent company, DMG Media, after a three-week hiatus during which Johnson had sought to install him as the supposedly impartial chairman of the media regulator, Ofcom. The *Guardian* reported at the time that he had 'flunked' the final interview and that 'individuals with knowledge of the recruitment process say this was despite Dacre being offered guidance on what to say in the interview and how to meet the job description criteria'.[2] Despite Dacre being found to be 'not appointable' by the interviewing panel, Johnson and his secretary of state for culture, media and sport,

Nadine Dorries, elected to ignore the suitable candidates and award Dacre another bite of the cherry. He failed again and scurried back to the safety of the *Mail*.

Humbled and humiliated by a rare foray outside his self-constructed comfort zone, this scourge of the 'Establishment' and tribune of 'ordinary people' was now so devoured by desperation for a peerage that he sacrificed any last vestiges of journalistic integrity on the altar of his own ambition. Acutely conscious of the fact that only Boris Johnson would be sufficiently unscrupulous to put him in the House of Lords, he presided over the period in which the *Daily Mail* detached itself entirely from observable reality and became a Johnson fanzine. But despite Johnson's best efforts, Dacre's bid for the Upper House crumbled after the launch of legal actions over alleged intrusion into privacy by the *Mail*'s publisher.

Coincidentally, I'm sure, Dorries, a vicious online troll who routinely used parliamentary privilege to abuse critics, became a *Daily Mail* columnist in April 2023 and would soon be railing against her own failure to secure a peerage promised by Johnson. The disgraced former prime minister himself followed her on to the paper in June, the day after publication of the Committee of Privileges report that found him to be in repeated contempt of parliament and an egregious serial liar.

It was not, however, mere vanity and hunger for honours that saw Paul Dacre do more than any other individual in the United Kingdom to create the ecosystem in which austerity, Brexit, Boris Johnson and Liz Truss could happen. That story starts much earlier and runs much deeper and darker.

If I had a different job and did not deal with its results every day, I would be sceptical that a single newspaper editor could have exerted such a malign influence over a population. But the callers who regale me with fact-free diatribes about immigration or the EU, impassioned paeans to incompetent or morally bankrupt politicians, and callous dismissals of the financially insecure, display a furious certainty that can only be explained by their daily residence in the Dacre echo chamber. Until they end up on my show, these largely decent people have literally never been asked to explain what they mean by the term 'woke', or asked precisely what 'EU laws' they object to, or what elements of 'immigration' they are desperate to 'control' and why.

When I first heard callers use the phrase 'cultural Marxism', for example, I had no idea what they were talking about. It is, I learned, a conspiracy theory widely regarded as far right and anti-Semitic that accuses an unidentified intellectual 'elite' of being embarked upon a secret international mission to replace Christian and conservative values with ill-defined 'liberal' ills. Clearly crackers and deeply dangerous (the Nazis used the phrase 'cultural Bolshevism' to similar effect), Dacre was already banging this particularly ugly drum when he gave the Hugh Cudlipp memorial lecture on 22 January 2007, claiming: 'The BBC exercises a kind of cultural Marxism in which it tries to undermine conservative society by turning all its values on their heads.'[3]

This is not normal. A national newspaper editor, ostensibly at the top of his game and in the process of being feted by his peers, was deploying inciteful language favoured by white-supremacist conspiracy theorists *in 2007.* It gets worse. The 'proof' that the BBC, an obviously imperfect institution that ties itself in knots in pursuit of 'impartiality', is a corrupt force lay not in evidence or detail but in their unspecified support for 'Labour, European Federalism, the State and State spending, mass immigration, minority rights, multiculturalism, alternative lifestyles, abortion and progressiveness in the education and the justice systems.'[4] The BBC does not, indeed cannot, endorse any of these positions but it does, on the handful of programmes that invite 'opinion', air them. That is what Dacre's *Mail* spent nearly three decades decrying: any form of challenge to his own carefully curated conspiracy theories was to be dismantled by painting his foes in ludicrous hyperbole.

There is nothing new here. In the fortnight following his infamous and profoundly racist 'Rivers of Blood' speech in Birmingham on 20 April 1968, Enoch Powell received some 100,000 letters of support. Many of his correspondents reflected Dacre's later views of the BBC: 'Why is BBC [*sic*] allowed to get away with being so biased? It is said to be riddled with communists' (woman from Ascot, Berkshire); 'The immense propaganda machine of the B.B.C and the press are against the people' (unidentified constituent); 'I now find the B.B.C is a platform for every self-acknowledged enemy of Britain' (woman from Bath).[5] Historically, totalitarian leaders need to impose media in which their warped version of 'truth' is the only one available to the people and anyone challenging it is a fifth columnist or 'enemy within' (another of Powell's favourite tropes). They normally have to enlist tame editors to deliver these alternative realities. Paul Dacre did it unprompted. And if Murdoch did away entirely with the notion of moral compasses in public life, Dacre created the toxic myth that he was using the only authentic one to protect the public from, inter alia, 'political correctness', 'cultural Marxism', communists and foreigners. Always foreigners.

Perhaps the best way to understand his contribution to public discourse in the United Kingdom is to see him as a precursor to Twitter trolls, except with an enormous inherited follower count that dwarfed anybody else on the platform and no interest in engaging with replies. He has spent his career spewing baseless invective about imagined enemies and threats to an audience kept permanently cowed by the commoditisation of fear. Crucially and quite deliberately, he never exposed himself to proper scrutiny or even mild questioning about his myriad unhinged claims and so, by the time of the Brexit referendum, ten years after that ridiculous Cudlipp lecture, swathes of the country shared his nonsensical fear of the BBC, 'progressiveness' and foreigners. Always, always foreigners.

Seven false articles of faith were preconditions for the breaking of Britain. First, that the international economic collapse of 2008 was somehow caused by public spending in the UK. The comedian Alexei Sayle put it best in 2019 when he described 'the idea that the 2008 financial crash was caused by Wolverhampton having too many libraries'.[6] Second, that leaving the EU would somehow improve the UK in materially measurable ways – whether by freeing up £350 million a week to spend on the NHS or ushering in cheaper food and higher standards of living. Third, the belief that people coming here from other European Union countries to provide much-needed labour in pretty much every sector were somehow to the detriment of the national interest. Fourth, that international and domestic institutions designed to protect populations and safeguard societies were secretly dedicated to damaging or destroying them. Fifth, that politicians and other public figures on the right side of Brexit or confected 'culture wars' or the immigration 'debate' should be exempt from the scrutiny and standards to which everybody else must be exposed. Sixth, that the pursuit of heretics, unbelievers and 'enemies of the people' should be vicious and unstinting. And seventh, the publication of blatant lies and the promotion of obvious liars. Nowhere did all seven preconditions meet as completely as in the pages of the *Daily Mail*. And if Boris Johnson was to prove the Messianic apotheosis of this horror show, Paul Dacre was his John the Baptist.

There is some crossover with the focus of the last chapter: here, Dacre's 2018 SoE speech echoes James Murdoch's self-serving desperation to believe that commercial success brought about by pandering to readers' worst impulses somehow justifies the abandonment of standards and truth: 'Freed from the obligation of having to connect with enough consumers to turn a shilling, such media organisations lose contact with the real world, and have little idea how money works (and, indeed, are suspicious of profit). Often hijacked by ideologues, invariably from the Left, they almost always regard with contempt the mass selling papers which need to appeal to large audiences in order to survive commercially.'[7] But, again, Dacre did not peddle his invented enemies, mythical conspiracies and bogus victimhood because it was good for business. He did so because he believed implicitly, albeit absurdly, that people like him really were under mortal threat from, say, the *Guardian*.

Consider, for a moment, how many people you can name today who both fit Dacre's description of hugely influential 'ideologues' here *and* enjoy a sizeable media platform from which to share their views. Guest slots and Twitter do not apply, only big circulation newspaper columns or TV and radio shows. Ask around. Maybe make a list. It is highly unlikely to get anywhere close to double figures and yet, as we have seen and will continue to see in these pages, there are legions of loud and powerful voices on Dacre's side of every argument.

Tragically, and very repetitively for a newspaper man, he expounds the same conspiracy in each of the three major speeches he gave in his career – the Cudlipp and two to the SoE. There is a rather obvious reason why, with the exception of the former *Guardian* editor Alan Rusbridger, he always fails to name a single individual in these diatribes. It is the same reason why he could never make these claims in a forum where he would be required to do so. There is no existential threat to his post-Powell propaganda, there is barely any challenge at all to it across the entire UK media landscape. And yet still he, his imitators and his readers cower in fear of invented foes. Such unchallenged cant is both a cornerstone of democratic corruption and the dominant hallmark of Dacre's *Mail*.

It will never be possible to measure how many people were seduced into this grimly timorous worldview by his or Murdoch's titles. How much of their work engendered jingoistic fearfulness, for example, and how much merely pandered to it. But either way, Dacre remains fascinating and uniquely important to understanding our unfolding national tragedy because he is both a major driver *and* an almost perfect exemplar of the prejudices, falsehoods and hypocrisies that lie at its heart.

Such is the nature of gaslighting that this is all much easier to see from the outside. In February 2017, the unpaid and anonymous editors of Wikipedia voted overwhelmingly to ban the *Daily Mail* as a trusted source for the website, describing it as 'generally unreliable' and calling for 'its use as a reference is to be generally prohibited, especially when other more reliable sources exist'.[8] Wikipedia founder Jimmy Wales later explained to CNBC in America: 'I think what they've done brilliantly in this ad funded world [is] they've mastered the art of click bait, they've mastered the art of hyped up headlines, they've also mastered the art of, I'm sad to say, of running stories that simply aren't true. And that's why Wikipedia decided not to accept them as a source anymore. It's very problematic, they get very upset when we say this, but it's just fact, so there you go.'[9] Neither the original decision nor Wales's comments were widely reported in the UK.

The more evidentially challenged callers to my radio show may all sound like *Daily Mail* columnists but they will, of course, not necessarily be *Daily Mail* readers. They are all Dacre's people, though. The untrue stories and the unfounded opinions that proliferate in the public space can almost always be traced back to the sort of journalism he pioneered. And while it can make for compelling – and commercially popular – radio to tug at a single loose thread of their certitude and then watch the whole shoddy outfit unravel, Dacre himself is painstakingly careful never to expose himself or his henchmen to comparable treatment. His behaviour in the office may have been tyrannical. His use of the expletive 'cunt', for example, was reportedly so liberal that his hysterical critiques of underlings became known as the 'vagina monologues'.[10] But as we have seen, outside the office, where he would have to engage with people not reliant on his favour for their livelihoods, he has spent his entire professional life in hiding. There, he created an organ entirely in his own image, forging a template subsequently copied by both newspapers and broadcasters. To understand his modus operandi is to understand how his brand of hate-filled propaganda became so pervasive.

At its root is the intimidation and silencing of all critics while claiming that it is, again, the 'other side' that is really pursuing this censorial course. Because barely anybody fits the description of supposed foes, this constantly evolving paranoia has seen, in recent years, Dacre's successors and acolytes in politics and journalism resort to attacking the spectacularly unspecific 'woke mob', the 'blob', the 'new liberal elite' and even the 'tofu-eating wokerati'. They do so because the landscape created by Dacre's weaponised paranoia – in informal partnership with successive Conservative governments and Rupert Murdoch's media empire – demands enemies. Stab-in-the-back mythologies demand people wielding daggers. Consider the philosophical and intellectual impossibility of inhabiting any sort of 'leftist echo chamber' in a UK where newspapers exert enormous influence on news coverage, not just on sympathetic broadcast outlets but also on the supposedly impartial BBC. *Daily Mail* editorials will be mentioned on BBC 'newspaper reviews', their nonsenses cited as genuine news by journalists who lack the independence and freedom of anonymous Wikipedia editors.

One of the most frequently recurring themes on my show is how the length of the metaphorical queue for the funfair ghost train will always dwarf the queue for the speak-your-weight machine. Humans often seem to favour fear over facts. Horror films, moral panics and front-page warnings about the imminent invasion of our island nation by 'swarms' of foreign-born humans all support the idea that we actively enjoy being frightened. I could fill a whole book with examples, but here are a few helpful earlier Dacre-era headlines: 'How using Facebook could raise your risk of cancer' (19 February 2009); 'How Labour threw open doors to mass migration in secret plot to make a multicultural UK' (10 February 2010); 'One out of every five killers is an immigrant' (31 August 2009); 'Britain is the country of choice for many "feckless" Poles' (7 November 2006); 'THE "SWARM" ON OUR STREETS' (31 July 2015). Dacre didn't merely exploit or pander to this impulse to be terrorised. He lived it. He truly believes not only that 'the problem with the Echo Chamber is that its inhabitants increasingly haven't a clue what real people in Britain, outside the M25, are thinking',[11] but also that he is their champion, a paragon of anti-elitism and a tireless critic of the Establishment. We will shortly examine his credentials for this claim.

Another part of his 'genius' lay in telling people what to be furious or frightened about while simultaneously claiming that his readers don't care about precisely the issues that fill his pages daily. When you develop the ability to step back from the fray, the results of this entirely unconscious dissonance veer from the ridiculous to the rancid. His columnists and editorials whined endlessly about the very issues that Dacre insists 'real people in Britain' completely disregard. 'I'll tell you what those people aren't talking about,' he promised in the 2018 SoE speech. 'They aren't obsessing about the "Me Too" movement or Transgender rights or equal pay for BBC women journalists.'[12] In fact, his readers are often to be found obsessing about precisely these issues but only because Dacre's lackeys portray them as threats or dangers. I don't think he realises how egregiously he is lying when he makes these claims. He is too far gone for that.

Let's look very briefly at his newspaper's coverage of the 'Me Too' movement. In the unlikely event that you are unaware of it, a helpful explanation was provided by *Mail Online* (editor-in-chief: P. Dacre) some seven months before he claimed that people weren't talking about it:

> In the wake of sexual misconduct revelations about Harvey Wein-stein, millions shared their stories about being sexually harassed and assaulted. The movement began in October 2017 after actress Alyssa Milano followed on a suggestion from a friend of a friend and tweeted: 'If you've been sexually harassed or assaulted write "me too" as a reply to this tweet.'[13]

In 2022 alone, the *Mail* reported in print or online that the actress Joanna Lumley had 'candidly voiced her opinions on the #MeToo movement and claimed it is "mad" that people are now calling them-selves "victims".' Minnie Driver spoke out 'about her "complex" feelings surrounding the #MeToo movement, admitting that while it was "satisfying" to see many female colleagues receiving justice, she also struggled watching "disingenuous" women discuss their experience.' 'Mia Wasikowska shared her #MeToo story after turning her back on Hollywood: "I was young, I didn't know how to protect myself".' Oscar-winning director Oliver Stone 'said sexual assault allegations against colleague Paul Haggis are possibly a result of the #MeToo movement.' Margot Robbie 'revealed that there are still problems with abuse in Hollywood following the #MeToo movement.' Dame Emma Thompson said that 'Amber Heard's blockbuster sex assault libel battle against Johnny Depp was "not representative" of the wider MeToo movement.' 'Beyoncé "is running #MeToo checks on producers and artists for her album Renaissance after one of her former collaborators was arrested on sexual assault charges".' Emily Ratajkowski 'claims Me Too movement has NOT "changed things" because men are only "afraid of consequences" and don't change their behaviour.' We could go on, only pausing to wonder how much coverage would be given to an issue in which his readers *were* interested?

On 3 January 2013 – over five years *before* Dacre's claim that his readers, his people, were not interested in stories about 'Transgender rights' – Lucy Meadows, a transgender primary school teacher from Accrington, Lancashire, complained to the Press Complaints Commission (PCC) of 'harassment from the press'. She specifically cited a *Daily Mail* column written by Richard Littlejohn on 20 December 2012. Among other baseless slurs, Littlejohn had accused Meadows of 'putting his [*sic*] own selfish needs ahead of the wellbeing of the children'. The then star columnist on a newspaper whose readers, according to Dacre, did not care about the issue at all went on to describe, entirely without evidence, the 'devastating effect' that Meadows's gender reassignment might have on her young pupils.

On 19 March 2013, Meadows took her own life. At the inquest into her death, Coroner Michael Singleton accused the *Daily Mail* of 'ridicule and humiliation' and a 'character assassination' of Lucy Meadows, concluding: 'I will be writing to the government to consider now implementing in full the recommendations of the Leveson Report in order to seek to ensure that other people in the same position as Lucy Meadows are not faced with the same ill-informed bigotry as seems to be displayed in the case of Lucy. And to you, the press, I say shame – shame on all of you.'[14]

Helpfully, Dacre shared his thoughts on Leveson in the SoE speech, calling it 'that massive misjudgement and over-reaction by a Prime Minister trying to save his skin after his insistence, against all advice, on taking a crooked, disgraced *News of the World* Editor to No 10 as his media adviser.'[15]

In at least one way, Littlejohn embodies Dacre's claim to represent the interests and sensibilities of people 'outside the M25'. He has spent much of his career as a *Daily Mail* columnist writing from his home in Florida. The newspaper initially defended this column, even deploying Dacre's time-honoured penchant for bogus victimhood: 'It is regrettable that this tragic death should now be the subject of an orchestrated twitterstorm, fanned by individuals – including former Labour spin doctor Alastair Campbell – with agendas to pursue.'[16] (Apart from Rusbridger, who stopped editing the *Guardian* in 2014, Campbell, who left Tony Blair's government in 2003, is the only person ever cited by Dacre as evidence of an enormous, influential cabal of prominent media and political figures.) Littlejohn's column was later quietly removed from the *Mail* website.

In January 2004, Dacre gave a vanishingly rare interview to Sue Lawley on *Desert Island Discs*. Asked what his staff likely thought of him, he replied: 'I think they'd say he's a hard bastard, but he leads from the front.'[17] He is, of course, nothing of the sort. Like all bullies, he is a coward and like all cowards he avoids confrontation at all costs. Another of Adrian Addison's *Mail Men* sources recalls: 'It always amused me that his shoe leather never wore out because every day he was on a carpet in the office; he strode out the door and was in a car which deposited him either at home or a restaurant. He would be horrified at what modern Britain had become – but he was never part of it.'[18]

Addison, incidentally, begins and ends his book with an invitation to Dacre to be interviewed. It will never happen – partly because of innate gutlessness and partly because of the length of the charge sheet against him. When, for example, Miriam González Durántez, the international trade lawyer and wife of former deputy prime minister Nick Clegg, guest edited BBC Radio 4's *Today* programme at Christmas 2015, she invited Dacre to discuss the treatment of women by the media. Again, he declined, cognisant no doubt of the way he had treated her. 'It started on the first day of the 2010 general election campaign,' she wrote later in response to reports that Boris Johnson wanted to install him as the head of Ofcom,

when he sent a photographer to my home to stand there for weeks from dusk to dawn taking pictures every time I left the house, regardless of whether I was going to my office or to buy a pint of milk. Dacre used those pictures in all sorts of ludicrous articles. It went on for years: articles about the shape of my 'derriere'; about my role as a wife and mother; he suggested my dead father was a fascist; and even claimed I benefited from human rights abuses in a Northern African country ... With time, I realised that it was just a tactic to tame people, a sheer demonstration of power: flexing his muscles to let my husband, Nick Clegg, see how much damage he could inflict on his family.[19]

Prince Harry explained this tactic further in his witness statement to the phone-hacking trial of Mirror Group Newspapers in June 2023. It is important to remember the former *Mirror* editor Piers Morgan is a former Murdoch editor, a current Murdoch employee, a former *Mail* columnist and a former 'editor at large' of the *Mail Online* website. 'Unfortunately,' Harry alleged, 'as a consequence of me bringing my Mirror Group claim, both myself and my wife have been subjected to a barrage of horrific personal attacks and intimidation from Piers Morgan, who was the editor of the *Daily Mirror* between 1995 and 2004, presumably in retaliation and in the hope that I will back down, before being able to hold him properly accountable for his unlawful activity towards both me and my mother during his editorship.'[20]

Dacre's treatment of Ed Miliband's family was arguably even worse. In 2013, the then Labour leader was riding high in the polls and in with a decent chance of winning power within the next two years. Despite his personal disdain for the incumbent Conservative prime minister, David Cameron, the prospect of Ed Miliband as PM clearly appalled Dacre. One of his most loyal attack dogs, Geoffrey Levy, was duly charged with putting the frighteners on him, just as González Durántez described. The resulting article remains one of the most outrageous ever to appear in a British newspaper. It also marks a major acceleration of Dacre's decline from blatantly bigoted but 'brilliant' editor into the unhinged hysteric who would shortly be traducing anything and anyone perceived as being an obstacle to the mythical 'good' Brexit. The article appeared under the headline 'The

Man Who Hated Britain' on the 27 September 2013 and contained a character assassination of Miliband's father, Ralph, a Jewish refugee who fled to Britain before the Second World War and died in 1994. Miliband junior, who had called for a review of media ownership laws shortly after becoming Labour leader, defied convention by publicly and strenuously objecting to the article. It is worth setting the opening paragraph of Levy's obloquy alongside Ed Miliband's defence of his father, published in characteristically graceless fashion by Dacre three days later.

Drawing on an adolescent diary entry made by Miliband senior in 1940, Levy wrote:

On a hot summer day, a young man made his way alone to Highgate Cemetery in North London to make a lifelong vow. Solemnly, he stood at the grave of Karl Marx at a moment when, in his own words, 'the cemetery was utterly deserted … I remember standing in front of the grave, fist clenched, and swearing my own private oath that I would be faithful to the workers' cause'.

Referring to the three years his father had spent serving in the Royal Navy, something glossed over by Levy in a single line, Miliband responded:

It was June 1944 and the Allies were landing in Normandy. A 20-year-old man, who had arrived in Britain as a refugee just four years earlier, was part of that fight. He was my father. Fighting the Nazis and fighting for his adopted country.

That Miliband was afforded a right of reply at all marked a departure from Dacre's normal way of doing business. The context in which it appeared, by contrast, was entirely on brand. Miliband's moving attempt to redress the abuse heaped upon his dead war-hero father appeared above a reprint of Levy's original attack and alongside an editorial, headlined 'An evil legacy and why we won't apologise', that explained Miliband had 'stamped his feet and demanded a right of reply'. It insisted; 'Today, we stand by every word we published on Saturday, from the headline to our assertion that the beliefs of Miliband Snr "should disturb everyone who loves this country".'

The deeply unsavoury episode also provided a helpful illustration of why Dacre never exposes himself to interview and prefers his executives to observe a similar form of purdah. A hapless deputy, Jon Steafel, appeared on *Newsnight* in the midst of the furore and was forced to admit that an online version of the story featuring a photograph of Ralph Miliband's gravestone and a crass pun had been wrong and subsequently changed. 'That did not appear in the paper,' he pleaded. 'It may very well be an error of judgement.' As far as I have been able to establish, Steafel's appearance, on 1 October 2013, was the last time an executive from Dacre's *Mail*, whether during his time as editor, chairman or editor-in-chief of parent company DMG Media, voluntarily exposed themselves to public scrutiny in this way. It is, as we have seen, easy to understand why. And yet still they insist that it is everyone else who inhabits an 'echo chamber'.

Disgusting though it was in isolation, the Ralph Miliband episode – and particularly the deployment of the phrase 'evil legacy' in relation to a man who actively fought the Nazis – is significant for another, even more troubling reason. We must tread carefully here. The intention is not to suggest that the current owner of the *Daily Mail*, or any of its editors, should be held responsible for the views of their ancestors and predecessors. They could perhaps do more to repudiate or acknowledge them but we will leave this sort of lazy, dishonest imputation to Dacre and his crew. Rather, it is to highlight the double standards and moral bankruptcy required to malign the memory of one man's dead father in a newspaper owned by a man whose own forebears didn't fight the Nazis but feted them.

In 1938, the *Daily Mail* published an article under the headline 'GERMAN JEWS POURING INTO THIS COUNTRY'. The language is eerily reminiscent of that deployed in Dacre's headlines about 'feckless Poles' or 'THE "SWARM" ON OUR STREETS'. The opening paragraphs of the article arguably even more so:

'The way stateless Jews and Germans are pouring in from every port of this country is becoming an outrage. I intend to enforce the law to the fullest.' In these words, Mr Herbert Metcalfe, the Old Street Magistrate yesterday referred to the number of aliens entering this country through the 'back door' – a problem to which The Daily Mail has repeatedly pointed. The number of aliens entering this country can be seen by the number of prosecutions in recent months. It is very difficult for the alien to escape the increasing vigilance of the police and port authorities.

In June 1934, the owner of the *Daily Mail*, Viscount Rothermere (Harold Harmsworth), wrote an article for his newspaper headlined 'Hurrah for the Blackshirts'. It was an encomium to the British fascist leader, Oswald Mosley, and his 'populist' movement. And while Rothermere later withdrew support from Mosley's party, he remained an enthusiastic supporter of Adolf Hitler. In June 1939, he wrote to him: 'My Dear Führer, I have watched with understanding and interest the progress of your great and superhuman work in regenerating your country.'[21] Ten days later, on 7 July 1939, he wrote to Joachim von Ribbentrop, Hitler's foreign minister: 'Our two great Nordic countries should pursue resolutely a policy of appeasement for, whatever anyone may say, our two great countries should be the leaders of the world.'[22]

These are just two in a series of fawning telegrams sent by Rothermere to senior Nazis in the months leading up to the Second World War. They emerged in papers released from Foreign Office intelligence files in April 2005 and received rather less coverage in the *Mail* than the unknown refugee Ralph Miliband's teenage diaries from the same era would eight years later. 'Czechoslovakia is not of the remotest concern to us,'[23] Rothermere also wrote in his paper as Hitler's intention to annex Sudetenland crystallised. And when Britain and France accepted Hitler's demands at Munich in September 1938, the *Mail* insisted that appeasement 'brings to Europe the blessed prospect of peace'.[24]

Support for appeasement was not confined to the *Mail* in British newspapers of the time and, again, it would be quite wrong to suggest that the current Viscount Rothermere be held in any way responsible for or hostage to his great-grandfather's views. At least as wrong, for example, as insisting that Ed Miliband be held responsible for his father's altogether less alarming ones ...

. . .

Back in the twenty-first century, the *Daily Mail*'s output on the days immediately prior to the 2016 Brexit referendum would no doubt have titillated the Old Street magistrate, Mr Herbert Metcalfe. An excellent and often oddly lyrical analysis by Tim Adams in the *Observer* on 14 May 2017 found that Dacre elected to put immigration scaremongering on his front page on 17 of the 23 weekdays leading up to the vote on 23 June. Adams wrote:

Read in sequence, those front pages have something of the shape of the opening pages of *Great Expectations*. First there is a series of front pages about Britain's 'wide-open borders'. These stories are sparked by a coastguard's interception of a boat of 18 Albanian asylum seekers off the coast at Dymchurch. It follows with the splash that the boat had been bought on eBay. The following day, by implication, we get an extrapolation of what this boat portends. The headline identifies 'EU killers and rapists we've failed to deport' and details, in the manner of Trump and Mexico, that 'thousands of violent thugs and rapists from the EU are walking Britain's streets', a number 'equivalent to a small town' flooding in through Kent. The following week, we have our first view of Magwitch himself, Avni Metra, 54, who is surprised at his flat in Borehamwood in the proximity of a kitchen knife, and apparently wanted for murder two decades ago in Tirana. He is not alone: there is also the 'one-legged Albanian double killer' Saliman Barci in Northolt. Though Albania and Kosovo (where the killers claim to come from) are not members of the EU, and it is not clear how leaving will do anything to prevent their arrival in Britain, the implication is clear. Cameron and his remainers are bringing a townful of knife-wielding Albanian murderers to the home counties. The 2,500 reader comments under this story speak with one voice: 'Get them out now and get us out now!'

And out we jolly well went, although on 7 August 2022, some six years later, the *Mail on Sunday* front page claimed: '4 IN 10 BOAT MIGRANTS ARE FROM WAR-FREE ALBANIA'. If the anti-immigration Brexit Dacre sold to his readers had been covered by the Trades Description Act, they would surely be entitled to some sort of refund.

Improbably, the pre-Brexit headlines that presaged Dacre's fears that Brexit might elude him proved even more shocking after the referendum. We will examine some of the most offensive – and one truly reprehensible and frankly incomprehensible editorial decision – to illustrate both the depths that were plumbed and the lasting damage done to our democracy by a newspaper editor riding roughshod over everything from the rule of law to the memory of an assassinated MP. It matters because without this hideous groundwork and the cover it afforded, the political triumph of a pathological liar like Johnson would have been inconceivable.

On 22 March 2017, Lord Thomas of Cwmgiedd, who as lord chief justice was then the most senior judge in England and Wales, told a parliamentary committee of a remarkable episode in his long and distinguished professional life. 'It's the only time in the whole of my judicial career that I've had to ask for the police to give us a measure of advice and protection in relation to the emotions that were being stirred up,' he said. 'And I think that it is very wrong that judges should feel it. I have done a number of cases involving al-Qaida, I dealt with the airline bombers' plot, some very, very serious cases. And I have never had that problem before. The circuit judges were very concerned. They wrote to the lord chancellor [Liz Truss] because litigants in person were coming and saying "you're an enemy of the people".'[25]

His testimony, and particularly that final phrase, refer to a front page that appeared in the *Daily Mail* on 4 November 2016. Written by James Slack – who as we know would go on to work for Theresa May and Boris Johnson before retreating to the *Sun* – it featured photographs of three High Court judges and the enormous headline 'ENEMIES OF THE PEOPLE'. In Dacre's eyes, Lord Thomas and his colleagues, Sir Terence Etherton (described as 'openly-gay' elsewhere in the *Mail*'s coverage) and Lord Justice Sales, had committed the unpardonable offence of handing down an independent judgement that he did not like. Namely, that Theresa May's government would need parliamentary consent to trigger Article 50 of the Lisbon Treaty and so start the process of exiting the EU. The challenge had been brought by Gina Miller, a British-Guyanese investment banker described in the *Sun* as a 'foreign-born multi-millionaire' (as opposed to owner Rupert Murdoch who is, of course, a foreign-born billionaire). In one of those twists of irony and hypocrisy that would come to typify the *Mail*'s attempts to rationalise the reality of Brexit, as opposed to the fairy-tale they had sold to their readers, Miller's mission was motivated by a desire to uphold the sovereignty of parliament. After the government appealed to the Supreme Court, Miller's case succeeded and the triggering of Article 50 was subject to a parliamentary vote.

But the legacy of that toxic headline lingers still. The Right Reverend Nick Baines, Lord Bishop of Leeds, told the BBC: 'The last time we saw things like the photographs of judges on the front page of a newspaper described as enemies of the people is in places like Nazi Germany, in Zimbabwe and places like that.'[26] It had already been compared on social media to a front page published in a 1933 German newspaper, which used the headline 'Traitors of the people' to accompany photographs of people whose citizenship had been revoked by the Nazi regime.

'The judiciary of England and Wales felt attacked personally,' said David Neuberger, president of the Supreme Court of the United Kingdom in his evidence to the March 2018 parliamentary committee. Both Neuberger, who described the coverage as 'undermining the rule of law', and Thomas had looked in vain to Liz Truss – justice minister at the time – for protection from Dacre's incitements. She had initially insisted that it would be wrong for a politician to criticise journalism but, following heavy flak, issued a statement late the following day that failed to criticise the *Daily Mail* but insisted that 'The independence of the judiciary is the foundation upon which our rule of law is built and our judiciary is rightly respected the world over for its independence and impartiality.'[27] You do not have to be Miriam González Durántez to work out whom Truss was thinking about when she defied her sworn oath to uphold and protect the independence of the judiciary. Five and a half years later, during her brief and calamitous period as prime minister, Dacre's *Mail* greeted her disastrous 'mini budget' with another enormous front page headline: 'AT LAST! A TRUE TORY BUDGET'.[28] And you do not have to work too hard to establish whether her claimed reluctance to criticise journalists was sincere. During the leadership contest that would see her briefly seize the Downing Street keys, she appeared on a television station infamous for hosting COVID-19 conspiracy theories and told the presenter: 'I always thought you had high quality standards at GB News. It's not the BBC you know, you actually get your facts right.'[29]

In October 2019, Dacre wrote a spectacularly unconvincing column for Andrew Neil's *Spectator* magazine under the headline 'Paul Dacre: Do I regret the "Enemies of the people" front page? Hell no!' In it, he complained that the *Telegraph*'s treatment of the same story had escaped comparable criticism to his own; that Britain's top judges could not possibly have conducted themselves in a neutral fashion over Brexit-related cases because 'the wife of one tweeted that the referendum result was "mad and bad'; and that the then Commons speaker John Bercow was 'Britain's real head of state'. It ended with a threat that judges' 'days hiding in penumbral obscurity are now numbered.' He is, unsurprisingly, yet to explain these extraordinary claims in public. Andrew Neil became a *Daily Mail* columnist shortly after the piece appeared.

On 19 April 2017, Dacre had another rush of blood to the head. This front page was prompted by Prime Minister Theresa May's decision to call a snap election and saw him once again abandon any semblance of journalistic responsibility. Featuring a close-up photograph of May against a black backdrop, it trumpeted, 'In a stunning move, Mrs May calls bluff of the "game-playing" Remoaners (including "unelected" Lords) and vows to ... CRUSH THE SABOTEURS.' While not as obnoxious as the 'Enemies of the People' effort, this is interesting for three reasons. First, the fact that Dacre's hypocrisy easily extends to denigrating the '"unelected" Lords' whose ranks he remains so desperate to join. Second, the fact that he once again proved to be an absolutely appalling reader of political runes. May, who actually called the election to shore up support from her own benches rather than 'crush' Labour or LibDem 'saboteurs', was 20 points ahead in the polls when campaigning began. When it ended she had 13 fewer seats than she had started with while Labour leader Jeremy Corbyn, benefiting from a misplaced belief that he might start offering meaningful opposition to Brexit, gained 30. Her 'stunning move', in other words, turned out to be an unmitigated disaster that sounded a death knell for her entire premiership. As we have seen, Dacre also failed to understand this. And third, unlike Truss, May was prepared to take a stand against his obvious incitement. Asked whether she agreed with the tone of Dacre's 'splash', she replied: 'Absolutely not, politics and democracy are about, of course, people having different opinions, different views. It's important in Parliament that people are able to challenge what the government is doing, that there is proper debate and scrutiny of what the government is doing – and that's what there will be.'[30]

Oddly, Dacre elected not to mention May's misgivings when his leader column launched an attack on some of the front page's other critics in the following day's paper. He preferred to focus on the Labour shadow chancellor, John McDonnell, an unidentified 'Guardianista' and, perhaps inevitably, Gary Lineker, who had tweeted: 'This kind of hate and aggression is the last thing the country needs.' Parenthetically, the second piece on the page was a fond farewell to the former chancellor, George Osborne, who had just announced his intention to leave parliament. He could, we were told, 'look back with pride on a remarkable record for a man not yet 46'.[31] Four and a half years later, on 19 November 2021, Osborne would tweet: 'I admired Dacre's forceful editorship of the Mail even if I was often on the wrong end of it. Can't quite understand why he – like others of his ilk – wielded such power, got the government, the PM and the Brexit he wanted, and still thinks the system is stacked against him.' It is a question for the ages.

There is plenty more evidence of the unhinged bile with which Dacre would liberally pepper the public space during this period. On 26 October 2017, he took aim at both academic independence and freedom of expression. Under the headline, 'OUR REMAINER UNIVERSITIES', readers were breathlessly informed that 'The extent of anti-Brexit bias at some of Britain's best known universities was laid bare last night amid a furious row.' The 'furious row' had been prompted by a bizarre letter sent by a Tory whip, Chris Heaton-Harris, to the vice-chancellors of higher education institutions. It is worth reproducing in full.

I was wondering if you would be so kind as to supply me with the names of professors at your establishment who are involved in the teaching of European affairs, with particular reference to Brexit.

Furthermore, if I could be provided with a copy of the syllabus and links to the online lectures which relate to this area I would be much obliged.

I sincerely hope you are able to provide me with such and I look forward to hearing from you in due course.[32]

Heaton-Harris has never revealed the motivation behind this bizarre and potentially chilling request. It seems unlikely that he was considering taking up a place on one of the courses dedicated to promoting the understanding of 'European affairs, with particular reference to Brexit'. It would, after all, have been too late: he had voted to leave the EU in 2016. And by 2023, as secretary of state for Northern Ireland, he was trying to unravel some of the damage done to both the peace process *and* the unionist cause that his vote had helped to bring about.

Paul Dacre, by contrast, was characteristically clear. Academics sharing the fruits of a lifetime's learning with their students were to be roundly condemned and, ideally, curtailed if their conclusions and opinions did not tally entirely with his own. 'Yesterday,' we were told, 'the Daily Mail uncovered a string of examples of senior figures at universities explicitly speaking out in favour of Remain.' It gets worse. 'Before the vote, a raft of senior academics spoke publicly to urge their students to back staying in the EU.' And worst of all: 'Last night, one student campaigner revealed a professor had stormed up to him at a Vote Leave stall in Durham – and compared Brexit campaigners to Nazis.' The same student, Tom Harwood (who unremarkably went on to work for both the extreme right-wing blog 'Guido Fawkes' and the conspiracy theory-platforming GB News), admitted later in the article that the professor had written a letter of apology. And rightly so. Comparisons with Nazis are almost always hyperbolic. In the following day's paper, Dacre invited students to inform on their teachers. Accompanied by a dedicated email address, a headline asked: 'Have you – or do you know anyone who has – experienced anti-Brexit bias at university?'

Theresa May's Downing Street was quick to disown Heaton-Harris, insisting that he had not been acting in his capacity as a member of government, but he and Dacre were not without heavy-weight support. Andrew Bridgen, who would later be accused of lying under oath by a High Court judge and expelled from the Conservative Party for comparing COVID-19 vaccines to the Holocaust, told the paper: 'I'm sure Chris Heaton-Harris wouldn't have got this explosive and very defensive response if he'd enquired about the syllabus on advanced pure mathematics.' But the last word must go to Professor Thom Brooks, dean of Durham University's Law School, who correctly called the story 'dog whistle politics at its worst'. Speaking to HuffPost UK, he added: 'It shows how badly Brexit negotiations are going that any kind of criticism of how things are is now being treated as treason. It might as well have said "enemies of the people" on the front page.'[33] The *Daily Mail*, it should be noted, has subsequently become a staunch defender of 'free speech' on university campuses. But only when the speakers are gender critical.

Perhaps the most telling example of Dacre's dangerous decline does not involve a *Daily Mail* front page but rather the absence of one. On 23 November 2017, Thomas Mair, the white-supremacist terrorist who had assassinated the Labour MP Jo Cox five months previously, was convicted of her murder. At the time of the killing, in the middle of that extraordinary run of pre-referendum front-page immigration scaremongering detailed by Tim Adams in the *Observer*, the paper had pursued a curious course. Despite the killer saying, 'This is for Britain', 'keep Britain independent' and 'Britain first' while attacking Jo, Dacre elected to focus on him being a 'loner with a history of mental illness'. (He was later examined by a psychiatrist, who could find no evidence that he was not responsible for his actions as a consequence of poor mental health.) Books found at Mair's home and an investigation of his internet history revealed obsessions with Nazis, white supremacy and apartheid-era South Africa but, according to Dacre's *Mail* on 24 November, the police were concentrating on mistakes made by social services that had left his depression untreated. And the paper's coverage of the case would get curiouser still.

Handing down a whole-life sentence, Mr Justice Wilkie, contrasted the killer with Jo, a passionate pro-immigration campaigner and staunch Remain supporter who had previously worked for Oxfam, saying: 'In the true meaning of the word, she was a patriot.' In reference to the killer, he added: 'It is evident from your internet searches that your inspiration is not love of country or your fellow citizens, it is an admiration for Nazis and similar anti-democratic white-supremacist creeds. Our parents' generation made huge sacrifices to defeat those ideas and values in the Second World War. What you did … betrays those sacrifices.'[34] But Dacre's *Daily Mail* article on 24 November reported that 'he feared losing his council house to an immigrant family'.[35] And it did so on *page 30.*

No fewer than 41 articles were deemed by Paul Dacre to deserve more prominence than the conviction and sentencing of a neo-Nazi terrorist responsible for the first murder of a sitting MP in 26 years. Their headlines included: 'My sherry-fuelled snog with long-haired hippy chancellor'; 'Fury over quango doom-mongers'; 'Brexit means 80,000 fewer migrants a year'; 'Why a UK worker takes five days to do what a German does in four!'; 'Why DO left-wing "comics" think it's so hilarious to make filthy jokes about the Queen?'; 'The Santa fib can damage your children, say academics'; 'The laughing migrants'; 'Now FIFA probes Wales ... because fans wore poppies in stands'; 'Baguette that fits your bag'; 'Pretty women "prefer gay men friends"' and 'Feminine wiles make male monkeys keen for a fight'.

When attention finally turned to the sentencing of Jo's killer, it appeared under the headline 'HE WANTED TO KILL HIS OWN MOTHER'. A story on the adjacent page asked 'Did neo-Nazi murder Jo over fear he'd lose council house he grew up in?' The killer, we learned, 'may have murdered MP Jo Cox because he feared losing his home of 40 years to an immigrant family'. Mr Justice Wilkie certainly didn't consider this to be the case. His verdict that he killed her due to his violent white-supremacist ideology was clear and unequivocal. Law professor James Chalmers tweeted persuasively, 'turns out there really is nothing the Daily Mail can't blame on immigrants'.

So why would Paul Dacre relegate such a harrowing and significant story to the back of what journalists call 'the book'? A clue, perhaps, can be found in an article he published eight days previously. It began: 'Tory Remainers were branded "collaborators" last night as they threatened to side with Labour to frustrate Brexit in Parliament.'[36] As with 'saboteurs' and 'enemies of the people', the use of the word 'collaborators' is provocative and even perhaps fascistic but by now Dacre was beyond caring about such niceties. Unlike 'saboteurs' and 'enemies of the people', however, 'collaborators' was a favoured word of Jo Cox's killer and there can be no doubt that he considered her to be one of their number. Asked to confirm his name at his first court appearance, he replied: 'My name is death to traitors, freedom for Britain.'[37]

In 1999 Mair had written to a right-wing magazine called *SA Patriot in Exile*: 'I was glad you strongly condemned collaborators in the white South African population. In my opinion the greatest enemy of the old apartheid system was not the ANC and the black masses but white liberals and traitors.'[38] In a previous missive to the same magazine he revealed: 'I still have faith that the white race will prevail, both in Britain and in South Africa. I fear that it's going to be a very long and very bloody struggle.'[39]

As established, it is highly unlikely that anyone will ever get the opportunity to ask Dacre about his decision – or that he will ever address the issue in one of his vanishingly rare, question-free speeches or *Spectator* magazine columns. We are left with mere speculation. We will never know.

We do know that, at the peak of his powers, the most influential newspaperman of his generation thought nothing of attacking judges, journalists, academics and elected politicians. Or, more pertinently, the rule of law, freedom of expression, academic freedom and parliamentary sovereignty. We know that after Boris Johnson fled that parliament in unprecedented disgrace and under multiple counts of contempt, Paul Dacre elected to *reward* him with a lucrative columnist's contract. To knit together these two strands of epic hypocrisy, in his first SoE speech in November 2008, he described one judge, Mr Justice Eady, as 'amoral' because 'he rejected the idea that adultery was a proper cause for public condemnation'. Fifteen years later Johnson, the sexually incontinent serial adulterer, was on his payroll, reportedly to the tune of £500,000-a-year. We know that his enthusiasm for Brexit and Johnson and Truss has cost the country billions of pounds and will continue to cause pain for generations to come. We know that his obsession with foreigners and immigration has poisoned the population and divided families. And we know that he has done all of this, and more, while constantly congratulating himself on being a staunch upholder of British 'values'. The anti-Establishment figure who craved a seat in the House of Lords and sent both of his sons to Eton. The sworn enemy of the EU who took at least £460,000 in subsidies from it for his 20,000-acre hunting and shooting estate in the Scottish Highlands and his country estate in Sussex.[40] The self-described scourge of 'quangocrats' who was so desperate to chair the quango Ofcom that he very briefly fled the sanctuary of the offices where nobody is permitted to challenge him – but everybody runs the daily risk of being on the receiving end of a barked, spittle-flecked 'Cunt!' We know that he will never consent to a proper interview, but if anybody ever gets the chance to hold him to the vaguest account for his uniquely corrosive career, I hope they begin by asking him precisely what 'values' he believes he championed. I can't think of one.

Chapter 3
ANDREW NEIL

For a start he picks as his editors people like me who are gener-
ally on the same wavelength as him: we started from a set of
common assumptions about politics and society ...

Andrew Neil on Rupert Murdoch[1]

ANDREW NEIL MAY NOT seem an obvious person for inclusion in this book, but both his career and his impact are a perfect illustration of what has happened to this country. To set the context for the unique influence he casts, I want to start with a seemingly unrelated story.

. . .

On 19 April 2023, a 25-year-old member of the BBC's Political Research Unit made his debut on the *Politics Live* discussion programme. Oscar Bentley, a fact-checker, provided an evidence-based analysis of claims Rishi Sunak had made during that day's Prime Minister's Questions (PMQs). Sunak had stated that: 'Since 2010, crime is down by 50 per cent under the Conservative Government.'[2] Bentley explained that Sunak's boast, based on figures from the Office for National Statistics, excluded fraud or computer misuse offences, which accounted for 4.4 million out of 9 million total offences in 2022. He added, quite correctly, that 'If you take crime actually recorded by police forces, that's actually gone up.' Similar statistical sleight of hand had already seen Boris

Johnson face rebuke from the then head of the UK Statistics Authority (UKSA) in February 2022. Johnson had claimed that crime had fallen by 14 per cent over a two-year period, prompting Sir David Norgrove to respond: 'If fraud and computer misuse are counted in total crime as they should be, total crime in fact increased by 14 per cent between the year ending September 2019 and the year ending September 2021.' (The room for these deliberate misinterpretations exists because the ONS only started counting crimes of fraud and computer misuse in 2015.) Bentley's conclusion, that Sunak was *technically* just about entitled to make the claim but was nonetheless playing fast and loose with the numbers, was beyond reproach. A straightforward, evidence-based analysis of a government claim.

The next day's newspapers were united in outrage. Not, however, at the mischievous misrepresentations of Rishi Sunak, but at the student activities of Oscar Bentley. 'BBC is accused of "obvious bias" as it emerges new political fact-checker is Labour activist', bellowed the *Daily Mail*, before revealing a catalogue of alleged offences including the revelations that Bentley had canvassed for the Labour Party while at the University of York, that he had once uploaded an image of a terrier to his social media with a caption endorsing 'dogs for Corbyn', and even, perish the thought, 'shared advertisements for Veganuary'. They were still fulminating the following day when journalist Guy Adams demanded: 'How impartial is the BBC's "impartial" fact checking unit?' Rather than trying to critique his actual analysis, Adams instead informed readers that 'the 25-year-old Bentley is actually a dyed-in-the-wool Labour supporter who canvassed for the former party leader Jeremy Corbyn, and who has said you should "never trust a Tory".'

The *Daily Express* reported the 'story' as if Bentley had been somehow hiding in his own office: 'BBC caught in bias row as Labour activist found working as political fact checker'. Rupert Murdoch's TalkTV, where genuine bias is a business model, raged: 'BBC fact checker canvassed for Jeremy Corbyn and smeared Conservatives'. The *Daily Telegraph* was initially a little less excitable, preferring the headline: 'Claims of bias as BBC hires Labour activist who said "never trust a Tory" as political fact-checker'. But by the next day they were fully on board with the hysteria, asking: 'How can we trust the BBC, if its political "fact-checker" is a Labour activist?' The *Telegraph*'s stablemate in the Barclay family's media empire, the *Spectator*, reported 'BBC hires Corbynista political fact checker' and asked: 'Can the BBC ever get it right?'

The answer to that final question, incidentally, is a resounding 'yes'. The very media outlets ostensibly disgusted by the student activities of a very junior 25-year-old recent recruit to the BBC had previously spent the best part of three decades supremely untroubled by the fact that one of the Corporation's most senior political broadcasters – a former *presenter* of *Politics Live* no less – was one of the most obviously and proudly opinionated individuals in the British journalistic firmament. The difference, inevitably, was that the biases and prejudices displayed by Andrew Neil at every stage of his long and illustrious career fit perfectly with those of the *Daily Mail*, where he currently writes a column, the Barclay family, for whom he was editor-in-chief of the Press Holdings newspaper group and later chairman of the *Spectator*, and Rupert Murdoch, for whom he edited the *Sunday Times* and was the founding chairman of Sky TV.

If Murdoch and Dacre were the chief architects of a media ecosystem in which the most basic truth could be abandoned on the altar of commercial or ideological interests, Neil is perhaps the finest example of the sort of journalist best placed to flourish within it. Vain beyond parody, his late-night Twitter rants and disastrous attempt to launch a new television station, GB News, perhaps blind younger generations to his once fierce intellect and erstwhile excellence as an interviewer of politicians. He remains of interest to us here for three reasons.

First, as we have already glimpsed, he embodies the epic double standards of the disproportionately powerful print media's attitude to BBC employees. This will remain important long after his departure from the broadcaster in 2020. Years of bullying and abuse of journalists perceived to be unsympathetic to, inter alia, neoliberal economics, Brexit and populist race-baiting masquerading as 'immigration concerns' have left the Corporation cowed and in many ways corrupted. We will see that Neil helped more than anyone to usher in an era where blatant Tory affiliations among staff go unremarked, while the vaguest hint of anti-Tory sentiment sees professionals effectively hounded out of their jobs. It also means, of course, that the BBC is fast becoming a place where anybody with a prior history of political engagement will think long and hard before applying for a job there. Unless, of course, that engagement was with right-wing politics. Crucially, throughout this period of unprecedented vilification of BBC staff, Neil signally failed to speak up for the idea that if someone as obviously possessed of pungent opinions as him can leave them at the studio door, then so could a colleague holding very different views. Instead, as we have already seen with the case of Oscar Bentley, writers on his payroll would enthusiastically side with the bullies.

Second, because Neil's tenure at the *Spectator* magazine saw him champion a coterie of spectacularly racist and gratuitously divisive commentators. Masters of the unhinged *ad hominem*, they leeched effortlessly into Murdoch's and Dacre's empires while Neil's patronage afforded a patina of respectability to Islamophobes, ethno-nationalists and other conspiracy theorists. All while Neil was supposedly abiding by the BBC's strict impartiality rules.

Third, because of the integral role he played in giving GB News credibility. These later misadventures in broadcasting show that far from being happy with a media landscape where opposing views are barely represented and where the BBC has been hollowed out from within, the right-wing billionaire class he represents is still not satisfied. They want even more domination and monopoly, and while Neil would humiliate himself trying to deliver it for some of them, the broader mission continues apace.

Keeping the response to Bentley's student activities in mind – and the clear implication that they should prevent him from working for the national broadcaster – consider just some of Neil's own pre-BBC positions. As a student at Glasgow University, he regularly attended the Federation of Conservative Students conferences. The former Tory minister Ann Widdecombe, who would end her career as part of Nigel Farage's Brexit Party freak show, remembered those days fondly in 2002: 'Andrew chaired things terribly well,' she told Ben Summerskill of the *Observer* on 28 July. 'He was evidently ambitious, but he worked well with others. Young people behaved respectably then and Andrew was responsible for late-night "noise and morality" patrols.' Upon graduating in 1971, he joined the Conservative Research Department (CRD). Founded by Neville Chamberlain in 1929, the CRD is effectively a 'think tank' operating within the Conservative Party to explore and formulate policy positions. Alumni include David Cameron, George Osborne and Enoch Powell. Two years later he joined *The Economist* and began his ascent up the greasy pole of journalism, culminating in the editorship of the *Sunday Times* in 1983.

There, by his own account, he was soon 'urging a market revolution more complete than even Margaret Thatcher was contemplating'.[3]

On 26 November 1989, Neil published an article in the *Sunday Times* magazine by the American political scientist, Charles Murray. Entitled 'Underclass: the alienated poor are devastating America's cities', it warned that the UK was shortly to be swamped by a 'population of working-aged, healthy people who live in a different world to other Britons ... whose values are contaminating the life of entire neighbourhoods'. Today, Murray's article reads like a template for the demonisation of the unemployed that would typify right-wing tabloid journalism in the following decades. He was paving the way for David Cameron's 'austerity', which left the UK woefully unprepared for the COVID-19 pandemic, and swingeing cuts to the benefits payments of society's poorest and most vulnerable families. Particular opprobrium was directed at single mothers and their children. Neil lapped it up. A *Sunday Times* editorial, 'The British Underclass', lambasted a social class 'characterised by drugs, casual violence, petty crime, illegitimate children, homelessness, work avoidance and contempt for conventional values'. By 1993, Murray, a researcher at a virulently right-wing 'think tank', the American Enterprise Institute, was calling for single mothers to be stripped of all state support and their children to be placed in 'well-equipped, carefully staffed orphanages'.[4]

Murray's work was regularly reprinted in pamphlet form by the IEA, the British 'think tank' that would later claim credit for Liz Truss and Kwasi Kwarteng's disastrous 'mini-budget'. Indeed, the first such collaboration boasted an introduction by David Green, the 'Director' of the IEA's 'Health and Welfare Unit' (remember the predilection for grandiose titles in these outfits). The relationship between the secretly funded pressure group and the *Sunday Times* was deeply symbiotic.

Neil would regularly report its activities in his newspaper and reprint its polemical pamphlets. In 1993, he was the keynote speaker at its annual conference.

These collaborations set the tone for one of the most damaging developments the British media has ever endured: the presentation of pressure groups dedicated to promoting the interests of their anonymous plutocrat sponsors as somehow independent or academic. The idea that one of their most enthusiastic cheerleaders and facilitators could become an 'impartial' BBC presenter is challenging. As we shall see, by the time Neil rocked up at the Corporation, this network of shady and deeply ideological outfits had infiltrated almost every corner of the British media, with its representatives enjoying more columns than the Acropolis and season tickets to every broadcast studio in the country. The basic requirement that anyone calling for cuts to state spending or a reduction in the regulation of industry should, at the very least, disclose the identity of their own sponsors has never been observed. In many ways, Andrew Neil set this discourse-disrupting ball in motion.

In 1994, Murdoch relieved him of his newspaper editing duties and brought him to New York, where he hoped his protégé would play a major part on the network that would become Fox News. That did not come to pass but Neil later told Martin Walker of the *Guardian* that he had wanted to challenge a 'great soggy liberal consensus on the big three networks'. In the same interview he also expressed a desire to 'expose the myth of AIDS'.[5] This despite having already offered the *Sunday Times*'s support to an ill-fated campaign to prove that HIV was not the cause of AIDS. 'At a time of moral panic,' wrote Summerskill later, in his 2002 *Observer* article, in a waspish reference to personal conduct that would likely have fallen foul of Neil's 'noise and morality' patrols, 'it was a reassuring viewpoint for many hetero-sexuals with colourful private lives.'

None of this presented any obstacle to Neil becoming a BBC politics presenter in 1998 or staying there, in an array of high-profile roles, until 2022. And he is not alone. Nick Robinson, a former political editor of both the BBC and ITV, currently presents BBC Radio 4's flagship *Today* programme. He is also a founder member of Macclesfield Young Conservatives and a former chairman of Cheshire Young Conservatives. At university, he was president of the Oxford University Conservative Association and, later, the chairman of the party's national youth wing, Young Conservatives. Whether or not this influences his work at the BBC is immaterial. The point is simply that Robinson, like Neil and anyone else at Broadcasting House with historic Tory loyalties, will never have their CV publicly picked over by powerful media forces dedicated to attacking anyone in the same building with historic Labour, Liberal Democrat, Green Party or Scottish National Party (SNP) loyalties.

In an article for the *New Statesman* magazine in April 2018, Robinson inadvertently highlighted another facet of this 'impartial-ity' problem. 'BBC programmes are not required to give equal airtime or weight to pros and antis in any debate,' he wrote in response to an article by the author warning that 'false equivalence' and a genteel reluctance to call out liars was leading the Corporation and the country into very dark places. 'Our rules make clear that we have to deliver "due impartiality". That word "due" makes clear that programme teams can and do make judgements on the validity of stories, chal-lenge facts and figures and acknowledge that different people speak with different levels of authority.'

More through complacency than malice, Robinson missed three crucial points. First, employees of the 'think tanks' described above are presented as honest brokers without any reference to their prove-nance or qualifications. With the right (secret) funding you could set one up tomorrow, crown yourself 'Director of Lifestyle Affairs' and be booked for an interview on the BBC by teatime. The abject failure to examine credentials or establish credibility drives a coach and horses through any notion of genuine 'impartiality'.

Second, the manufactured necessity of 'balance'. The former BBC presenter Emily Maitlis put it best when she described the 'Patrick Minford paradigm'.[6] Referring to EU referendum coverage, she described how 'it would take producers five minutes to find sixty econo-mists who feared Brexit and five hours to find a sole economic voice who espoused it'. For the BBC viewer or listener, the representative of, say, 1 per cent of expert opinion is presented as an equal and opposite force to the spokesperson for the other 99 per cent.

During a brief period of presenting Newsnight on the BBC, I once found myself poised to interview Pascal Lamy, a former director general of the World Trade Organization (WTO), about the remit and responsibilities of the WTO. It was during the post-referendum period when Brexiters were scrabbling around for anything to camouflage the idiocy of what they had ushered in, culminating in a demonstrably ludicrous claim that the UK would flourish with no free-trade agree-ments or trade deals 'under WTO rules'. Nobody on the planet was better qualified to examine this claim than Lamy but a BBC editor informed me that we would also need to interview someone else 'for balance'. The Conservative MP and Brexit-supporter Andrea Lead-som, who had no experience of international trade or knowledge of the workings of the WTO, accepted the invitation and proceeded to tell Lamy that his analysis of 'WTO rules' and the organisation he once ran was wrong. That Robinson, like Neil before him, cannot or will not see the absurdity that was so obvious to Maitlis (and, less importantly, me) might explain why he remains at the Corporation while she does not.

Finally, in an environment where those 'judgements on the validity of stories' are policed by national newspapers in a vicious and aggressive way, it is surely impossible for subconscious wariness not to creep in. Not only when booking and interviewing guests, but also when indulging the ridiculous practice of including comment pieces in BBC 'newspaper reviews' that turn the opinion-free national broadcaster into an amplifier of precisely the issues that Murdoch, Dacre & co. want to see dominating the news agenda. It doesn't occur to anyone that it is daft for the BBC to provide free advertisements for organisations dedicated to its own destruction because it is a completely normalised throwback to days when the print media was not so completely hell-bent on achieving ideological monopoly. And just as Paul Dacre presumably hoped to frighten judges into decisions by warning that their days of 'hiding in penumbral obscurity are now numbered', so BBC journalists and managers live in perpetual fear of the '*Daily Mail* treatment'.

We can hope that Oscar Bentley remains true to his calling in future appearances but, having seen his face and personal history plastered all over the national press in deeply unflattering terms, he could be forgiven for endeavouring to avoid a repeat performance in future. I have been unable to find any evidence of tireless student politician Robinson speaking out in defence of Bentley. And can you blame him? To do so would be to put a target on his own back. Not just from outside the Corporation but also, as we shall see, from within.

Robinson's colleague and successor as political editor of the BBC, Laura Kuenssberg, has also managed to escape being targeted by the

Murdoch press. On 19 February 2023, she provided a helpful clue as to why that might be. When the SNP's Westminster leader, Stephen Flynn, explained that Brexit-induced problems in Northern Ireland had taken Westminster by surprise 'because Boris Johnson lied', Kuenssberg immediately interrupted him, saying: 'That's quite a charge.' On the contrary, it was a statement of simple fact. Johnson had not only campaigned on a bogus claim that his 'deal' was 'oven-ready' but was also filmed telling business leaders in Northern Ireland that 'there will be no border down the Irish Sea – over my dead body'.[7] I don't know whether Kuenssberg felt the need to challenge a statement of incontrovertible fact because it made her uncomfortable or because, consciously or otherwise, she feared repercussions for not doing so. But, and this *is* quite a charge, it is a clear and characteristic dereliction of journalistic duty.

Speaking of derelictions, in his *Daily Mail* column on 24 June 2023, Neil himself would claim that before the referendum Remainers did not 'spend any time confronting the fact that Northern Ireland and its open border with the Republic of Ireland would constitute a major stumbling block to any clean break with the EU'. In fact, Sinn Fein had used the slogan 'Brexit means borders' during their campaign, and on a visit to Northern Ireland in June 2016, the then chancellor George Osborne explained that 'There would have to be a hardening of the border' if the UK was outside the EU. In the same month, former prime ministers John Major and Tony Blair both referred to the inevitability of an 'Irish Sea border' during a visit to Derry. In a public statement, Blair said there 'would have to be checks between Northern Ireland and the rest of the UK, which would be plainly unacceptable as well'. If, as Neil was still contending unchallenged in June 2023, there had been no mention of this 'stumbling block' one wonders why Arlene Foster, then first minister of Northern Ireland, referred to 'deeply offensive' scare stories from the Remain campaign and Theresa Villiers, then the Leave-supporting secretary of state for Northern Ireland, described any suggestion that Brexit would have a negative impact on the peace process as 'deeply irresponsible'.

While some fortunes rose at the BBC during this period of unprecedented pressure from politicians and rival media groups, others indubitably fell. A management faced with newspapers and government demands to 'rein in' their staff has two choices: look after power or look after the people speaking truth to power. Too often BBC panjandrums pursued the path of least resistance.

On 26 May 2020, Emily Maitlis delivered the customary monologue at the opening of that night's *Newsnight*. In it, she addressed a press conference given the previous day by Prime Minister Boris Johnson's chief adviser, Dominic Cummings. At issue was a 60-mile round trip he had made with his wife and child on 3 April from his father's farm in County Durham to Barnard Castle, a well-known tourist destination. At the time, car journeys for leisure pursuits were forbidden by the lockdown rules that Cummings had helped to formulate, and both he and his wife were supposed to be self-isolating due to contracting COVID-19 days previously. Indeed, his wife, Mary Wakefield, had previously provided a moving account of the family's experiences with the virus in an article for her employer, Andrew Neil's *Spectator* magazine. She mentioned neither the trip to Barnard Castle, nor the altogether longer car journey from London to County Durham after her initial symptoms appeared, describing instead her later emergence 'into the almost comical uncertainty of London lockdown'.

After a lengthy delay, presumably to allow government lawyers time to go over his statement with the finest-tooth comb, Cummings stepped into the Downing Street Rose Garden to present his novel defence. The family trip to the beauty spot on his wife's birthday, we learned, had been a rehearsal for the much longer journey back to London, necessitated by worries about his eyesight.

'My wife was very worried, particularly because my eyesight seemed to have been affected by the disease,' he explained. 'She didn't want to risk a nearly 300-mile drive with our child, given how ill I had been. We agreed to go for a short drive to see if I could drive safely.'

(Even here, Boris Johnson's strained relationship with the truth was soon on display. Despite there being no established links between COVID-19 and damage to eyesight, he told the daily Downing Street briefing: 'I'm finding I have to wear spectacles for the first time in years, I think because of the effects of this thing. So I'm inclined to think that's very, very plausible, that eyesight can be a problem associated with coronavirus.' Unfortunately, he had told an interviewer in 2014: 'I'm now so short-sighted, I'm blind! My eyes used to be fantastic but now ...'[8])

In retrospect, Maitlis's words that night seem mild. 'Dominic Cummings broke the rules,' she said. 'The country can see that and it's shocked the government cannot. The longer that ministers and the prime minister tell us that he worked within them, the more angry the response to this scandal is likely to be.' What followed makes more sense now that we know about the serial lockdown law-breaking in Downing Street itself and the willingness of law-breakers to lie about it. Even to the House of Commons.

'It was only the next morning that the wheels fell off,' Maitlis explained later.[9] 'A phone call of complaint was made from Downing Street to the *BBC News* management. This – for context – is not unusual. It wasn't unusual in the Blair days – far from it – in the Brown days, in the Cameron days. What I'm saying is it's normal for government spin doctors to vocalise their displeasure to journalists.

'What was not foreseen was the speed with which the BBC sought to pacify the complainant. Within hours, a very public apology was made, the programme was accused of a failure of impartiality, the recording disappeared from the iPlayer, and there were paparazzi outside my front door.

'Why had the BBC immediately and publicly sought to confirm the government spokesman's opinion, without any kind of due process? It makes no sense for an organisation that is, admirably, famously rigorous about procedure – unless it was perhaps sending a message of reassurance directly to the government itself? Put this in the context of the BBC board, where another active agent of the Conservative Party – former Downing Street spin doctor and former adviser to BBC rival GB News – now sits, acting as the arbiter of BBC impartiality.'

She is referring here to Robbie Gibb, a former producer on Andrew Neil's BBC programmes and another shining example of how compromised the BBC has become. Gibb's early career saw him shuttlecocking between jobs at the Corporation and within the Conservative Party, most prominently as chief of staff to the shadow chancellor, Francis Maude. By 2016, he was head of BBC Westminster and so responsible for much of the Corporation's Brexit coverage. On 19 April 2019, *Channel 4 News* reported that during Gibb's tenure the BBC had obtained evidence that Nigel Farage and Arron Banks's Leave.EU had used Facebook to deliberately target supporters of far-right organisations including the National Front and the British National Party. 'So why did the BBC never report this story?' asked the Channel 4 presenter Fatima Manji. Given Gibb's roles within both the Conservative Party and the BBC during the ensuing four years, it is worth examining this report at length.

Manji continued: 'The story the BBC had was true. But according to the emails we've seen, the response from Arron Banks [co-founder of the Leave.EU campaign] and Andy Wigmore [Banks's bag-carrier] wasn't. They decided to launch a full-on assault on the BBC, claiming the Corporation was biased and threatening them with legal action. And they appealed to the then head of BBC political programmes, Robbie Gibb. He's now Theresa May's top spin doctor ...

'Despite the Leave.EU social media team telling him otherwise, Banks writes back to the [BBC] reporter copying in Gibb: "It's wholly wrong to say we have targeted extreme right parties any more than say communist. It's anyone who has expressed an interest in leaving the EU. Your report needs to reflect this or it will be biased and we will take whatever legal action we need to protect our reputation." Then in a series of late-night emails to Robbie Gibb, Banks complained about their spokesman Richard Tice being dropped from a BBC programme, claiming this was all a smear campaign: "We do not specifically target the BNP or any other party or group and to say otherwise is wrong. Off the back of this Richard Tice ... has been bumped off the Marr show again! Why can't he go on and defend our position if necessary?" Half an hour later: "All this is an attempt to portray us as racist." Minutes after emailing Gibb, this is what he [Banks] told Richard Tice: "I don't think they will run it after all that lot. You will have a busy week next week since Robbie will react by giving us massive exposure."'

Banks later recalled the episode in his book about the Brexit campaign, published in diary form: 'I woke up to news that the Beeb is planning to run a smear story about our Facebook pages ... Robbie

Gibb is being quite helpful and says he's trying to hose it down.'[10] The BBC never ran the story. The *Sunday Times* reported elements of it on 2 May 2016, when Leave.EU told the paper that it had 'stopped promoting to far-right groups instantly' upon learning what had been happening. Robbie Gibb told *Channel 4 News*: 'These allegations are ridiculous and without merit. I remain proud of my contribution to the BBC's impartial coverage of the 2016 EU referendum campaign.'

On 4 January 2020, Robbie Gibb wrote an article for the *Daily Mail* (where else?) attacking the supposedly anti-Tory bias of BBC Radio 4's *Today* programme. Short on evidence but long on adjectives like 'negative', 'sneering' and 'haughty', Gibb (by now knighted for his services to Theresa May's brief premiership) accidentally said the quiet part out loud, expressing incredulity that a BBC editor with *similar political loyalties to his own* might prioritise objective journalism over keeping a Tory government sweet. He wrote:

> Interviewed on the BBC's *Feedback* programme over the Government's boycott of *Today*, its editor Sarah Sands declared the Government believes 'it's a pretty good time to put the foot on the windpipe of an independent broadcaster', while accusing No. 10 of 'Trumpian' tactics in its refusal to appear on the programme. This is extraordinary and unfortunate language coming from the former editor of the Right-wing *Sunday Telegraph* who championed Boris Johnson as Mayor of London when she was editor of the Evening Standard.

His outrage, in other words, is not that Sands criticised the government, but that she did so despite previously writing for a right-wing newspaper and supporting Johnson as London mayor. What is the point, Gibb appears to wonder, of having simpatico journalists in senior positions at the BBC if they are going to make trouble for the government?

Sands, previously a DMG/*Telegraph* stalwart, had been appointed to the editorship of *Today* in 2017. It looked at the time like a desperate and vain attempt by BBC bosses to soften the endless allegations of bias they had received from her previous employers. Gibb, we can presume, would have been delighted. But she proved an able and independent editor, and her early analysis of Johnson's 'Trumpian' tendencies now looks uncannily accurate. Again, the counterfactual is helpful here. It would once have been perfectly possible for the BBC to appoint a *Today* programme editor who had previously held a senior position on, say, the *Guardian*. By 2017, and in another chilling illustration of how complete the capture of the BBC had become, it would have been unthinkable. Indeed, the mooted appointment of one former *Newsnight* deputy editor, Jess Brammar, to a senior role at the BBC after a brief hiatus running the HuffPost website was furiously resisted by another former *Newsnight* deputy editor, Robbie Gibb.

Sixteen months after that *Mail* article, in which a BBC boss turned Tory spin doctor had berated a Tory newspaper editor turned BBC editor for not being sufficiently sympathetic to an obviously dishonest Tory prime minister, Boris Johnson put Robbie Gibb on the board of the BBC. The April 2021 appointment was rendered even more extraordinary by the fact that, until October 2020, Gibb had been a key figure behind the planned launch of GB News, and reportedly responsible for recruiting his similarly 'impartial' old colleague Andrew Neil to be chairman and 'face' of the channel. Its co-founder, Boston-based businessman Andrew Cole, had previously described the BBC as a 'disgrace'; 'bad for Britain on so many levels' and in need of being 'broken up'.[11] Nonetheless, Gibb bounced back to the Corporation and would quickly make his presence felt.

More than happy to work with Andrew Cole, Gibb was reportedly rather less happy to work with Jess Brammar. On 10 July 2021, the *Financial Times* reported that Gibb had sought to block her appointment to a new role overseeing the Corporation's domestic and international television channels. According to the *FT*, Gibb texted the BBC's director of news and current affairs, Fran Unsworth, to warn that she 'cannot make this appointment' as the government's 'fragile trust in the BBC will be shattered'. A 'source close to Gibb' denied using the words attributed to him but the *FT* was told by sources that Brammar's appointment had stalled since the intervention, described by the newspaper as 'highly unorthodox for a non-executive director at the BBC'. In normal circumstances, the *FT* explained, Brammar's candidacy would not even have been raised at board level.

Inevitably, the usual ghouls started salivating. On 21 August, the *Mail on Sunday* reported that she had 'posted a series of now-deleted tweets critical of Boris Johnson, Brexit and Britain's imperial past' and 'promoted a series of controversial opinions while she was working for the Huffington Post'. Jacob Rees-Mogg, apparently unaware of either the facts of this case or the recently completed three-year tenure of former *Daily Telegraph* deputy editor Sarah Sands at the helm of the *Today* programme, asked: 'When did the BBC last hire somebody from ConservativeHome to come and be their senior figure or from the *Daily Telegraph*?'[12]

The charge sheet was short. While *not employed by the BBC*, Brammar had taken to Twitter to accuse the serial liar Boris Johnson of lying in a TV interview and compared Brexit to the TV series *Better Call Saul*, 'but less funny or interesting or enjoyable'. She had also criticised the Society of Editors' response to claims by Meghan Markle of racism in the British press. 'I'm aware I won't make myself popular with my peers,' she tweeted on 9 March, 2021, 'but I'm just going to stand up and say it: I don't agree with [the] statement from my industry body that it is "untrue that sections of the UK press were bigoted".' In contrast, on 25 August 2022, Scotland's *National* newspaper printed screenshots of a Twitter exchange Gibb had enjoyed in June 2015, a year before the Brexit referendum and while Gibb was very much *employed by the BBC.* He was asked: 'You mean you will vote NO to the EU?' He replied: 'yes :)'.[13]

In May 2023, a former editor of the BBC's *The Andrew Marr Show*, Rob Burley, recalled an exchange with his then boss, Gibb, shortly after the referendum. In his excellent book, *Why Is This Lying Bastard Lying to Me?*, Burley revealed that Gibb had ordered him not to interrogate the infamous claim on the side of a Vote Leave bus that leaving the EU would somehow enable £350 million a week to be spent on the NHS. He wrote: 'All that was done, [Gibb] told me. It was time to move on. He thought that anything that looked back at the referendum would look to voters like an attempt to rerun it. It risked giving the impression that the BBC couldn't accept the outcome and wanted to discredit the result.' Recalling the exchange in Burley's book, Gibb said that the now completely discredited figure of £350 million 'was not a lie at all'. In September 2021, Brammar was appointed to the new role.

The dangerous absurdity of an obviously biased former BBC man, appointed to the board by the notorious liar Boris Johnson, policing the 'impartiality' of BBC journalism was perhaps best summed up by Lewis Goodall, a former policy editor on *Newsnight*. 'When I was at the BBC Robbie Gibb made my life really difficult day after day,' he said in March 2023 on the *News Agents* podcast. 'He made my life really, really hard at the BBC. You know, day after day I would hear from people saying, "Just watch it. Robbie's watching you …" By comparison to Robbie Gibb, my sort of grand summit within the Labour Party was vice-chair of Birmingham Northfields CLP and youth officer when I was seventeen years old. And I'm sitting there going "Hang on a minute, I'm being lectured about impartiality from a man who until about twelve months ago was – checks notes – literally Head of Comms in Downing Street."'

Goodall left the BBC in June 2022. His departure followed that of Emily Maitlis, whose position should have been ring-fenced and gold-plated after her epochal interview with Prince Andrew ended the disgraced royal's role in public life; the former US correspondent Jon Sopel, who had been offered the once prestigious job of political editor; and Andrew Marr, whose seminal Sunday morning programme would be taken over by Laura 'That's quite a charge' Kuenssberg. Sir Robbie Gibb remained on the BBC board throughout this unprecedented exodus of major on-screen talent.

· · ·

For all the double standards and hypocrisy his employment there embodied, Neil's work at the BBC was often impressive. As we have seen, the problem he highlights here is the impossibility of somebody possessed of opposite opinions enjoying similar success. This came to pass even as Fleet Street's chorus of critics shrieked endlessly about the Corporation being in the grip of unidentified 'leftists'. And yet Neil's greatest contribution to the creation of an ecosystem in which the United Kingdom could hobble herself came not at the BBC, but through his chairmanship of the *Spectator* magazine.

Ever since he appointed the hapless Fraser Nelson as editor in 2009, Neil's magazine deployed a phalanx of favoured scribes to violently coarsen discourse about immigration in general and Muslims in particular. They did so under the cover of the magazine's almost 200-year-old reputation for respectability. Indeed, until Nelson came along, *Spectator* editors would often quickly move on to become senior Conservative politicians (Nigel Lawson, Boris Johnson) or to edit national newspapers (Charles Moore, Dominic Lawson).

One of Neil and Nelson's favourite columnists, Panagiotis 'Taki' Theodoracopulos, became briefly infamous for publishing various paeans to the Greek neo-Nazi party, Golden Dawn. On 8 August 2015, he wrote:

> Migrants are the latest nuisance to invade Europe ... The only thing that stands between them and utter anarchy in the poor neighbourhoods are the youths of Golden Dawn. Golden Dawn is referred to as a neo-fascist political party, instead of a nationalist one, because it will not play ball with the people who have reduced the country to the state it's in today. A few of Golden Dawn's followers have made some extremely unfortunate remarks, which has made it easy for the jackals of the media to paint the third largest party in Greece as neo-Nazi. Take it from Taki: the party's strength lies in its youth movement and its incorruptibility, and it's as neo-Nazi as Ukip.

Perhaps apart from the unwitting truth of this last phrase, Theodoracopulos's assessment of the harmlessness of Golden Dawn didn't hold up to wider scrutiny. Prior to the publication of this piece, Greek media had identified several instances of Golden Dawn members appearing to give Nazi salutes. The party's campaign slogan during elections in 2012 was: 'So we can rid this land of filth'. In a picture taken on 14 September 2012, Panagiotis Iliopoulos, a Golden Dawn MP, showed his 'Sieg Heil' tattoo.[14] Another Golden Dawn MP, Artemios Matthaiopoulos, was previously the lead singer of a Nazi punk band called Pogrom, whose repertoire included a song called 'Auschwitz' with lyrics including 'fuck Anne Frank' and 'Juden raus' ('Jews out'). Yet another, Ilias Panagiotaros, had described Hitler as a 'great personality, like Stalin'. He also expressed opinions that, as we shall see, could easily have come from at least one of Neil's writers, describing most immigrant Muslims to Greece as 'jihadists; fanatic Muslims', and offering support for the notion of a one-race nation, stating, 'if you are talking about nation, it is one race'.[15]

On 10 January 2019, the journalist Owen Jones appeared on Neil's *This Week* programme and stated that the *Spectator* had 'defended Greek neo-Nazis'. A visibly rattled Neil responded: 'No, it hasn't.' The next day, however, he tweeted: 'For the record: I don't think Golden Dawn are neo-Nazi. They are totally Nazi. I think Taki was totally wrong. But I don't read him for political analysis. And it's the editor's decision what is published, not mine. I protect editorial freedom. Even when I profoundly disagree.'

Just two years later he would accidentally give the lie to the ludicrous notion that the magazine's editorial policy has nothing to do with him. On 8 October 2021, the *Financial Times* journalist Janine Gibson suggested to him that, of all his media interests, the '*Spectator* has always been [his] favourite. "Yes! It's ... well, I'm in overall charge," he says, laughing loudly and pointedly. "The editor reports to me and the commercial [side] reports to me, so if things go wrong in the end it's my responsibility."'

This self-confessed responsibility is why Jonathan Portes, professor of Economics and Public Policy at King's College, London, prefers to refer to Neil as 'editor-in-chief' of the magazine instead of simply 'chairman'. He has spent years chronicling *Spectator* contributors' endorsements of ethno-nationalism and flirtations with far-right politics. He told me: 'With Andrew Neil as editor-in-chief and Fraser Nelson as editor, the *Spectator* has – by Neil's own admission – published an open endorsement of a Nazi party. But that's not all – it continues to employ not just well-known anti-Semite and Nazi sympathiser Taki, but also the self-confessed racist liar Rod Liddle, and white ethno-nationalist Douglas Murray, and has published assorted far-right provocateurs, from Gavin McInnes of the Proud Boys to [Dutch far-right politician] Thierry Baudet. While the *Spectator* also publishes many competent and professional journalists, it's impossible not to see this as a deliberate strategy to legitimise the far right, for both ideological and commercial reasons.'

Liddle and Murray, both 'associate editors' of the magazine and both prolific contributors to Murdoch and/or *Mail* and *Telegraph* titles, are perhaps the best examples of precisely the kind of Neil-sponsored journalists who now prosper in the UK. I want to take a little time to look deeper at each of them in turn.

After deciding against a career in teaching because he 'could not remotely conceive of not trying to shag the kids',[16] Liddle rose through the BBC ranks to become editor of the Radio 4 *Today* programme and a columnist for the *Guardian*. Somewhat surprisingly for someone who would end up all over right-wing media (he has columns in the *Sun* and the *Sunday Times*), his position at the BBC became untenable after he used his *Guardian* column to lampoon members of the pro-hunting Countryside Alliance. The incident Portes refers to above relates to the revelation that he had contributed to an independent Millwall Football Club message board using the username 'monkeymfc'. On 17 January 2010, the *Mail on Sunday*, following up an investigation by the Liberal Conspiracy website, reported that: 'Liddle initially claimed any controversial remarks left by monkeymfc had been placed by a hacker. However, he admitted last night to making most of the comments.'

In October 2009, Liddle joined a debate about whether the BNP should admit non-white members. He wrote: 'There's thousands of organisations catering exclusively to black and Asian minorities. ✶✶✶✶ 'em, close them down. Why do blacks need a forum of their own? As a power base and cash cow for ✶✶✶✶s and in order to perpetuate the myth of widespread discrimination.' Later that month, 'monkeymfc' contributed to a thread entitled 'Channel 4 claiming blacks are thick'. The *Mail* reported: 'In comments Liddle strongly denies writing, the contributor says: "On average a little under 10 per cent thicker than whites; 15 per cent thicker than east Asians. I thought everyone knew, too. Some argument about cultural bias of tests, but same results come up in US."' Sunny Hundal, the editor of Liberal Conspiracy, later commented:

> Liddle denied making racist comments, saying that others sometimes logged in under his account and posted comments with his username. Oddly though, we couldn't find any comments complaining about others doing this, though. Must be an oversight ... BUT we did find DOZENS of racist/sexist comments made by 'monkeymfc' on that Millwall site. We asked Rod Liddle if he had made these comments, and how hackers had gotten his password. He didn't respond.[17]

By 13 June 2014, the 'strong denials' and the claim that he had been 'hacked' were forgotten. In an interview with Simon Hattenstone of the *Guardian* he insisted that his comments had been 'taken out of context'. Asked about saying that black people have lower IQs than white people, he replied: 'It's true that 97 per cent of intelligence tests put whites 7 per cent ahead of black Africans, and that we're behind Asians and particularly east Asians. And I then said there's a greater division in races than between races. And you can't trust any of them because they're culturally determined. I'm merely being accurate.'

Other comments posted by 'monkeymfc' included: 'Someone kick her in the cnt'; 'Fcking outrageous that you can't smoke in Auschwitz'; 'the correct term would be niggermeat, rather than wogmeat? You've got to get your terminology correct' and 'Semi-house trained Muslim savages'. Two months after the 'monkeymfc' scandal, the Press Complaints Commission upheld a complaint about a December 2009 *Spectator* blog in which Liddle, under his own name, had written: 'the overwhelming majority of street crime, knife crime, gun crime, robbery and crimes of sexual violence in London is carried out by young men from the African-Caribbean community'. This claim was, to use a technical term, bollocks. The PCC adjudged that the article 'contained inaccurate information in breach of Clause 1 (Accuracy) of the Editors' Code of Practice.' But even now he's still at it, revealing in a recent column: 'I have spent the morning trying to draw a cartoon of a black person without it being racist. It's bloody difficult. Especially the lips.'[18]

Of all the opinion engineering that made the UK ripe for the rhetoric of a pound-shop demagogue like Nigel Farage, perhaps the most outrageous was the idea that racism or its euphemistic cousin 'legitimate concerns about immigration' were somehow 'working class'. If Liddle's language hadn't been so toxic, his desperation to see himself as somehow of the 'street' would be almost endearing. Referring to the sort of journalists who dream of editing the *Today* programme or writing a column for the *Guardian*, he told Hattenstone: 'I thought about my mates at Millwall Online, God I respect them so much more than these other people, these ghastly fucking people.' In reality, the anti-immigrant animus that would drive so much of Brexit and do so much lasting damage to social cohesion was much more 'Home Counties' than 'Red Wall'. If Paul Dacre's *Daily Mail* provided the brawn, Andrew Neil's *Spectator* cast itself as the brains, dressing base bigotry in the clothes of academia and using flowery language to mask the ugliest rhetoric. Unfortunately for British Muslims, and perversely because no EU countries are majority Muslim, Islamophobia would prove to be the most effective way for right-wing media to persuade voters that we could not 'control our borders'.

Few British commentators have done more to inflame Islamophobia than Liddle's *Spectator* colleague, Douglas Murray. Another denizen of the incestuous 'think tank' network, Murray's Centre for Social Cohesion (CSC) was set up in 2007 with funding from Civitas, which had itself been formed from the remains of the IEA's Health & Welfare Unit. An erstwhile colleague of Murray's at the CSC, James Brandon, wrote in January 2009: 'My time there was a constant struggle to "de-radicalise" Murray and to ensure that the centre's output targeted only Islamists – and not Muslims as a whole.'[19] It's fair to say that Brandon was not entirely successful.

In 2008, the CSC was incorporated by yet another think tank, the Henry Jackson Society (HJS). On 18 February 2017, one of the original founders of the HJS, Matthew Jamison, wrote of being ashamed at what the organisation had become: 'The far right anti-Muslim racist nature of the HJS has helped to lay the intellectual groundwork for much of what President Trump and his Breitbart reading "alt-right" movement is attempting to do against Muslim people and immigrants in the United States.' Breitbart London, the British iteration of Steve Bannon's online hatefest, was founded in 2014 and headed, inevitably, by yet another *Spectator* regular and Andrew Neil protégé, James Delingpole. But it was for Murray that Jamison reserved particular disgust:

> Its Associate Director, the white supremacist, racist anti-Muslim bigot, Douglas Murray is the most ugly and offensive example of this vicious, racist anti-Muslim campaign. Mr. Murray is full of venom and hatred for Muslims. He seems to have a perverse and deranged obsession with all things Islam related. In a ghastly speech in the Dutch parliament in 2006 Murray stated: 'Conditions for Muslims in Europe must be made harder,' and 'all immigration into Europe from Muslim countries must stop.'[20]

Unsurprisingly, Murray would later offer support for Donald Trump's so-called Muslim ban, which very deliberately targeted 'Muslims as a whole'.

If the 'white supremacist' accusation seems a little strong, it is worth noting something Murray wrote in 2013: 'To study the latest census is to stare at one unalterable conclusion: mass immigration has altered our country completely. It has become a radically different place, and London has become a foreign country. In 23 of London's 33 Boroughs, "white Britons" are now in a minority.'[21] I'm not sure how this can be read as anything but an implicit insistence that non-white Britons are somehow 'foreign' and therefore not *properly* British.

According to Paul Goodman, then the shadow communities minister, Murray was offered an opportunity to disown his Dutch parliament comments but refused, prompting the Conservative front bench to sever relations with him and the CSC. Goodman later wrote:

> The solution seemed to me to be obvious. Murray should disown his remarks. He could, for example, say that 'I realised some years ago how poorly expressed the speech in question was', and confirm that 'my opinions have also altered significantly'. The Conservative front bench would then be able to enjoy normal working relations with his Centre for Social Cohesion, which my colleagues now demanded should be curtailed altogether – reasonably enough. I went to see Murray and put this suggestion to him. He would have spared himself a great deal of time and trouble if he had taken it. And such an apology would have been a sign of strength, not weakness. But in this case strength was wanting. Our meeting ended without agreement.[22]

There would be no such schism at Andrew Neil's *Spectator*, where Murray continued to delight readers with insights boasting headlines such as 'Donald Trump won't be as bad as you think' (9 November 2016); 'Why do politicians refuse to tell it how it is on immigration?' (25 March 2018); 'Turning the tide: how to deal with Britain's new migrant crisis' (31 July 2021) and 'The cost of mass migration' (6 May 2023). Or, over at the *Telegraph*, 'American and British voters are being failed by the same big immigration lie' (19 May 2023); 'It's in the UK's national interest for Trump to triumph' (28 August 2020) and, my personal favourite, 'Of course Donald Trump deserves the Nobel Peace Prize' (10 September 2020). There is clearly an audience for this stuff. In addition to his *Spectator* and *Telegraph* duties, Murray writes books describing Enoch Powell's (him again) 'prophetic foreboding' and warning about the imminent immolation of white-majority countries as well as regular columns for Rupert Murdoch's *Sun*, *Times* and *New York Post*. Inevitably, he also pops up in the *Mail*.

Admiration is not confined to Neil, Murdoch, Dacre and their acolytes. The following appeared on the now defunct website of the English Defence League, a viciously Islamophobic and racist movement once euphemistically described by Murray as 'a grassroots response from non-Muslims to Islamism':[23] 'Luckily there are a few members of the middle and establishment classes who believe that the EDL at least deserve a fair hearing. One of these is the British writer and former director of the Centre for Social Cohesion, Douglas Murray. It's a pity there aren't more public figures like Douglas Murray. Thank you for being right Mr Murray.'[24]

Appreciative audiences can sometimes cause problems of their own, even for veteran purveyors of what is best described as 'gentrified xenophobia'.[25] In London in May 2023, basking in the warm embrace of the creepily titled National Conservatism Conference, Murray issued a heartfelt plea for more British nationalism, explaining, 'I see no reason why every other country in the world should be prevented from feeling pride in itself, because the Germans mucked up twice in a century.' Referring to the First and Second World Wars, and by implication to the state-sponsored murder of 6 million Jewish people, as well as disabled, Roma and LGBTQ+ people, as Germany having 'mucked up' prompted understandable disgust in some quarters. On 16 May, Professor Tanja Bueltmann, a professor of migration and diaspora history at the University of Strathclyde, tweeted a clip of the speech with the following commentary:

79 years ago today, the Nazis began the main phase of extermination of Hungarian Jews. Three trains arrived in Auschwitz that day in 1944, with 9000 deportees murdered in gas chambers. 79 years later, NatCon speaker Douglas Murray refers to Nazism as a 'mucking up'. Minimising the Holocaust in this way and conflating Nazism with feeling pride in one's country – it is as ahistorical as it is shameful. The deliberate Nazi policy of exterminating those deemed unworthy is not a 'mucking up'. It is genocide.

Inevitably, the outrage barely dented Murray's popularity with commissioning editors. Two months later he was back in the *Telegraph*, writing about racism in English cricket under the satire-proof headline: 'The left now wants the utter abolition of Britain as we know it' (1 July 2023). It was an accidentally insightful, though wholly unoriginal, sentiment. The previous week, Richard Littlejohn's *Daily Mail* column had rejoiced in the headline 'These days only one world view is permissable [*sic*]: Ultra-woke, pro-migrant, anti-Brexit and anti-Boris.' By the middle of 2023 both Murray and Littlejohn, along with most of their fellow members of the Brexit/Johnson/Trump fan clubs, had realised that the gig was up and begun the laborious business of trying to blame the inevitable failures of their heroes on the people whose warnings about those failures had gone unheeded. As we have seen, they will not be short of platforms from which to do so.

· · ·

On the evening of 13 June 2021, Neil launched the channel that he hoped would finally deliver him media-mogul status, saying: 'We are proud to be British – the clue is in the name.' Chairman and chief presenter of GB News, on a contract reported to be worth £4 million, he had been characteristically dismissive of anyone suggesting that the project looked like a bid to become a British Fox News. It would not, he insisted, 'slavishly follow the existing news agenda'. Instead, it would cover 'the stories that matter to you and those that have been neglected' and deliver 'a huge range of voices that reflect the views and values of our United Kingdom'. It was, to be kind, an unmitigated disaster.

Neil's penchant for wearing a black jacket (to mask, apparently, his proclivity to perspire profusely) against a black background left him looking like a disembodied head on screen. Technical problems abounded and his promise that it would not be an 'echo chamber' withered a little more with every appointment of a contributor with a long history of hating, in no particular order, immigration, Meghan Markle, footballers taking the knee and the EU. Neil lasted just eight shows and resigned entirely from the network in September 2021, saying he did not want to be a part of a 'British Fox News'. In an interview with the *Daily Mail* about the experience, he started crying and confessed: 'I came close to a breakdown'. It was a very sad career culmination for a man who once used one of his countless BBC programmes to ask: 'Are we raising Generation Snowflake?'[26]

GB News did not fall with Neil's tears. On the contrary, despite making monumental financial losses (£31 million in its first year on air) it went on to become precisely the sort of 'echo chamber' that Neil and his fellow right-wing commentators claim to despise. It is bankrolled by hedge fund manager Paul Marshall, a Brexit-backing Tory donor, and Legatum, a Dubai-based investment fund founded by New Zealand-born billionaire Christopher Chandler. Like Rupert Murdoch's TalkTV, their schedule is packed with right-wing politicians and self-styled 'anti-woke' presenters, plucked from the pages of the *Sun*, *Mail*, *Telegraph* and *Spectator*, dedicated to ensuring that right-wing talking points are amplified to deafening levels. Tory MPs are regularly to be found interviewing Tory MPs and while the audiences remain negligible, the attention they receive from right-wing newspapers is unsurprisingly disproportionate. It is as if a dangerous new front has been opened in the war against the fractured but precious impartiality of the BBC. Andrew Neil fired the first shot.

Chapter 4
MATTHEW ELLIOTT

*We need to learn from our European colleagues and the
Tea Party movement in the US ... It will be fascinating
to see whether it will transfer to the UK. Will there be the
same sort of uprising?*

Matthew Elliott[1]

ON 3 JULY 2018, a largely unknown figure called Matthew Elliott was
interviewed on the BBC by its then political editor, Laura Kuenssberg.
The encounter was remarkable for two reasons. First, Elliott – the chief
executive of Vote Leave, the official Brexit campaign group – was in the
studio to respond to an imminent Electoral Commission (EC) investigation into his organisation's alleged breaking of electoral law some two
weeks *before* the EC's official findings would be published. Aware that
his organisation was to be found guilty on at least four charges, he had
tried to mark his own homework by submitting a 500-page dossier to
the EC attempting to rebut its conclusions before they were even
published. Affording Elliott this unprecedented opportunity to launch
a pre-emptive strike on the commission left Kuenssberg unable to properly challenge Elliott's version of events or establish whether or not he
was telling the truth. Unfortunately for BBC viewers, Elliott's attempted
self-exculpation was presented as an enviable scoop. Second, it left his

unfounded allegations and conclusions about the EC investigation unchallenged for two weeks in the public domain – and plastered across all the right-wing, Brexit-supporting newspapers.

When the report was published on 17 July, Vote Leave was reported to the police and fined £61,000: £20,000 for exceeding its spending limits by hundreds of thousands of pounds, £20,000 for failing to comply with the commission's investigation and another £20,000 for filing false information; throw in a £1,000 fine for failing to produce invoices in support of its own spending claims and we arrive at the grand total. It is a pittance in the context of the £7.5 million it spent on campaigning but a serious sanction nonetheless.

So what? The referendum was done and dusted. All's fair in love and war, and the febrile pro-Brexit atmosphere in media *outside* the BBC ensured that, apart from a few howls of outrage from a handful of 'Remoaner' journalists and the crusading barrister Jolyon Maugham of the Good Law Project, the story would be summarily dismissed as sour grapes or evidence of the 'Establishment' conspiring against Brexit. The report even acknowledges that if it hadn't been for Maugham, the journalism of Carole Cadwalladr at the *Observer*, openDemocracy and others, the investigation would likely never have been reopened. Consider, though, the second of those fines – for *failing to comply with the investigation* – in the context of what Elliott was able to claim unchallenged to Kuenssberg a full fortnight before the verdict came in.

He said: 'They haven't followed due process. They listened to one side of the story. So these so-called whistle-blowers who came out in March, you know, they've been in to the Electoral Commission to have interviews. We've offered to go in for interviews, both at a board level and also at staff level, but they haven't accepted any interviews from our side. They also haven't accepted the fact that we're doing an internal investigation into all of this. We've got outside IT experts in to look at all of our emails. We've had several teams of lawyers to actually piece together what happened two years ago during the referendum. And actually, when we look at all the evidence, all the facts, actually they stack up on our side.' Under remarkably gentle questioning from Kuenssberg regarding emails that would prove crucial to the EC's conclusion about unlawful coordination between ostensibly separate campaign groups, he insisted: 'And all of those emails are completely fine. We followed the rules at all times.' The interview concludes with a visibly perspiring Elliott insisting: 'So we followed, yes, the letter of the law, but also the spirit of running a positive campaign.'[2]

The EC's response to seeing the subject of its investigation invited by the BBC to rubbish its findings before anyone else had seen them was diplomatic: 'The commission has concluded its investigation and, having reached initial findings, provided Vote Leave with a 28-day period to make any further or new representations. That period ended on Tuesday 3 July. The unusual step taken by Vote Leave in sharing its views on the Electoral Commission's initial findings does not affect the process set out in law.'[3]

Two weeks later, the EC was rather more forthright. In a direct contradiction of Elliott's previously unchallenged claims, the commission's full report said that Vote Leave had repeatedly refused to attend interviews. The detail of the report was damning in the extreme. Interviews were requested in November 2017 and Vote Leave indicated that it could cooperate. Despite this, it did not respond to a request to set interview dates in December 2017 and January 2018. Instead, Vote Leave sent legal letters to the Electoral Commission threatening to judicially review the opening of the investigation. Two further offers of interview dates were made but Vote Leave 'began to repeat procedural questions we had already answered'. Elliott and his colleagues were then issued with a formal investigation notice to provide certain documents but did not reply by the deadline or produce the documents, saying instead that they could be inspected at their own lawyer's office. Subsequently, Vote Leave offered to let the EC inspect the documents as long as it was permitted to discuss why the investigation should be closed, an offer the commission described as neither appropriate or helpful. When the documents were finally made available, they were found to be incorrect or incomplete.

It is impossible to calculate the damage done to proper coverage of the EC's case, or to the public interest, by the BBC's extraordinary decision to allow the convicted party free rein to malign its investigators weeks before their conclusions were published. Had Kuenssberg waited for the full report, Elliott's protestations could at least have been countered by the EC chief executive, Claire Bassett, who said: 'Over a three-month period we actually made five attempts to interview Vote Leave and we were unable to. We have in fact issued a record fine for failure to cooperate with a statutory notice because we found it so difficult to get Vote Leave to work with us in this investigation.'[4]

As we have established, the BBC had long been a place where journalistic misjudgements favouring the Brexiter cause were far from a punishable offence. And Kuenssberg could be confident that rolling out a metaphorical red carpet for Elliott would not see her end up on the wrong side of her bosses, the wrong end of newspaper hatchet jobs or accused of impartiality by the usual media Rottweilers. (The High Court would later agree with the Electoral Commission's conclusion that Vote Leave had broken the law, and find the watchdog had misinterpreted the rules in pre-referendum advice it gave to Vote Leave.)

'I think the BBC profoundly failed,' said Christopher Wylie, the Canadian data consultant who first revealed that Cambridge Analytica had been collecting data from millions of Facebook users and using it to target political advertising. 'They initially refused to cover it, and when they did, they talked to the people who had committed the unlawful act, not the people who submitted the evidence.'[5] We shall see that this interview was the apotheosis of a process where legions of unaccountable, unelected, largely unqualified, self-appointed 'experts' from a dizzying array of so-called 'think tanks' were carefully cultivating journalists, placing 'stories' and being permanently available to fill broadcast guest slots. Without the building of that process, Elliott would not have been let through the studio door that day, let alone permitted to use the BBC as a soapbox from which to spout his self-serving drivel.

A normal country, with a normal media and vaguely normal politics, would indubitably have made much more of the scandal, and the role of the BBC's political editor in it. But by July 2018 nothing about Brexit Britain was normal. Theresa May was still in Downing Street and two of her senior advisers, Stephen Parkinson and Cleo Watson, had held senior roles at Vote Leave. Her spokesman simply, and irrelevantly, said: 'The PM is absolutely clear that this was the largest democratic exercise in our country. The public delivered a clear verdict and that is what we are going to be implementing.'

Over at the Metropolitan Police, to whom the Electoral Commission had referred the case, the response was even less impressive. Nearly six months after the Met received a dossier of evidence of potential crimes, the openDemocracy journalists James Cusick and Adam Ramsay enquired into the investigation's progress. They reported: 'Following inquiries by openDemocracy, the Met revealed it has yet to start any formal investigation, and has remained effectively stalled for months in "assessing evidence". Pushed on why there has been no progress, or no formal case logged, a Scotland Yard spokesman admitted there were issues and "political sensitivities" that had to be taken into account.[6] Almost exactly a year after the Electoral Commission found Vote Leave had broken electoral law, the man who fronted its campaign, Boris Johnson, would become prime minister.

So who is Matthew Elliott, why did he hold a position of such influence despite his relative anonymity and how has he ended up on this book's cast list of rather better known people? We are not here to relitigate Brexit. That the referendum victory was built largely on lies and, as we have seen, law breaking is now barely debatable. Reversing the damage is a generational challenge and not one, for now, that can be undertaken at the ballot box or in a courtroom. Brexit remains of enormous interest not just because of what it continues to do to our economy, trade and international reputation but also because of what it can teach us about the public discourse and political landscape that needed to be in place for its champions to triumph. And an absolutely crucial part of that involved a decades-long mission to insinuate the most extreme 'free market' or 'libertarian' ideologies into every corner of the British news media and, later, government itself. The secretly funded vessels through which this was achieved style themselves 'think tanks' or even 'educational charities' but, despite frequent protestations to the contrary, effectively operate as lobby groups tirelessly promoting policies that allow businesses, or wealth, to operate with as little regulation, taxation or scrutiny as possible. And Matthew Elliott is a primary example of the pernicious effects of these organisations.

Although many of these think tanks were born from the 'economic liberalism' espoused by the Austrian philosopher and economist

Friedrich Hayek, as their influence has increased so their adherence to any substantive intellectual credo has crumbled. Hayek challenged the post-war Keynesian consensus that state planning and public spending could and should be utilised to stabilise economies, reduce unemployment and protect populations from the violent vicissitudes of 'boom and bust' economics. But by the twenty-first century, the UK and US 'free-market think tanks' ostensibly founded in his image were essentially dedicated to promoting greed, protecting greed and serving the interests of the greedy. As such, newspaper owners love them as organisations who can reliably provide soundbites to undermine the socialised healthcare of the NHS or the welfare state and champion rampant corporate profiteering. Elliott, who founded the so-called 'TaxPayers' Alliance' (TPA) in 2004, is a latter-day admiral of this little fleet, which is centred on Tufton Street in the heart of Westminster.

According to its own website: 'The TaxPayers' Alliance (TPA) was launched by Matthew Elliott and Andrew Allum in early 2004 to speak for ordinary taxpayers fed up with government waste, increasing taxation, and a lack of transparency in all levels of government.' The word 'ordinary' is doing an extraordinary amount of work here. Early backers included David Alberto, co-owner of the serviced offices company Avanta, who gifted Elliott free serviced office space around the corner from the House of Commons worth an estimated £100,000 a year. Anthony Bamford, the Brexit-supporting Tory donor and JCB tycoon who would later let a disgraced Boris Johnson live in his Cotswolds garden, made minor donations in a private capacity. Malcolm McAlpine, scion of the Robert McAlpine construction empire, was another donor, explaining: 'Our family business ... advocates value for money government and we, for some years, supported the Taxpayers Alliance, which brings to general attention a large number of instances of apparent excessive and unproductive expenditure of public funds.'[7] Intriguingly, at the time of this statement his company was engaged in building London's Olympic Stadium while the TPA was a frequent critic of the £9.3 billion of public money slated to be spent on hosting the 2012 games.

Today, the funding transparency website Who Funds You? gives the TPA an E, the lowest transparency rating, but in their early years they were more open about their donors. The spread-betting tycoon Stuart Wheeler was one. He also gave £5 million to the Conservatives before switching allegiance to Nigel Farage's UKIP and later becoming co-treasurer of Vote Leave. The Tory donor and hotelier Sir Rocco Forte was another. By 15 May 2023, the Brexit he had enthusiastically backed was proceeding so well that he told *The Times* he was thinking of moving to the EU, saying: 'I am of Italian origin, I speak Italian, a large part of my business is in Italy and if I was in Italy I'd be able to expand quicker than I could sitting here in the UK'.

By 2009, the organisation was reported to have been quoted by the *Daily Mail* in 517 articles *in a single year*.[8] The *Sun* was not far behind, quoting an outfit founded by Elliott, the 25-year-old former political researcher for a Conservative MEP, on 307 separate occasions. This, of course, was the year in which Rebekah Brooks was writing to David Cameron about 'rooting for you tomorrow not just as proud friend but because professionally we're definitely in this together!' Indeed, the imminent party conference speech to which she refers here was greeted enthusiastically by Elliott, who said: 'The idea of tearing down the walls of big government as Cameron did in his speech on Thursday is something we have been talking about for years. The Tory party has moved onto our agenda.'[9] It could, of course, be the case that the interests of the billionaire Rupert Murdoch's chief representative on earth (Brooks), an assortment of extremely wealthy Brexit-supporting businessmen, the Conservative prime minister behind a catastrophic programme of 'austerity' and the grandly titled TPA 'chief executive', Matthew Elliott, were entirely aligned with those of 'ordinary taxpayers'. But it seems unlikely to me.

This remarkable synergy notwithstanding, Elliott has always rejected claims that the TPA is a Conservative front organisation. You can often judge a man by the company he keeps. Over the next decade, he would set up Big Brother Watch, a civil liberties campaign group. Its founding director was Alex Deane, a former chief of staff to David Cameron who later failed in his attempt to become a Conservative parliamentary candidate. In 2012, Elliott was also a founding member of Conservative Friends of Russia (CFoR), which was launched in August in the Russian ambassador's garden. Other attendees included the Conservative minister John Whittingdale and his aide, Carrie Symonds, future mistress and wife of Boris Johnson. Three months later, in November, the *Guardian*'s Luke Harding reported that the group's diplomatic contact, Sergey Nalobin, was the son of a former KGB general and the brother of a serving FSB officer. In April 2011, in an email published by the *Guardian*, Nalobin wrote to a contact: 'We've received instructions from Moscow – to discuss the perspective of co-operation between British Conservatives and United Russia in the parliamentary assembly of the Council of Europe. With whom would it be best to discuss this question?'[10] Sixteen months later it was, presumably, Ferrero Rocher all round at the CFoR launch.

In 2013, Elliott founded Business for Britain, a Eurosceptic campaign group. Three years later, after the referendum result, he wrote an article for the Brexit Central website, which he also founded, titled: 'How Business for Britain helped change the course of history in three short years'. Its first editor, Jonathan Isaby, had previously co-edited the website ConservativeHome (founded by Tim Montgomerie, a former speech writer to two Tory leaders, chief of staff for one and future *Times* comment editor) and served as 'political director' of the TPA. A ConservativeHome columnist at the time, Chloe Westley, had previously been Vote Leave's head of social media and a 'campaign manager' at the TPA. In 2019, she would join Boris Johnson's Downing Street staff as a 'special adviser' while Montgomerie briefly became his 'social justice adviser'. In March 2023, it was reported that Elliott would be nominated for a peerage in Liz Truss's resignation honours.[11] He found himself in familiar company. Big Brother Watch board member Mark Littlewood was also reported to be on the list. He, of course, is the 'director general' of the IEA and also the 'think tank's 'Ralph Harris fellow'. It is worth taking a moment here to find out a little more about Harris.

In 1955, a British farmer named Antony Fisher read an article by Friedrich Hayek in the *Reader's Digest* magazine. It was a 'condensation' of Hayek's book, *The Road to Serfdom*. In it, Hayek argues that interventionist governments ostensibly dedicated to organising society in the hope of promoting freedom and improving the lives of citizens would instead end up destroying the very things they professed to value: freedom and democracy. Fisher was convinced that the UK was heading towards disaster. He visited Hayek at the London School of Economics, where he was a professor, and sought advice on how best to contribute to the resistance. He recorded the advice: 'He explained his view that the decisive influence in the battle of ideas and policy was wielded by intellectuals whom he characterised as the "second-hand dealer in ideas".'[12] In 2011, the documentary maker Adam Curtis described the meeting:

Hayek told Fisher to set up what he called a 'scholarly institute' that would operate as a dealer in second-hand ideas. Its sole aim should be to persuade journalists and opinion-formers that state planning was leading to a totalitarian nightmare, and that the only way to rescue Britain was by bringing back the free market. If they did this successfully – that would put pressure on the politicians, and Fisher would change the course of history.[13]

Somewhat improbably, Fisher would first make his fortune as a pioneer of battery farming chickens and then use it to set up the 'Institute of Economic Affairs'. But he couldn't do it alone. Curtis explains: 'Fisher and [Oliver] Smedley had met at a fringe organisation called The Society of Individualists. They became friends because they were both convinced that the innocuous-looking, state-run Milk Marketing Board and Egg Marketing Board were actually the enemies of freedom.' It's worth noting the similarities here to the paranoid convictions that would later animate so many Brexiters. Smedley, who had previously set up the 'Council for the Reduction of Taxation' and would later found an anti-Common Market pressure group, 'Keep Britain Out', urged caution on his co-founder. Concerning the first draft of the IEA's aims, he wrote to Fisher that it was

Imperative that we should give no indication in our literature that we are working to educate the Public along certain lines which might be interpreted as having a political bias. In other words, if we said openly that we were re-teaching the economics of the free-market, it might enable our enemies to question the charitableness of our motives. That is why the first draft is written in rather cagey terms.[14]

The wider story of Fisher and Smedley is, incidentally, absolutely riveting and told in characteristically engrossing fashion in Curtis's blogs. The former would, by Curtis's reckonings, go on to found 150 so-called 'free-market think tanks' around the world. His granddaughter, Rachel Whetstone, was political secretary to Michael Howard when he was Tory leader and married to Steve Hilton when he was director of strategy to Conservative prime minister David Cameron. Smedley, by contrast, would go on to establish a pirate radio station that would later merge with Radio Caroline, and stand trial for manslaughter. But this is not their story.

In 1957, Fisher and Smedley appointed a young leader writer from the Glasgow *Herald* to run their two-year-old 'think tank'. Ralph Harris, another Hayek disciple, had mounted two unsuccessful attempts to become a Conservative MP but would abandon his political ambitions for an altogether more influential, albeit less prominent, role in the Tory high command. He was 'general director' of the IEA from 1957 to 1988 and then founding president from 1990 until his death in 2006. Harris seems a rather more high-minded and likeable figure than his successors in the 'Tufton Street' ecosystem. Ennobled by Margaret Thatcher in 1979, he elected to sit in the Lords as a crossbench peer and voted Labour in both 1974 general elections. Nevertheless, his modus operandi established what would become the template for the flotilla of ideologically aligned 'think tanks' that would follow in the IEA's wake. One obituarist wrote: 'He was indefatigable in phoning newspapers to remind them of the next IEA pamphlet coming off the press. He ran informal luncheons, which mixed up patrons with journalists and academic writers. These always featured a discussion on some current topic or a new publication, all conducted by Harris, good-naturedly encouraging all the company to have their say. He would finish by gently reminding those present that the Institute needed support in its mission of letting markets operate effectively.'[15]

From 1988 to 2001, Harris was also an independent director of Rupert Murdoch's Times Newspaper Holdings. We have already seen the symbiotic relationship between the IEA and the *Sunday Times* under Andrew Neil's editorship. Harris took things further, offering the IEA's full-throated support to Murdoch's bid to move into broadcasting. In 1990, for example, the IEA's 'research and editorial director', Dr Cento Veljanovski wrote *The Media in Britain Today*, a furious rejection of the argument that allowing newspaper barons to move in to satellite TV would pose a profound threat to media diversity and competition. The 91-page pamphlet was published by Murdoch's News International. 'The alliance between the IEA and News International, a major news media corporation, was remarkable,' wrote David McKnight in *Murdoch's Politics*, 'as it involved newspapers and television outlets being used as vehicles to publicise the think tank's political and intellectual agenda.'

Even more remarkable, and even less understood by most of the British public, is how completely that agenda would come to be embraced by the Conservative Party. When Margaret Thatcher became prime minister in 1979, she wrote to Fisher and described him as having 'created the climate of opinion which made our victory possible'.[16] To Ralph Harris she wrote: 'It is primarily your foundation work which enabled us to rebuild the philosophy upon which our Party succeeded.'[17]

Forty years later, on 28 July 2019, the IEA sent an email to its supporters:

This week liberty-lovers witnessed some exciting developments as newly elected Prime Minister Boris Johnson appointed possibly the most liberal, free-market oriented cabinet since the days of Margaret Thatcher. The IEA is delighted to note that no less than 14 cabinet members and cabinet attendees are alumni of IEA initiatives, the 'Free Enterprise Group' and 'FREER', both designed to champion ideas of free enterprise and social freedom.

It went on to boast that 'FEG alumni now make up three of the four great offices of state, including Chancellor of the Exchequer Sajid Javid, Foreign Secretary Dominic Raab, and Home Secretary Priti Patel.' Smedley's heirs no longer had to worry about being 'cagey' – they were in power.

The same email contained a round-up of the media appearances IEA members had made during the previous week. It was a remarkable roster, although business as usual for the individuals concerned. There is now barely a political programme broadcast or newspaper printed that does not contain contributions from a representative of either the IEA or one of the similar outfits formed in its image. This proliferation was inevitable. Even the Murdoch/Dacre/Barclay axis would balk at platforming the same secretly funded, unaccountable organisation several times a week.

The more, it would seem, the merrier: the Centre for Policy Studies (CPS) was co-founded by Margaret Thatcher, Alfred Sherman and Keith Joseph in 1974; the Adam Smith Institute (ASI) was established in 1977; Civitas, an IEA offshoot, appeared in 2000; the TaxPayers' Alliance in 2004; and Policy Exchange in 2007. Other players come and go but these five organisations form the backbone of a neoliberal cabal that exerts extraordinary influence over government and media alike.

But don't take my word for it. 'We propose things which people regard as being on the edge of lunacy,' said Madsen Pirie, president of the ASI. 'The next thing you know, they're on the edge of policy.'[18] The future *Guardian* editor Alan Rusbridger was an early chronicler of their influence, writing in 1987: 'Early papers proposed the contracting out of local government services (1980), the compulsory tendering of local government services (1983), the contracting out of hospital ancillary services (1982), the fundamentals of the poll tax (1981–1985) and the deregulation of road transport and privatisation of the National Bus Company (1980).'[19]

Pirie has also provided a very helpful account of how these successes were achieved. 'We slipped easily into working with the IEA, the CPS and the National Federation of Small Businesses,' he wrote in his 2012 memoir, *Think Tank: The Story of the Adam Smith Institute.*

It was a huge help that we had some press support. The *Telegraph* sketch writers, John O'Sullivan and Frank Johnson, were very much on side, as were leader writers from the *Telegraph*, *The Times*, the *Daily Mail* and others. We had hardly any friends in radio or television, however.

A group of us took to meeting at Saturday lunchtime in the Cork and Bottle wine bar just off Leicester Square, owned by New Zealander Don Hewitson. We would colonise one of the barrel-vaulted alcoves and plan strategy for the week ahead. Those meetings always included the ASI and someone from the IEA and the CPS, plus people from *The Times* and *Telegraph*, from Margaret Thatcher's research staff and later the No. 10 policy unit ... Typically we would decide how we could focus the policy agenda on to specific subjects during the coming weeks and try to co-ordinate our activities to make us more effective collectively than we could have been individually. One or more of the think tanks might arrange a publication; another would organise a seminar; the journalists would endeavour to have the subject covered in leader columns; while the research staff would ensure it was drawn to the attention of the appropriate members of the shadow Cabinet.

Almost 50 years later, three very important things have changed. Now, the think-tank staffers mostly *write* the newspaper articles themselves; Pirie's plaintive complaint that 'We had hardly any friends in radio or television' has been comprehensively reversed, and the infiltration of their personnel into the very heart of government exceeds even the wildest dreams of Fisher, Smedley, Pirie and Elliott. In that week of Boris Johnson's installation, the aforementioned IEA email disclosed that:

> This week IEA spokespeople were across the media discussing whether the new PM and cabinet will deliver positive pro-market reforms and usher in a competitive and free economic environment. Our Associate Director Kate Andrews [shortly to join Andrew Neil's *Spectator*] penned several articles, including one for *The Telegraph* arguing that the PM and International Trade Secretary must hurry up and pursue free trade deals around the world, regardless of a deal or no-deal Brexit. Kate also wrote for City AM, compelling Boris Johnson to stick to his pledge to restructure social care delivery, looking at pre-funded systems around the world; and for the Times Red Box about how a battle of ideas could play out – the newly established socialists versus the 'libertarian comeback kids'. Kate also spoke to LBC, CNN, and BBC World Service about the changes in Whitehall. Meanwhile, our Head of Communications Nerissa Chesterfield appeared on Sky News to

discuss the benefits of Brexit, including the ability to strike bilateral trade deals, and for the cabinet to create a more pro-business atmosphere in the UK.

This, it must be stressed, is a *perfectly typical* schedule for IEA staff. Director General Mark Littlewood has a weekly column in *The Times*. He was also secretly recorded in 2018 telling an undercover reporter that the IEA was in 'the Brexit influencing game' and that IEA donors could get to know government ministers on first name terms. He said: 'The people running our international trade team are talking to [Gove] definitely once every three or four days ... along with David Davis, Boris Johnson, Liam Fox.' And while pitching for funding, Littlewood explained that funders could shape 'substantial content' of any research commissioned.[20]

Christopher Snowdon is the IEA's 'head [inevitably!] of lifestyle economics' and describes himself as a 'scourge of nanny statists'. In 2019, the *British Medical Journal* reported that 'The IEA keeps its funding sources private, as it is legally allowed to do, but *The BMJ* can reveal today that it is part-funded by British American Tobacco. In the past, it has also taken money from the gambling, alcohol, soft drinks and sugar industries.'[21] Coincidentally, Snowdon moans regularly about anti-obesity, anti-alcohol and anti-smoking policies in the pages of the *Telegraph*, *Spectator* and *Mail*. He also pops up in the *Critic* magazine, founded in November 2019 and funded by an asset management tycoon, Jeremy Hosking, because, presumably, the print media did not previously lean heavily enough towards its brand of Brexit fetishisation.

Another former Tory donor, Hosking was a major backer of Nigel Farage's Brexit Party and, in 2021, became the founding donor of the Reclaim Party, an eccentric little 'anti-woke' outfit fronted by an actor, Laurence Fox, best known for his more famous relatives and for being 'the lad from [the ITV drama] *Lewis* who isn't Lewis'.[22] It seems unlikely that Hosking expects proximity to political power in return for his £1 million investment in the party.[23] In May 2021, Fox ran for London mayor, lost his £10,000 deposit and secured under 2 per cent of the vote. In July 2023, he stood in the Uxbridge and Ruislip by-election necessitated by Boris Johnson's resignation as an MP. Again, Fox lost his deposit, securing 714 votes.

Snowdon's colleague, Kristian Niemietz (head of political economy), is less prolific but often published in the same places.

Over at the CPS, where board members include Lord Bamford and Fraser Nelson, the current 'director' is Robert Colvile. A former comment editor at the *Telegraph* titles, he also worked on the Conservatives' 2019 election manifesto and has a column in the *Sunday Times*. He is also 'editor-in-chief' of the think tank's spin-off, CapX, a website dedicated to disseminating Tufton Street dogma. In February 2023, *Byline Times* reported that Richard Sharp (the one who would shortly step down as BBC chairman after failing to disclose that he had facilitated an £800,000 loan for Boris Johnson, who appointed him) had given tens of thousands of pounds to right-wing organisations in the UK via his personal charity. The Sharp Foundation made donations to *another* 'think tank', the Institute for Policy Research, which in turn gave money to the CPS, the TPA and, bizarrely for a future BBC chairman, 'News-Watch', an organisation dedicated to critiquing the BBC and accusing it of political bias. Sharp, a former CPS board member, also gave £42,400 directly to Colvile after the tragic early death of his wife. There is no suggestion that the money was anything other than a generous and thoughtful gesture. Colvile himself explained: 'The money went into a trust to support my children as they grew up, and help ensure that I wouldn't have to worry so much about education and living costs as a widower.'[24] It is worth wondering, though, how the sort of newspapers that Colvile and Littlewood write columns for would report such largesse from a future BBC chairman if the recipient did not share their politics. It is, of course, also evidence of the network of extremely close relationships between ideological bedfellows who could, in the skewed ecosystem under examination here, rise all the way to the top of the BBC. *Byline Times* reported that, during the period of Sharp's donations, the CPS 'published several reports criticising the so-called bias at the BBC against Brexiters and the right. Around the same time, CapX published articles calling for the abolition of the licence fee.'[25]

These connections may seem complex at times, and even difficult to follow, but that merely reflects the extent of the think-tank/media/political hybrid network and its influence on British society. The interconnectedness is almost as opaque as the funding. The revolving doors between the think tanks and the UK media have, as we have seen, been spinning for decades. Whether insinuating their secretly funded 'research' in to our daily newspapers, contributing to discussion programmes without disclosing their allegiances or penning opinion pieces, the sole basis for their implied authority is, circularly, their membership of the think tank. The current 'chief executive' of the TPA, for example, does not appear to have worked *anywhere* else. The website entry for John O'Connell reads: 'John O'Connell joined the TPA as an intern in 2009. Since then he has worked at every level of the organisation which made him uniquely qualified to become Chief Executive beginning August 2016.' Nevertheless, 'John frequently represents the TPA on television and radio, including prominent appearances on flagship broadcast programmes and documentaries.'

O'Connell's former colleague, 'research director' Duncan Simpson, once wrote an article for the *Daily Mail* entitled: 'How we can stop The Blob: The vaccine tsar is right – our stultifying civil service has been holding Britain back for years.'[26] The byline 'Taxpayers Alliance research director DUNCAN SIMPSON has a bold plan for real change' shows exactly how mere membership is presented as some sort of qualification. Simpson's CV provides few clues as to what his actual qualifications for providing such bold analysis might be. 'Prior to working at think tanks,' it tells us, 'Duncan worked for Douglas Carswell as his parliamentary assistant.' Carswell, lest we forget, was the backbench Conservative MP who achieved brief notoriety by defecting to Nigel Farage's UKIP in 2016 and winning the subsequent by-election in Clacton. He was also a co-founder of Elliott's Vote Leave. Such was Carswell's dedication to the people of Clacton, not to mention his determination to enjoy the fruits of Brexit, that he now lives in Jackson, Mississippi, where, I kid you not, he is currently the president and CEO of a 'free-market, conservative think tank'.[27] Incidentally, Duncan Simpson is no longer at the TaxPayers' Alliance. He is now 'executive director' of the Adam Smith Institute. It is unlikely that he misses the company of his former colleagues too much. At least not on Tuesdays. Of which more shortly.

So whereas a previous revolving door existed between think tanks and the media, the *new* revolving door leads from think tank to government and, sometimes, back again. If the ease with which publicly known Dacre and Murdoch personnel can now slide in and out of Downing Street roles is alarming, the more recent government infiltration of 'Tufton Street' types has proved downright dangerous. In August 2020, the secretary of state for international trade, Liz Truss, appointed Tom Clougherty, 'head of tax' at the CPS and formerly 'executive director' of the ASI, to advise on possible locations for new 'Freeports', special areas within the UK's borders where different economic regulations apply.[28] He was joined on the panel by Eamonn Butler, co-founder and director of the ASI. In October that year, Truss announced a raft of new appointments to the 'Strategic Trade Advisory Group'. Littlewood and Colvile were in, as was a former 'deputy director' of the ASI, Matt Kilcoyne, who has frequently written for the *Spectator*. Daniel Hannan, a ridiculous Brexiter who was inevitably rewarded with a peerage by Boris Johnson, was included both there and as an adviser to the Board of Trade. By now, the former MEP had achieved the holy grail of having his own think tank, the Initiative for Free Trade, which had previously shared an address with Colvile's CPS, 57 Tufton Street.

At the time, Truss was embarked upon a programme of presenting cut-and-paste trade agreements with former EU partners or suboptimal new arrangements with territories as triumphs of diplomacy and her own political acumen. It proved mightily popular with Conservative Party members, who regularly placed her at the top of cabinet popularity polls, but, as with almost everything Brexit-related, rather flew in the face of objective evidence. On 15 June 2021, for example, she hailed a new deal with Australia as 'win–win'.[29] In November 2022, George Eustice, who held the farming brief when the deal was struck, said in the Commons: 'Since I now enjoy the freedom of the back benches, I no longer have to put such a positive gloss on what was agreed. Unless we recognise the failures the Department for International Trade made during the Australia negotiations, we will not be able to learn the lessons for future negotiations. The first step is to recognise that the Australia trade deal is not actually a very good deal, which was not for lack of trying on my part.'[30]

Former UKIP member Eustice who, unlike Truss, campaigned for Brexit and is from a farming family, added, 'Overall, the truth of the matter is that the UK gave away far too much for far too little in return. We did not actually need to give Australia nor New Zealand full liberalisation of beef and sheep. It was not in our economic interests to do so. And neither Australia nor New Zealand had anything to offer in return for such a grand concession.'

On 1 June 2023, as the deal came into force, Australian media was even less impressed by the British position. A laughing Karl Stefanovic, co-host of the Nine Network's breakfast programme, *Today*, asked studio colleagues: 'So what else do they actually have? There's black pudding, Cumberland sausages. That's about it.' One colleague added 'Spice Girl CDs and English breakfast tea' to the list while another explained: 'It's about what we sell to them, Karl. It's a good thing for us. A good thing for us because we get to sell more beef and that's great for everybody in Australia.' On the same day, *Politico* reported that Boris Johnson's personal intervention had made the deal even worse than expected. It is worth reproducing the salient part in full.

After three intensive hours of talks the dinner was reaching a 'crescendo,' a former Australian official said, with the Aussies pressing Johnson to give them what they wanted on beef. To their amazement, Johnson gave way on tariffs and product weights. [George] Brandis, the [Australian] high commissioner, moved like a flash, writing down Johnson's pledge on a piece of paper and then excusing himself to go to the washroom. On his way to the toilet he handed the paper to an aide, the same former Australian official added. The aide digitally scanned the note and sent it instantly to the Australian High Commission on the Strand, where a waiting colleague quickly turned it into a formal trade document. This was sent back and – remarkably – printed out inside No. 10, and then placed by the Australian team into an official-looking folder. The folder was handed back to Brandis as he headed back into the dinner. As the meal continued, Brandis and Morrison pulled out the new documents, asking Johnson to sign an Agreement in Principle for the U.K.-Australia trade deal which would formalize his verbal concession on beef. 'Of course,' said Johnson, signing the documents before those present. In doing so, the British prime minister said, he hoped such a favorable deal would 'make up for' the U.K. joining the EU back in 1973, according to three people directly familiar with the events … Liz Truss was "livid" when she learned of the agreement over breakfast the following morning … 'Your boss has already conceded the whole kingdom,' Dan Tehan, Australia's chief negotiator, told Truss gleefully, according to one former senior U.K. minister involved in the negotiations, as Truss attempted to reopen the talks minutes before the deal was made public.[31]

Minette Batters, general secretary of the National Farmers' Union, was outraged. '[It] was a real breach of trust and confidence for farmers,' she said. 'The anger is still visceral.'[32]

When Truss arrived in Downing Street, the appointment of think-tank types accelerated exponentially. Her chief economic adviser was Matthew Sinclair, who, like John O'Connell, went straight from university to the TPA, where he eventually became 'chief executive'. Sophie Jarvis, a former 'head of government affairs' at the ASI became her political secretary. Caroline Elsom, previously 'head of education and enterprise' at the CPS became her health adviser. Ruth Porter, formerly the IEA's 'communications director', was appointed deputy chief of staff. James Price, another former TPA 'campaign director', became chief of staff to the chancellor of the Duchy of Lancaster in the Cabinet Office. Over at the Foreign and Commonwealth Office, Giles Dilnot became a special adviser. He had previously been 'director of communications' at yet another 'libertarian think tank', the Legatum Institute, where Matthew Elliott was once a 'senior fellow'. This one was set up by Christopher Chandler of Legatum Foundation fame, currently haemorrhaging millions over at GB News. Price was joined at the FCO by Victoria Hewson, fresh from a stint as 'head of regulatory affairs' at the IEA and another Legatum Institute alumnus. Radomir Tylecote adorned Jacob Rees-Mogg's mercifully brief tenure as business secretary. He had previously been 'director of defence and security' at Civitas and a fellow of the IEA. Callum Price, a former 'head of communications and external affairs' at the CPS and previous intern at the IEA and TPA, became an adviser at the Department of Levelling Up, Housing and Communities. He was joined there by Jack Airey, formerly 'head of housing' at Policy Exchange. A new arrival at the Department for Education was Robyn Staveley, a former 'head of communications' at the CPS. Over at Work and Pensions appeared *another* former 'head of communications' at the CPS, Lauren Maher. She was joined there by a former 'head of welfare and opportunity' at the CPS, James Heywood. Danielle Boxall, a former TPA 'media campaign manager' became an adviser in the Wales Office.

It is likely this list is not exhaustive, but only one journalist in the UK, Sam Bright, the former investigations editor at *Byline Times*, has even tried to keep track of these appointments. I have drawn heavily on his tireless work here and heartily recommend his book, *Bullingdon Club Britain: The Ransacking of a Nation*. When you consider how much effort the Murdoch, Dacre and Barclay family press, not to mention Truss and her political allies, put in to inflating bogus notions of conspiracy and secretive collusion between people in positions of power, it is frankly astonishing how lonely Sam's work has been and how little attention has been paid to a very real and unaccountable 'Blob' of interconnected characters operating with 'Common Purpose' and in plain sight at the heart of UK government. And it is unlikely that we would know the relatively little we do about how they operate without the extraordinary courage of another man, someone once described by Matthew Elliott as a 'fantasist'.

Like Christopher Wylie, Shahmir Sanni was one of the 'so-called whistle-blowers' contemptuously referred to by Elliott during that fateful BBC interview with Kuenssberg. And like Wylie, he would be completely vindicated by events. The personal cost to Sanni, however, would prove almost unbearable. On 24 March 2018, he gave an interview to the *Observer* in which he shared 'concerns that the masterminds behind the 2016 vote – including key figures now working for Theresa May in Downing Street – may have flouted referendum spending rules and then attempted to destroy evidence'.[33] Sanni, a 21-year-old recent graduate who had moved to the UK from Pakistan ten years earlier, was motivated by a touchingly simple faith in what he considered to be British values: 'This is the one country where no matter what is happening, people will stand in a line,' he explained. 'People here, there is a core ethos of what it means to be British: to do it right. To wait your turn. To never cheat or lie your way to get to the front. It's what it means to be British.'[34]

One of the 'masterminds' named in the original story was Stephen Parkinson, a former 'director of research' at the CPS and by then Prime Minister Theresa May's political secretary. In response to the *Observer*'s enquiries, Parkinson issued a statement revealing that he had been in a romantic relationship with Sanni and so could understand 'if the lines had become blurred for him'. Dominic Cummings, campaign director for Vote Leave, published the statement on his infamous 'blog'. Sanni's lawyer successfully lobbied Cummings to take down the statement but it was given to the *New York Times* by a Downing Street official later that day. 'At that point, it was clear to us that there was no containing that information any more,' said Sanni's lawyer, Tamsin Allen. 'That email, to us, meant that he had effectively been outed in a statement from an official Downing Street email.'[35]

A gay man, Sanni was not out to his family in either the UK or Pakistan and urgently tried to contact them, 'though my aunt and uncle in Birmingham found out by a *Mail on Sunday* journalist going up to them and asking them what they think of me being gay'.[36] The ensuing front-page headline was 'PM's aide in toxic sex row over pro-Brexit cash plot'. The stakes could hardly have been higher. 'The Home Office [where Parkinson had been a special adviser] says people get killed for being gay in Pakistan,' Sanni explained later. 'This was an act of violence. But I don't think the majority of the public or parliament got this. They don't understand the gravity of outing someone who is a Pakistani Muslim. If they did, Theresa May would be out of a job.'[37]

Instead, on 13 April 2018, less than three weeks after his allegations were published, it was Sanni who found himself out of a job, sacked from his post-referendum position at Matthew Elliott's TaxPayers' Alliance. It was his employment tribunal claim for unfair dismissal that provides us with an all too rare insight into how the network of 'think tanks' collude and collaborate to deliver the twenty-first-century equivalent of what Madsen Pirie and co. were cooking up in that Leicester Square cellar almost 50 years previously. The 'nine entities' referred to here are mostly familiar to us: The

TaxPayers' Alliance; the office of Peter Whittle (a former leader of the UKIP); Civitas; the Adam Smith Institute; Leave Means Leave; the Global Warming Policy Foundation; Brexit Central; the Centre for Policy Studies and our old friend the Institute for Economic Affairs.

'Meetings take place at 55 Tufton Street every other Tuesday ("The Tuesday Meetings"),' Sanni claimed.

> Attendance at the Tuesday Meetings varies, but is usually attended by all or substantially all of the Nine Entities. The Respondent [TPA chief executive John O'Connell] and its staff lead the Tuesday Meetings, which are typically chaired by Mr Isaby [Jonathan, former TPA chief executive turned editor of Brexit Central]. The purpose of the Tuesday Meetings is to agree a common line on political topics in the news between the Nine Entities, and to co-ordinate the public messaging that the individual organisations can then issue on that topic.

He later expanded:

> Discussion centres around a simple idea that anything funded by the state is wrong. Many of these people reiterate the same one-liners to each other so much that they are convinced that there is no other way. I have heard public [sector] workers depicted as enemies of progress, the civil service conveyed as pointless and many key public services that make Britain what it is referred to as a nuisance. Whether it is care workers, teachers, nurses, doctors, civil servants, it does not matter – all of their roles can be replaced by the private sector and, in the eyes of many Conservative politicians, they should be. 'The NHS doesn't need reform,

it just needs to be sold-off,' is a phrase I have heard used at these private dinners. Along with: 'Publicly-funded care workers aren't essential, if people are getting old they should have worked hard when they were younger. Why should taxes pay for their laziness?' There is a deep-rooted culture, disseminated by influential lobby groups who are platformed by the media, of seeing public funding as an enemy of progress. It is purely ideological, based not in economic theory or academia, but entirely on a regurgitation of political statements.[38]

Sanni's lawyers had told the tribunal that they intended to demand disclosure of communications between the nine organisations linked to 55 Tufton Street. On 12 November 2018, the TPA admitted to illegally sacking him while claiming to the BBC that the decision to concede was taken on 'pragmatic grounds'.[39] In fact, the failure to fight the case left the TPA accepting all of Sanni's allegations: unfair dismissal, wrongful dismissal, direct discrimination and 'dismissal by reason of a philosophical belief in the sanctity of British democracy'.

Sanni's lawyer, Peter Daly of Bindmans, described the 'extreme public vilification' Sanni had endured. The 'derogatory statements' made by Elliott to the media included the claim that Sanni was 'completely lying' on Sky News, that he was a 'fantasist' on Channel 4 and, where this chapter began, a 'so-called whistle-blower' on the BBC. Talking about the TaxPayers' Alliance, Chris Milsom, a barrister who specialises in whistle-blowing cases, told the *Observer*:

It is incredibly unusual for a respondent to make a complete concession on liability as the respondent has here. To wave a white flag to avoid disclosing documents and giving evidence in court is really unusual. They conceded everything. How does an ostensibly private company come to be working with Downing Street? What is their relationship? Who are their funders? If this had been fully ventilated in a public trial we could have found these things out. The effect of these admissions, however, is that Mr Sanni was dismissed both because he blew the whistle on electoral crimes and because of his philosophical belief in the sanctity of democracy. We must now ask: is that an entity that is fit to be on the BBC ostensibly speaking on behalf of all 'taxpayers'?[40]

Milson's question has still not been answered. The TPA, along with the rest of the 'Tufton Street' crew, still pops up in BBC studios with unerring regularity. Stephen Parkinson was made Baron Parkinson of Whitley Bay in Theresa May's resignation honours in 2019 and Matthew Elliott is, at the time of writing, reportedly set to join him in the House of Lords at Liz Truss's behest.

Shahmir Sanni, the man whose life they turned upsidedown because, in part, of his 'belief in the sanctity of British democracy', moved back to Pakistan after lockdown. Speaking to me from Karachi in July 2023, he reflected on the scandal and the subsequent, very mixed, fortunes of its protagonists. Two things were particularly striking. The compassion and decency he retains despite his uniquely hostile treatment by all three pillars of the toxic ecosystem under scrutiny here: the Conservative Party, the 'think tanks' and the right-wing media. And the sheer happenstance of how he found himself at the very heart of a story that signalled a complete subversion of the British values that an idealistic young man, working in London for the first time, believed that everybody shared. I resolved to tell the whole story here because it remains largely misunderstood and because, despite the best efforts of Carole Cadwalladr and others, few people have been more profoundly let down by the UK media than Shahmir.

I told a friend that I was desperate to get out of Birmingham [he laughs]. I was working in Topman and worried about getting stuck. He had political contacts and suggested that getting involved in Brexit would be a great way to make contacts and establish a foothold that could lead to work as an adviser or a consultant or a civil servant or something. He reached out to some friends in the Remain campaign and some friends working for Vote Leave. The Remain lot didn't get back to him but Vote Leave invited me to London for an interview. So I had an interview with Stephen Parkinson at the very start of the campaign. I got the train from Birmingham and was so nervous. I was petrified. I didn't know how to talk. I didn't know how to work in a professional environment. I was 21 but they were, like, 'Sure, you start next week.' So I started off as a volunteer.

Did I know about the difference between Conservatives and Labour? Sure. Did I think that Vote Leave was a right-wing organisation? Hell, no! The first person I made friends with was in the Green Party. I've always loved the Green Party and that got me excited, you know. Then slowly but surely the Green Party members, the Labour Party members started to leave. In the beginning I thought: 'This is great. Everyone in England is nice because everyone here is progressive.' I didn't have any idea about the more extreme right-wing nature of some Conservatives in the UK. Coming from Pakistan, my understanding of fascism was very, very different. I grew up during the time of [Nawaz] Sharif. Karachi was hell. Bomb blasts every week. *Time* magazine called it

Asia's most dangerous city. I had a very privileged upbringing so was insulated from much of the violence but the experiences forged my understanding of politics. So I would never conceive of Vote Leave being some kind of evil organisation. I think I saw it as some white people doing white people shit who had no idea what it was like in real politics, you know? Where people get murdered. I say all this because oftentimes people held me to some sort of moral standard. They would say that I should have known better. Well I didn't. I was 21. I didn't know any better. I was trying to figure out who I was. I was desperate for a job. I was unemployed. And I didn't even get paid by Vote Leave at the start!

I was groomed into it. I use that word intentionally. There were all these very influential people within the political sphere. I had no idea who they were but everyone around me kept saying: 'This person is amazing. This person's really powerful.' I mean I knew who Boris Johnson was, but Priti Patel? No. I was so distanced from it all at the start and then I think I eventually started drinking the Kool-Aid. Brexit will help the Commonwealth. It will build more connections with black and brown people. I just drank it. And also, I didn't have much of an option. I was in this space, my first actual real work environment, straight out of university. I thought that I was useless. I had deep impostor syndrome, being one of the only brown people there. Probably the only one actually doing work. And so each day I think I was trying to work out how to assimilate myself, how to lay the foundation stones for a career. And then I found out about the money. That's when I remember thinking: 'Oh, that's a bit weird.' I remember when Darren [Grimes, the 22-year-old fashion student who chaired BeLeave] told me that Cummings and Stephen Parkinson had suggested that all this money goes to AggregateIQ. I was like: 'OK, fine.' I don't have any power here. I don't have any say.

The 'money' is the £675,000 payment that BeLeave, described as a 'Vote Leave Outreach Group' on the official Vote Leave website, paid to AggregateIQ, the Canadian data company that ran Vote Leave's digital campaign. The most piercing note of Shahmir's later whistle-blowing addressed the fact that coordination between campaign groups is, quite simply, illegal. Shahmir, by now treasurer of BeLeave, alleged that his organisation's activities were controlled and directed by senior Vote Leave staff and that the £675,000 was paid to AggregateIQ through BeLeave because Vote Leave was already close to exceeding the £7 million limit on its own campaign spending. The Electoral Commission would, as we know, later find that Vote Leave had indeed exceeded the limit by funnelling the money through BeLeave. Even now, the successful suppression and dilution of this scandal by the key culprits and client journalists is shocking. On the *same day* that Elliott was smearing Shahmir on the BBC with the help of its political editor, Shahmir told *Channel 4 News* what they both knew to be the truth:

> It doesn't matter what Matthew Elliott has to say, all everyone needs to do is look at the evidence. According to electoral law you cannot coordinate between two different campaign groups and you have spending limits. Spending limits keep elections and campaigns and referendums fair. Vote Leave used BeLeave as a way to overspend, and they lied by saying there was no coordination. As secretary, treasurer and research director of BeLeave, [I know] there was coordination, it was a coordinated campaign. There is evidence to show BeLeave was created by Vote Leave. There are emails that

show that Vote Leave was coming up with the mission statement of BeLeave … there is more than enough evidence of there being a coordinated campaign and that is against electoral law.

Watching the interview now, there is a righteous indignation to his manner but also a quiet resolve. The advice of both legal professionals and the journalists who had helped him to come forward was that the revelations were of sufficient seriousness to bring the entire referendum result into question. It had been won, after all, through law breaking. And while he may have expected the Brexit-supporting media, the Conservative Party and his former colleagues to close ranks and come after him, he was not prepared for at least one element of what followed. A deeper knowledge of how the same vested interests had conspired to scupper Leveson or leave the *Sun*'s Hillsborough lies uncorrected for decades would, perhaps, have served him well.

> I remember sitting in that room with National Crime Agency [NCA] officers. Me and Chris [Wylie] had been taken in to separate rooms and were talking to very senior people. I remember the reactions the investigators had when I gave them the evidence. Yes, they're trained professionals who aren't supposed to react to what you're providing, but I remember them going: 'Whoa. This goes deeper than we thought.' These are the words and language they were using, as I was turning my laptop around with my lawyer sitting beside me, going: 'This is the video. Here's some audio. Here's the clip to the data.'

As we know, the investigations eventually went nowhere because of 'political sensitivities' and, crucially, the tactics of Shahmir's exposed detractors. As we have seen, they could not interrogate his evidence so they came after him instead with terrible consequences. Today, he is surprisingly sanguine about the saga. The darkest times are hopefully behind him and, still just 29, he is determined to look forwards not backwards. But he allowed me a final insight in to why he risked everything on a point of principle in a country that had only been his home for a decade.

I look back at that person and I understand him. I understand what I was saying. I was trying to appease this belief I genuinely had that justice prevails in the United Kingdom. I believed in British society because British society had provided my family with a safety net outside of Karachi, Pakistan. And so I think I almost believed that I owed England, that I owed the country. I had a dedication to fixing it, to helping it. I don't believe that any more. There is a part of me that still believes that people, no matter whether they're British or Pakistani, have the capacity for kindness and compassion and change. I still believe that, but I guess now I'm not so invested. That's not for me. The real injustice was that the evidence and the work that I had provided in my first revelations as a whistle-blower, against Vote Leave, and the Conservative Party, were on a scale that should have either put them in jail or banned them from politics permanently.

In an ideal scenario, I would have been vindicated and remembered as someone who had protected Britain from total decimation. In my egotistical fantasy part of me wanted that and to prove to myself that we – me, Chris, Carole [Cadwalladr], Jess [Search, former commissioning editor at Channel 4] and others – could actually help change people's lives for the better. But I'm happy now and I can't say that for any of those guys. They got everything they thought they wanted. The big jobs, Downing Street, the lordships, and I can't say that they're happy because I know that they're miserable. And I know that they're deeply unhappy. And I know that they will never find fulfilment because they're so bitter, they're so resentful, they're so angry. From Matthew Elliott and Dominic Cummings to Boris Johnson, with all these people I look at them now with pity.

How jarring it is, as we survey the 2023 political landscape, to read of a young Pakistani-born Muslim man feeling a debt of honour to the UK because of the sanctuary and opportunity it provided for his family. On 13 July, Prime Minister Rishi Sunak announced that a long-delayed pay offer for public sector workers would be funded by increasing the already punitive fees that foreign-born workers and students must pay for temporary visas and access to the NHS. In the same week, an immigration minister, Robert Jenrick, ordered that cartoon murals at a processing centre for unaccompanied child asylum seekers be painted over because they were 'too welcoming'.[41] A month previously, a splinter group of particularly unpleasant Conservatives had called for a cessation of the issuing of *all* visas for foreign-born workers in the care sector, where vacancies already stood at 165,000. We have seen how media created the environment in which immigration could be successfully weaponised to achieve political goals like Brexit and sell newspapers or magazines like the *Sun* and the *Spectator*. But the absolute abandonment of the values that Shahmir describes came about because the explicit racism of Enoch Powell, once so violently rejected by his party, is today in the very heart of the Conservative Party. And it is there, largely, because of one man's unique ability to communicate it not through threats of violence or 'Rivers of Blood' rhetoric, but through nudges, winks and beery bonhomie.

Chapter 5
NIGEL FARAGE

Why does anyone have time for this creature?
He's a dimwitted racist.

Professor Alan Sked, founder of the UK Independence Party[1]

ON 22 OCTOBER 2009, the leader of the fascist British National Party, Nick Griffin, appeared on the BBC's flagship political debate programme, *Question Time*. The previous week's edition had seen the Labour home secretary, Alan Johnson, badger the presenter, David Dimbleby, to rescind Griffin's invitation. 'You may like to consider your invitation,' he said. 'There isn't a constitutional obligation to appear on *Question Time*. That gives [the BNP] a legitimacy they do not deserve. These people believe in the things that the fascists believed in the Second World War, they believe in what the National Front believe in. They believe in the purity of the Aryan race. It is a foul and despicable party.' Griffin, who had been convicted of inciting racial hatred in 1998, was cock-a-hoop, telling *The Times*: 'I thank the political class and their allies for being so stupid. The huge furore that the political class has created around it clearly gives us a whole new level of public recognition.'[2] He went on, describing a fellow panellist, Baroness Sayeeda Warsi, as the 'Token Asian, Muslim woman on the Conservative team. They were always likely to play a stunt like that.'

181

The BNP, founded by the former National Front chairman John Tyndall in 1982, was a veritable box set of far-right bigotries: homophobia, anti-Semitism to the point of Holocaust denial (Griffin once dubbed it the 'Holohoax') and, obviously, racism. Obsessed with notions of racial purity and ethno-nationalism, the party's central dogma was that white Britons were under threat of extinction from ethnic minorities and immigration. It is another mark of how far we have fallen that, barely a decade later, the 'Great Replacement' conspiracy theory would find a home in relatively mainstream media on both sides of the Atlantic. Most notably, on Rupert Murdoch's Fox News[3] and in Andrew Neil's *Spectator*.[4]

Accordingly, the BNP was violently opposed to mixed marriage and initially in favour of the compulsory repatriation of non-white Britons. In 2005, its 'senior legal officer' and a close ally of Griffin, Lee Barnes, wrote:

> The immigrant communities in Britain are ... colonies filled with colonists. They are alien islands inside our towns and cities with their own laws and cultures. They will never integrate as they did not come here to integrate, but to re-create their own cultures in our country. The fact is that the only solution to Multi-Culturalism is not some asinine and bogus attempt to impose British cultural values on immigrants, but simply to commence repatriating them.[5]

When Griffin, a former 'national organiser' for the National Front, defeated his mentor Tyndall to become leader of the party in 1999, he styled himself a 'moderniser'. Repatriation of ethnic minorities would now be voluntary; 'the three Hs: hard talk, hobbyism and Hitler' would be excised from the party vocabulary and Islamophobia would take precedence over anti-Semitism. A Cambridge graduate who emphasised his family-man status, Griffin had a much better grasp of how to achieve electoral success than most of his fascist forebears, writing: 'Of course we must teach the truth to the hardcore ... [but] when it comes to influencing the public, forget about racial differences, genetics, Zionism, historical revisionism and so on ... we must at all times present them with an image of moderate reasonableness.'[6]

Cultivating that 'image of moderate reasonableness' would prove absolutely crucial to the successful seeding of far-right, overtly racist ideology into the heart of British politics. But despite understanding this so implicitly, Griffin was not, in the end, the man to accomplish it. However hard he tried to appear 'to the manor born' during the *Question Time* appearance that would mark the beginning of the end of his political relevance, he couldn't quite cultivate the required characteristics or escape the shadow of his earlier allegiances. To do so would require levels of disingenuousness, dishonesty and desperation for approval that eluded him. This was either because he was, ultimately, more fascist ideologue than cynical opportunist, or simply because he lacked the easy superficial charm with which British public schools have been inculcating mediocre young men for centuries. He was, in a way, more saloon bar than golf club, and therefore destined never to cut through to the *Telegraph*- and *Spectator*-reading – and, more importantly, *writing* – classes.

Griffin's 1998 conviction for inciting racial hatred, for example, was for writing articles that not only denied the Holocaust but also praised the Waffen SS. And yet in May 2018, Andrew Neil's *Spectator* published *another* column by the Greek shipping heir and socialite 'Taki', this time headlined: 'In praise of Wehrmacht: The real story of D-Day is the heroism of the German soldiers who were vastly outnumbered but fought nobly and to the death'. It prompted the *Times of Israel* to report that 'A far-right race baiter who works as a columnist for a respected weekly British current affairs magazine wrote a piece sympathising with the Wehrmacht, the unified armed forces of Nazi Germany.'[7] The crucial word here is, of course, 'respected'. The reputation of the organ in which such bile appears inevitably sanitises opinions that would be beyond the pale in other contexts. We have already seen Taki's *Spectator* colleagues routinely equate ethnic minority status with being 'foreign' in the context of Britishness, in a similar vein to Griffin and the BNP's view of 'alien islands inside our towns and cities'. Ultimately, Griffin's Achilles heel was not the odium he attracted from people who abhorred his views, but the snobbishness of people who shared them.

For the British liberal, perhaps the biggest shock of the last decade has been the warmth afforded a less obviously obnoxious man, possessed of many of Griffin's views, by many across the media and political spectrum. In retrospect, we should not have been remotely surprised. I have already shown how the media landscape was, after years of casual othering, immigrant blaming, Islamophobia and xenophobia, perfectly primed for such a character. Understand this and it's not a surprise to see the subsequent rise of a public-school educated pantomime 'toff' who could sing from Griffin's hymn sheet in a wholly different accent – favouring the same tunes but with subtly different words. And given how much of the Murdoch/Dacre/*Telegraph* media was, as we have seen, already riddled with 'respectable' racism, it was probably inevitable.

Griffin's appearance on *Question Time* saw a tripling of the regular audience figures to 8.2 million but was, largely for the reasons just examined, widely judged to be a disaster for the BNP man. He failed to engage with the audience or successfully deflect the aggressive questioning of his fellow panellists. His eligibility for appearing on the programme was undeniably electoral if not, in the view of many commentators, particularly moral. On 4 June 2009, Griffin had been elected to the European Parliament alongside BNP colleague Andrew Brons, a former chairman of the National Front and former member of the neo-Nazi National Socialist Movement. Staunchly anti-EU, there was an irony in seeing a strain of political legitimacy afforded to the BNP by its members' election to a European Parliament it sought to leave or even abolish. Griffin was not the first 'Eurosceptic' far-right politician to exploit the opportunity afforded by membership of a parliament he sought to depart. Nor would he be the last. Cometh the hour, cometh the con man: Nigel Farage, one of the most frequent *Question Time* guests of all time.

People *like* Nigel Farage. Entire books have already been written about his rise to unearned prominence and his impact upon the political landscape. But the most simple and important element of his appeal *is* his appeal. He effects the demeanour of a mildly sozzled City gent, dresses like a city-dwelling social misfit's idea of a country squire and reassures people it is fine to be discomfited by the nationality of their new neighbours, fellow passengers speaking different languages on their train or the 'hordes' of unidentified and unwelcome foreigners they never personally encounter but keep reading about in their morning newspaper. Throw in a Dulwich College education and the bonkers British deference that commands, and the essence of that appeal is distilled. Unlike Nick Griffin or Enoch Powell, Farage was always desperate to be liked and, crucially, expected to be. He will, in almost all circumstances, back himself to bluster his way out of trouble and studiously avoids any circumstances where he might not.

His friend and ally, the convicted sex offender Donald Trump, is a master of the same dark arts.

This is why it's so rare to see their masks fully slip. Both Farage and Trump thrive on the failure of unsympathetic political journalists to recalibrate for their deliberate dilution of common decency and even truth itself. The established checks and balances were simply unprepared for how far these men would go. When Trump abused a disabled journalist or boasted of serially sexually assaulting women (defended, incidentally, by Farage), decent people presumed that outrage and disgust would shame him into retreat. They did not conceive of a character surfing the wave of opprobrium, revelling in the outrage, celebrating his supporters being dubbed 'deplorables' by Hillary Clinton.

Similarly, when Farage spoke of wanting to choose his neighbours according to their nationality or, emboldened by the referendum result, received a standing ovation at an Alternative for Germany (AfD) election rally, there was a lazy presumption that standards had been breached, that consequences would surely follow. The crucial point here is that the media ecosystem presided over by Murdoch, Dacre and the Barclay family's proxies had already, without most of us noticing, torched those checks and balances. Violent inconsistency and contempt for genuine 'traditional British values' went unpunished because, with the BBC cowed and contorted by bogus 'balance', there was nobody in the Fourth Estate left to uphold them.

Farage's invitation to address the far-right German party had, for example, followed his insistence that Barack Obama had no business involving himself in the politics of another country. The invitation was issued by one of AfD's MEPs, Beatrix von Storch, the granddaughter of Adolf Hitler's finance minister, Lutz Graf Schwerin von Krosigk. They were, inevitably, united by their hatred of immigration. 'I regard

Beatrix as a friend, I believe we have strong shared values,' Farage told the rally. Indeed, in April 2016 she had joined the Europe for Freedom and Democracy group in the European Parliament (chaired by Farage). Her welcome followed her expulsion from the European Conservatives and Reformists Group after she said that border guards should shoot at women and children trying to cross the border 'illegally'. As Farage also revealingly told the rally, 'Once you are able to speak the unspeakable, people will begin to think the unthinkable and that is how you beat the establishment.'

Whether 'racist' or not, discomfort with immigration is a constant background hum and, whether we like to admit it or not, everybody knows at least a little of what it feels like. If the person pushing in front of you in a supermarket queue speaks an unrecognisable language or wears a hijab or simply looks *different*, the initial offence at their conduct can be easily compounded by the thought that 'they' have somehow less right to be there in the first place than 'you'. It is, obviously, bunkum. Since ancient times, the most successful societies have been the most diverse, and therefore the most attractive to 'rootless Cosmopolitans', as Stalinists might have described them, or 'citizens of nowhere', as Theresa May dubbed them during her dismal attempt to ride the racist tiger through Brexit to Downing Street. But although someone will always tell you that immigrants are to blame for anything wrong with your life, it's rubbish. And the more oxygen this view receives, regardless of facts, the more people will be intoxicated and comforted.

You can blame the failures of the NHS on foreign-born people, as Farage did in April 2015, saying nonsensically: 'I wanted to make people think and understand why their grandmother who is 85 finds it very difficult to get drugs for breast cancer but anybody can get on a plane from anywhere in the world, be HIV tested in London and receive antiretroviral drugs.'[8] He would later deploy another favoured weapon from his arsenal of absurd but effective claims and add: 'It is a sensible Christian thing to look after your family and your own community first.'[9] In fact, you can blame all personal dissatisfaction with a public sector that had, by 2015, already been gutted by Cameron and Osborne's so-called 'austerity' on immigrants. In the run up to that year's general election, the UKIP website maintained that: 'Immigrants must financially support themselves and their dependants for five years. This means private health insurance (except emergency medical care), education and housing – they should pay into the pot before they take out of it.'

In the hands of the immigrant blame culture's most pungent practitioners, you can even blame them for traffic jams. On 7 December 2014, Nigel Farage explained why he had failed to attend a drinks reception in Port Talbot two days earlier. The reception was being held for members of UKIP, the party he had been leading, on and off, since 2006. 'It took me six hours and fifteen minutes in the car to get here. It should have taken three and a half to four,' he told the BBC's *Sunday Politics Wales*. 'That has nothing to do with professionalism. What is does have to do with is a country in which the population is going through the roof, chiefly because of open-door immigration, and the fact the M4 is not as navigable as it used to be.'

By now, before the decision to hold a Brexit referendum had even been made, Farage had made a lucrative career out of blaming immigration for everything. It's possible, but far from certain, that the right-wing media would have been less kind to Farage if he hadn't been providing cover for the failing policies of the Conservative government it had helped to install. His usefulness to the Tories, however, would prove limited and short-lived. Like Boris Johnson, Farage would always be largely motivated by a deep and abiding commitment to attracting attention and his own self-interest.

Earlier that year, on 28 February 2014, he had set out the stall that would eventually propel UKIP to victory in the European elections and Farage into the nightmares of Tory leader David Cameron. 'In scores of our cities and market towns, this country in a short space of time has frankly become unrecognisable,' he told an audience in Torquay. 'Whether it is the impact on local schools and hospitals, whether it is the fact in many parts of England you don't hear English spoken any more. This is not the kind of community we want to leave to our children and grandchildren.' Asked about this outlandish statement later, he claimed to have recently boarded a train at Charing Cross station in London. 'It was a stopper going out and we stopped at London Bridge, New Cross, Hither Green,' he explained. 'It was not until we got past Grove Park that I could hear English being audibly spoken in the carriage. Does that make me feel slightly awkward? I don't understand them ... I don't feel very comfortable in that situation and I don't think the majority of British people do.'

All racists are liars. It goes with the territory. You simply cannot contend that skin colour makes one person superior to another in any way without telling a fundamental and demonstrable untruth. This is why, 60 years after its delivery, Martin Luther King's dream for a country that would put Donald Trump in the White House remains so poignant: 'I have a dream that my four little children will one day live in a nation where they will not be judged by the colour of their skin but by the content of their character.' Regardless of character, Farage was happy publicly to judge people by not just the colour of their skin, but by the languages they spoke on trains, by their country of birth and by their religion. And, just like Trump, he understood that trumpeting the 'big lie' – that accidents of birth *do* convey innate, biological superiority – would endear him to followers desperate to believe in their own victimhood so much that any other lie he uttered would be not just forgiven but embraced. Understand that this sense of victimhood extends to the editorial floor of national newspapers and, latterly, television stations forged in their image (Farage is currently a presenter on GB News), and you understand why episodes that would have ended other political trajectories barely dented Farage's.

The examples of his dishonesty are legion but perhaps the most arresting evidence of the ease with which he can spin a fallacious yarn involved a claim in 2016 that he had been the target of an assassination attempt. In the days before the self-styled man of the people acquired a chauffeur, he was driving through France when a wheel fell off his Volvo, prompting Farage to tell the *Mail on Sunday* that police and mechanics had told him the wheel nuts had been deliberately loosened. Asked by the newspaper why he was convinced sabotage was the cause, he replied: 'The mechanics that looked at it were absolutely certain of it. The French police looked at it and said that sometimes nuts on one wheel can come a bit loose – but not on all four.'[10] Questioned about the allegation on the radio, he added: 'Someone clearly had loosened the nuts on all four of the tyres of my car, which led to a slightly unfortunate incident with the wheel coming off, and it wasn't very nice.'[11]

The story understandably gathered pace and was reported across Europe, prompting the French newspaper *Libération* to contact Philippe Marquis, the mechanic who had examined the Volvo. He told the newspaper that the wheel nuts were loose because of bad repair work. He also explained that the pair had been unable to communicate verbally because Farage, self-appointed scourge of people living in England without being able to speak the language, could speak no French despite living and working as an MEP in the French city of Strasbourg for the best part of 20 years. 'We only spoke with our hands,' said a baffled M. Marquis. Farage then undertook an extraordinary, but characteristic, reverse ferret and claimed: 'I never mentioned any mechanic.'[12]

The *Mail on Sunday*, which at that point was still sometimes endeavouring to hold Farage to account, responded on 9 January 2016 by reproducing the transcript of their original interview.

MoS: Who do you think might have done it?

Farage: Haven't got a clue. Quite frankly, with the way my life's been over the last two-and-a-half years, nothing surprises me.

MoS: Have you had death threats before?

Farage: Of course. It's not a particularly easy game, this. So it was looked at, the French police and mechanics looked at it but I have made no formal report in this country.

MoS: It's almost like out of an Agatha Christie … someone loosening the nuts on a wheel.

Farage: The mechanics that looked at it were absolutely certain of it.

A spokesman for the prosecution service in Boulogne-sur-Mer later told *The Times* that the police report made no mention of sabotage and that they would have started a criminal investigation if there had been any suspicion of foul play, explaining, 'In France, prosecutors can investigate even without the victim's agreement.'[13] No investigation was ever launched.

The episode may seem silly, although presumably not to Farage's children, but it is significant for at least three reasons: the abject dishonesty on display, the evident wriggling and obfuscation when challenged, and the bogus victimhood that underpinned the original lie. The basic deception about foreigners – whether they are somehow diluting our indigenous blood lines, ruling over us from Brussels or stealing our jobs – is so attractive to so many, the liar lying loudest earns a form of impunity that is close to impenetrable. It is, for example, easy to explain why Trump continues to claim that he won the 2020 election, but more baffling why so many continue to endorse his obvious lie. The answer, as with Farage, is that people want what he says to be true, regardless of how compelling the evidence may be that it is not.

This is almost impossible for the uninitiated to fully grasp. You can't make something true just by wanting it to be so. How can people ignore the evidence before them? Especially to the point where it motivates us to act, or vote, against our own and our children's interests? Why would we put our trust in obvious charlatans and abandon integrity or accountability in politicians? The answer almost always lies in the promise to protect us from ill-defined and often non-existent enemies. We overlook their shortcomings because they've told us to be scared and that they will protect us. The line from here to Boris Johnson's unprecedentedly corrupt premiership, where supporters, colleagues and client journalists would queue up to defend the indefensible and repeat his most blatant lies about 'Blobs' and 'Mobs' and 'getting all the big calls right' in the fight against COVID-19, could hardly be clearer.

Farage never intended to be Johnson's warm-up man. He believed, and possibly still does, that he would one day enjoy genuine political power. When Trump won the White House, he told young – usually female – colleagues at LBC, where we briefly worked at the same time, that he expected to become prime minister 'sooner rather than later'. He believed this even though a year prior he had just been an entertaining sideshow to some, a growing threat to others (including Cameron) and the obvious heir to the failures of Powell and Griffin to still more. He helped boost *Question Time* ratings, was a provocative presence in countless other studios and provided newspapers with plenty of copy. This last point should not be underestimated. The moment 'respectable' news journalists chose to treat Farage as a valid contributor to public discourse as opposed to an opportunistic, lying, racist grifter – simply to garner bylines or to help sell the Brexit their bosses wanted – something previously sacrosanct at the heart of British journalism shattered. It is yet to be repaired.

Indeed, he was always more of a media personality than a politician because his personality demanded that he always be the ringmaster. Even if it meant establishing his own circus. His ego and astonishing sense of self-importance would not countenance anything else. Not for him the slow climb through the ranks of an established party's structure or the graft and inspiration required for commercial success. This combination of laziness and conceit is the source of both his 'success' – his contribution to the referendum result – and his broader failure – a serial inability to get elected to any parliament except, like Griffin before him, one he didn't want British people to be in. Nigel Farage was never going to get anywhere in a 'proper' political party and it had become clear very quickly that he would never make a 'proper' fortune in the City.

To achieve the sort of status he sought, Farage had to create a small pond in which he could be the biggest fish. That it was a pond full of xenophobes, homophobes, misogynists, racists and reactionaries seemed, occasionally, to embarrass him. For example, he told me (quite dishonestly) in 2016: 'I'm perfectly happy for us to have a debate about our idiots and our people who are offensive. The frustration is this: all anyone wants to talk about are the idiots in UKIP.' But it was the only pond available and when it became clear that its inhabitants and their sympathisers could tip the balance of a referendum, Farage and his bigotries were afforded the attention he had always dreamed of by a media desperate to get Brexit over the line. And while many members of the Tory party may have shared his views about immigration or Muslims or even refugees, they were aware that to say so in public would, at least for now, be career threatening. They needed a foil, someone to 'speak the unspeakable' and to pretend that it was 'unspeakable' not because it was disgusting and false, but because it would somehow outrage the guardians of 'political correctness' or shame the undefined 'Establishment'. It was a role for which Farage had spent his whole life preparing.

On 4 June 1981, a young English teacher at Dulwich College, Chloe Deakin, wrote a long letter to the headmaster urging him to reconsider his appointment to prefect of a boy in the school, one Nigel Farage. It was unearthed by Michael Crick of *Channel 4 News* in September 2013 and still makes for extraordinary reading:

Dear Master,

I am happy to say that I am not acquainted with N. P. Farage of MSRY – happy because judging from the reports I have received he is not someone with whom I would wish to be acquainted; and because I am, therefore, able to write on the ground of no personal prejudice, but on that concerning principle.

You will recall that at the recent, and lengthy, meeting about the selection of prefects the remark by a colleague that Farage was 'a fascist, but that was no reason why he would not make a good prefect' invoked considerable reaction from members of the Common Room. Another colleague, who teaches the boy, described his publicly professed racist and neo-fascist views; and he cited a particular incident in which Farage was so offensive to a boy in his set, that he had to be removed from the lesson. This master stated his view that that behaviour was precisely why the boy should not be a prefect. Yet another colleague described how, at a CCF camp organised by the College, Farage and others had marched through a quiet Sussex village late at night singing Hitler youth songs; and when it was suggested by a master that boys who expressed such views 'don't really mean them', the College chaplain himself commented that, on the contrary, in his experience views of that kind expressed by boys of that age are deep-seated, and are meant.

Deakin went on to express horror at the headmaster's decision to appoint Farage as a prefect and described the announcement in assembly as being 'met with disbelief and derision' by his fellow pupils. Farage's response to Crick, who also reported that 'several Dulwich old boys have told me they recall Farage making racist remarks as a pupil, and voicing support for right-wing groups', was telling: 'Of course I said some ridiculous things, not necessarily racist things. It depends how you define it. You've got to remember that ever since

1968 up until the last couple of years, we've not been able in this country, intelligently to discuss immigration, to discuss integration, it's all been a buried subject and that's happened through academia, it's happened through politics and the media.'

'1968' is, presumably, a reference to Enoch Powell's 'Rivers of Blood' speech. Indeed, in his memoir, *Fighting Bull*, Farage explains the animosity of certain teachers towards him at this time as being a consequence of his public admiration of Powell. Note also, the tactic of pretending not to understand what 'racism' is.

On 14 May 2019, the *Independent* published *another* letter about Farage's schooldays. Its author, who remained anonymous, described himself as good school friend who had even stayed at Farage's home and enjoyed a 'great British breakfast' cooked by his mother. He explained that he had initially determined to share his memories after Farage unveiled his infamous 'Breaking Point' poster during the referendum campaign. Fearing 'repercussions', he changed his mind after Jo Cox was assassinated by a white-supremacist terrorist later the same day.

> I haven't chosen to write before, but I simply have to now. I now wonder if there is a connection between you at 16 and you at 52. I don't believe you have fascist sympathies now, but there are things that tell me your views might not have changed that much despite the many years …
>
> For I vividly recall the keen interest you had in two initials of your name written together as a signature and the bigoted symbol that represents from the many doodles over your school books. Nigel Farage, NF, National Front. I remember watching you draw it. Just a laugh, eh, Nigel?

As the son of an immigrant family, your frequent cry of 'Send em home' and mention of the name Oswald Mosley didn't mean much to me either until much later when I learnt of the British Fascists …

But I also remember something altogether more alarming: the songs you chanted at school. In her letter Chloe Deakin mentioned reports of you singing Hitler Youth songs, and when you were confronted by that, you denied it.

But I do remember you singing the song starting with the words 'gas them all, gas 'em all, gas them all'. I can't forget the words. I can't bring myself to write the rest of it for it is more vile that [*sic*] anything the teachers at Dulwich would ever have been aware of.

By 2019, Farage's response was ploddingly predictable: whataboutery, obfuscation and a complete failure to address the central allegations. 'To say that this is going over old ground is an understatement,' he said. 'The period during which I was at Dulwich was highly politically charged with the rise of Thatcherism to the Brixton riots just down the road. There were many people of that time who were attracted to extreme groups on both sides of the debate.'[14]

There is, of course, plenty of new ground. It remains largely ignored and unexplored by a media that has subsequently taken Farage to their hearts for two reasons: he remains so closely identified with Brexit that excusing his obvious awfulness became intrinsic to pretending that Brexit was not a ridiculous disaster and, once again, he provides acres of 'copy'. Consider just some of the public conduct that has been given a free pass by the media ecosystem described in the first three chapters of this book.

Imagine, for a moment, receiving an invitation to appear on a show presented by the notorious American conspiracy theorist and far-right provocateur Alex Jones. He is, perhaps, best known for claiming repeatedly that the 2012 Sandy Hook school shooting in Newtown, Connecticut, never happened, that the 26 shot dead did not die and that their grieving families were 'crisis actors' contributing to a covert US government attempt to push gun control on to the population. Closer to home, Jones also claimed that the London terror attacks on 7 July 2005 were a government plot. In 2022, his lies about Sandy Hook culminated in $1.487 billion damages being awarded to a first responder and families of victims.

Nigel Farage does not have to *imagine* receiving an invitation to appear on air with this abomination. He accepted one on at least six occasions between 2009 and 2018.[15] His appearances are riddled with casual references to 'globalists' and a 'new world order', both stalwarts of anti-Semitic rhetoric. The Community Security Trust, which monitors anti-Semitic sentiment in the UK, described Jones as 'a notorious conspiracy theorist who should be beyond the pale for any mainstream politician'. A spokesman added: 'Furthermore, for Jones's conspiracy-minded audience, Farage's references to "globalists" and "new world order" will be taken as familiar codewords for antisemitic conspiracy theories.'[16]

In October 2017, a caller to his LBC radio show told Farage that the pro-Israel 'lobby' in the US was as likely to have influenced Donald Trump's election as alleged Russian interference. Farage responded: 'Well the Israeli lobby, you know, that's a reasonable point, Ahmed, because there are about six million Jewish people living in America, so as a percentage it's quite small, but in terms of influence it's quite big.' He added: 'Well, in terms of money and influence, yep, they are a very powerful lobby,' and 'there are other very powerful foreign lobbies in the United States of America, and the Jewish lobby, with its links with the Israeli government, is one of those strong voices.' In 2018, Farage described the Jewish financier George Soros as 'the biggest danger to the entire Western world' and claimed that he wanted 'to undermine democracy and to fundamentally change the make-up, demographically, of the whole European continent'.[17]

It is interesting to note how right-wing individuals and outlets who professed outrage at the Labour leader Jeremy Corbyn's perceived anti-Semitic sympathies reacted to Farage's, reported in Israel as: 'The former leader of a nationalist political party in Britain with close ties to President Donald Trump said that American Jews have a disproportionate influence over politics.'[18] Spoiler alert: they mostly didn't.

An appearance on Jones's programme in April 2018 is particularly memorable. In it, Jones poses the following question to Farage: 'You've talked about ... the bigger EU plan to collapse the Middle East and North Africa and flood Europe with Islamicists ... You're a leading expert [author's note: !] on this. Why is the Left allied with radical Islam? Why are they trying to flood?'

Farage replies: 'Because they hate Christianity. They deny absolutely our Judaeo-Christian culture which, when you think about it, actually are the roots completely of our nations and our civilisations. They deny that. They also, don't forget Alex, want to abolish the nation state. They want to get rid of it. They want to replace it with a globalist project and the European Union is the prototype for the new world order. Do you know, if Hillary had won that election last year, she was going to sign America up to get really close to this kind of thing ...'

After the triggering of Article 50 in March 2017, Farage recorded himself raising a pint outside a London pub (he prefers wine when no cameras are around) and saying: 'Well done Bannon, well done

Breitbart. You helped with this. Hugely.' The Bannon referred to is Steve, Donald Trump's former campaign CEO who was indicted on charges of money laundering, fraud and conspiracy in September 2022. In the month preceding his appointment as Trump's campaign CEO, Bannon boasted that he had made Breitbart News 'the platform for the alt-right'. According to Reuters, 'alt-right' is

> a term popularised by white nationalist activist Richard B. Spencer to describe a loose coalition of far-right racist and white-separatist groups. Breitbart, ranked among the 50 most-viewed political websites before Trump's inauguration, also unabashedly boosted Trump's presidential candidacy with laudatory articles nestled among Islamophobic fables, false narratives about 'black crime' and anti-feminist screeds.[19]

The editor-in-chief of Breitbart London was Raheem Kassam, a former 'chief adviser' to Nigel Farage, while James Delingpole, the *Spectator*, *Telegraph* and *Mail* regular (who once managed to humiliate himself with an extraordinary show of ignorance on his own boss Andrew Neil's TV show), was its 'executive editor'. Bannon also had deep ties to Cambridge Analytica, as a board member and later executive chairman. After it emerged that the data firm had used the Facebook data of 50 million people without permission, the *New European* newspaper and other outlets reported that the clip of Farage thanking Bannon had 'disappeared from YouTube',[20] including from an article on the Breitbart site.

That Farage would trumpet his debt to Bannon and Breitbart so openly is another mark of his confidence that the right-wing Establishment was privately comfortable with the company he kept and the bile he spouted, even if they knew not to say so publicly. As ever, Boris Johnson was an exception to the rule, saying of Farage in 2013: 'A rather engaging geezer. He's anti-pomposity, he's anti-political correctness, he's anti-loony Brussels regulation. He's in favour of low tax, sticking up for small business and sticking up for Britain. We Tories look at him, with his pint and cigar and sense of humour, and instinctively recognise someone fundamentally indistinguishable from us.'[21] In 2019, Farage repaid the compliment by standing down candidates from his latest vehicle, the Brexit Party, in Tory-held seats, paving the way for Boris Johnson's landslide victory.

So apart from the silent patronage of proprietors (the owners of the *Telegraph*, the Barclay brothers, threw a 50th birthday party for him at their Ritz hotel in 2014) and politicians, how did Farage escape the consequences of actions and outbursts that would ordinarily have scuppered even his low-level political career? Part of the answer lies in his skill set. As with Trump and Johnson, the ability to lie without qualm or conscience is, in the political short term at least, a super-power. Similarly, the ability to pander to sinister and vicious prejudices without appearing sinister or vicious can deliver huge dividends. But a large part of the responsibility for his impunity, and his considerable contribution to the breaking of Britain, lies once again with the mainstream media and, specifically, with the BBC.

How much of what is detailed above were you already aware? None of it is new. All of it is publicly available and has been for years. How often have you heard or seen interviewers insist that Farage should be held to account for his previous pronouncements or associations before then allowing him to swerve the question? When it comes to the question of how UK media *should* have handled Farage, I can, I think, write with rare authority.

On 16 May 2014, Farage turned up in my radio studio somewhat unexpectedly. We are now accustomed to his dissembling and dodging but, at the time, it was still striking and even newsworthy. Some right-wing newspapers were still suspicious of him – indeed, the *Mail on Sunday* invited me to write about the encounter under the headline 'What you need to know about Nigel Farage before you vote this Thursday'. My interview with him remains interesting for three key reasons. First, it convinced some commentators that Farage's 15 minutes of infamy was up. The *Daily Telegraph* blogger, Dan Hodges, now a *Mail on Sunday* columnist, stated that it 'effectively finished Farage's career'. Conversely, a quick glance at my inbox after he was dragged from the studio by his own director of communications, an unctuous former *Daily Express* political commentator called Patrick O'Flynn, persuaded me that no amount of public embarrassment would see him lose any support from his racist base. It was a depressing moment. Second, all modesty aside, it showed just how easy it is to hold him to account, and therefore prompted the question of why so few political journalists endeavoured to do so subsequently. If they had, the course of British politics would quite possibly have run rather differently. And third, it shows just how casual his relationship with truth has always been and, crucially, how easily he dissembles and backtracks when presented with evidence of his own lies.

The interview came about in comical circumstances that have never been fully divulged before. My producer at the time, an enterprising and engaging young man called Michael Keohan, had received a mild dressing down for failing to come up with many subjects suitable for possible inclusion on that morning's programme. Without my knowledge (I was in the lavatory at the time), he called Farage directly and reminded him of a challenge he had laid down on a colleague's phone-in programme the previous week to debate me about the accusation that he was racist. On returning to my desk suitably refreshed and about ten minutes before we were due on air at 10am, Michael revealed that Farage would be coming into the studio shortly after 11 o'clock. I think he agreed because he, quite understandably, had little or no idea who I was. Nonetheless, I wasn't really up for it, having had no time to prepare. Michael was insistent that I'd been 'banging on' about Farage for long enough to convince him that I knew more than enough to conduct the interview cold.

It was, to say the least, an illuminating experience, although, ultimately, a futile one. In the context I've outlined here, where Farage is essentially Nick Griffin in a more palatable guise – an inveterate liar, a facilitator of far-right politics and overtly, albeit smilingly, racist – some moments stand out more than others. Given what would happen to him, and to the UK over the following years, it is an arresting listen. The first thing to note is how often he tries to shift the conversation away from the question asked and often towards his own bogus victimhood. The second, of course, is how easily he lies. Third, retrospectively, is that none of it ultimately mattered. When you look at political discourse in 2023 it is clear that his brand of obfuscation and evasion has proved far more successful than my attempts at highlighting lies and holding liars to account.

The interview, edited here but still available wherever you get your viral content, begins with me playing a clip of him complaining that 'idiots' in UKIP attract unfair levels of media attention before reading a tweet from a UKIP council candidate in Gloucester, John Lyndon Sullivan: 'I rather often wonder if we shot one poofter whether the next 99 would decide on balance that they weren't after all. We might then conclude that it's not a matter of genetics but rather more a matter of education.'

> **O'Brien:** Admittedly, fairly small fry in the UKIP machine. Not a description you could apply to your small business spokesman who, it turned out this morning, has employed seven illegal immigrants in the last year.

After bemoaning the frequency of 'people saying silly things', Farage immediately tries to deflect to 'other parties', saying: 'But hey, hang on a second, what's going on in the other parties?' Viewers and listeners are often perturbed by frequent interruptions and interviewers are consequently sensitive to the accusation. The answer to such concerns is to intervene swiftly and decisively when the subject is obviously not answering the question asked.

> **O'Brien:** I'll ask them when they're here, Nigel, but I'm talking about your party today.

> **Farage:** But that's the point. Nobody ever does ask them. And that's the point I'm making.

This is so obviously untrue it barely merits a response ...

> **O'Brien:** So what happens to [John Lyndon Sullivan] now?

> **Farage:** He will face a disciplinary charge on whether he's brought the party into disrepute.

O'Brien: [The tweet] was on the 17th of February. [Three months earlier.]

Farage: Was it? I don't know.

O'Brien: What about the small business spokesman who employed seven illegal immigrants?

Farage: Be a little bit careful on that story, you know. He founded a business which he's no longer a director of. His sons run it. They have got a big row going on …

Again, any reluctance to interrupt obvious obfuscation is a betrayal of journalistic standards that Farage has come to rely on. All you need to undo it is facts.

O'Brien: He resigned, to be clear, as a director of the company three days after the immigration raid.

Farage: Yah. Yah. I know that. He's resigned as a director.

O'Brien: After the immigration raid.

Note now how effortlessly he moves from an argument that failed, because it was spurious, to an entirely different one that doesn't stand up to scrutiny either.

Farage: Yah. But he wasn't responsible for the day-to-day running of it. However, I've spoken to him this morning. He says they made checks and are in dispute with the immigration authorities and they've gone to appeal so we'll have to see how that plays out. But that doesn't make him an idiot, you know.

O'Brien: What does it make him?

Farage: Well. Well. We don't know. You know, let's find out what happens here ... My argument, James, is this. Wherever we have found people who have had extreme, racist, unpleasant views, we've unceremoniously got rid of them. Furthermore, I've tried to protect the party by making it absolutely clear that anybody that had previously been a member of the BNP or organisations like that cannot even join as a member. And to hold up the views of a handful of people as being representative of UKIP frankly isn't the truth.

O'Brien: Well, OK. What about your associations with the BNP? If we go back to 1997 when you had lunch with a chap called [Mark] Deavin who, as you know, was responsible for writing an astonishing [article]. His exposé of Jews in the media was called 'Mindbenders'. You were photographed with him and it was reported at the time that you were a man who often used words such as 'nig-nog' and the n-word ... in the pub after committee meetings. And a month after that lunch Deavin wrote an article for the far-right journal *Spearhead* suggesting the BNP and UKIP get into bed together. How does something like that happen?

Farage: Because Mr Deavin was brought into the centre of UKIP by a chap at the time who was the leader. Um. And turned out to be something very different. And I've never seen him since that day.

O'Brien: No. The lunch you had with him was after he was exposed.

Again, note how quickly he abandons one ploy and moves immediately to another bout of bogus victimhood.

Farage: Yah, I wanted to find out why.

O'Brien: Find out why what?

Farage: Why somebody like him, who had been held up to me as a great academic who was going to make a very big difference ...

O'Brien: But you'd seen what he'd written. 'The Grand Plan: the origins of non-white immigration'.

Farage: I wanted to find out what on earth had made somebody change their point of view. Nothing more than that. I haven't spoken to him since. As for the allegations, you know, as to what I said in the pub after a committee meeting, you will not find a single other member of that committee who makes that allegation.

O'Brien: Alan Sked has. The founder of UKIP.

Farage: Yes I know. Well ... In politics all sorts of disappointments happen to people and they throw mud.

O'Brien: Yes, I know. So what about the mud that's been thrown about the far-right parties with which you sit in Europe? The Danish People's Party, the True Finns Party, the Dutch SPG. Perhaps most interestingly, the Lega Nord. I think you co-chair, don't you, that group with Francesco Speroni, who described Anders Breivik as someone whose ideas were in defence of Western civilisation?

Farage: No, he didn't actually – one of his members did and we kicked him out of the group.

O'Brien: No, no. You're thinking of Mario Borghezio, who went further and said in a radio interview that Breivik had some excellent ideas …

Farage: If you were to come with me to Italy, or Poland, or Slovakia, and listen to the political discourse, you would realise how incredibly different it is to what we would consider to be acceptable in this country … We have said that we will not sit with the Front National and parties like the Austrian Freedom Party. We are not a party that wants to be linked to the far right.

In March 2017, Farage conducted a radio interview with Front National leader, Marine Le Pen, in which he praised her 'connection with the French people' while she thanked him 'for showing us the way out of this huge prison'. She was referring to the EU, although, largely as a consequence of observing the reality of Brexit, her party's position on 'Frexit' soon softened to the point of disappearance.

O'Brien: I think the phrase you used [when challenging me to this 'debate'] was 'members of the political class and their friends in the media'. So let's run through that. You currently write columns in the *Express* and the *Independent* every week?

Farage: Yes … As for the political class. Look, you know, I was in business … I have actually given up and sacrificed a huge amount [to go in to politics].

O'Brien: Have you? Because the last business you were involved in, I think you resigned as company secretary six weeks before it was wound up by the Inland Revenue.

Farage: Er. No. That was … I … that was … The last company I was a director of, OK, the last company I ran was my own company which I ran for nine years and which closed down in good standing.

This nine years, as far as I can tell, is the sole foundation of his frequent insistence that he is somehow not a 'career politician'.

O'Brien: OK. So you weren't company secretary of Farage and …

Farage: I was company secretary …

O'Brien: And you resigned six weeks before …

Farage: I didn't make any money. It was a non-income related job. I wasn't paid a penny for being company secretary.

O'Brien: Presumably because if they owed 120 grand to the Inland Revenue there wasn't any money around to pay you anything? … Let me just move on then to that invitation to go overseas and listen to conversations in other countries where perhaps far-right politics are not viewed as askance as they are in this country. You've mentioned your discomfort at listening to foreign languages on a train recently?

Farage: I ... I made the point that I got on a train and went for several stops and there were a lot of people around me and no one spoke English. And, I thought, you know, this is ... I didn't object to it. I felt slightly uncomfortable ...

O'Brien: Your wife is a German speaker?

Farage: Well my children are too, yeah.

O'Brien: Does that make you feel uncomfortable?

Farage: No. No, because they can speak English.

O'Brien: Well how do you know those people [on the train] couldn't?

Farage: Well maybe they could but I got the distinct feeling that it certainly wasn't their language of choice and if you look at the primary school situation in the East End of London, you know, where you've now got schools where a majority don't speak English. Doesn't that say ...

O'Brien: The schools you refer to, the pupils you refer to are registered and recorded as having English as a second language. They're not registered and recorded as not being able to speak English ... Your own children would fit in to that category.

Farage: Uh, well, hopefully lots of people can speak lots of different languages. But the point I'm making is do we want to live in an integrated …

O'Brien: No, no. Forgive me but the point you're making is that schools in the East End are full of children who can't speak English. I just want you to recognise that's not true, what you've just said. The children who are typified as speaking English as a second language would include your own daughters. Their mother tongue being German.

Farage: They come from homes where English is most definitely not the first language and in too many cases is not the language at all.

O'Brien: But no one's counted how many people are in the second category?

Farage: They haven't, no. And it would be very helpful and useful if they did and perhaps we'd be even more surprised and even more shocked.

O'Brien: Or perhaps we'd realise that most bilingual children in this country are children like yours.

Farage: Let's turn it round the other way shall we?

O'Brien: Yes, let's.

Farage: Let's talk about immigration …

O'Brien: If that was the debate that you'd offered to have on this programme we'd have it now but what the caller asked you was why so many people think you're racist … And part of the answer would be that you talk about children who can't speak English as a first language without mentioning that it includes your own children.

Farage: I mean, what is racism? You know, is racism between races?

O'Brien: Don't you know? How can you say you're not something when you don't know what it is?

Farage: Is race about colour? Is … is … is race about race or is it about nationality. You know, I made a comment there that wasn't intended to say any more than that I felt uncomfortable about the rate and pace of change and numbers of people …

O'Brien: No, you felt uncomfortable about people speaking foreign languages despite the fact that presumably your own wife does when she phones home to Germany.

Farage: I don't suppose she speaks it on the train, you know. And that's the point I was making.

O'Brien: Well, why not? Is she not allowed to? And what about the line about not wanting to live next door to Romanians?

Farage: I was asked if a group of Romanian men moved in next door to you, would you be concerned?

O'Brien: What about if a group of German children did? What's the difference?

Farage: The difference, and you know what the difference is.

O'Brien: No, I honestly don't and I think this is the disconnect between your position and mine.

The difference, of course, is that racists throughout history have insisted that certain minorities have a particular proclivity to criminality, that it is somehow in their DNA. It is most often seen in the context of defending the disproportionate and indiscriminate use of 'stop and search' powers against young black men. Farage's entire career has been built on variations of the same theme. Accordingly, he was soon talking about Roma criminals and people traffickers ...

O'Brien: I asked you a question about Romanians and you started talking about people traffickers ... Why didn't you say people are perfectly entitled to say that they feel uncomfortable about living next door to people traffickers, wherever they're from? Why do you say Romanians?

Farage: I didn't say Romanians ...

Fleet Street was united in describing the encounter as a 'car crash' and potentially career ending (for Farage!). The *Sun*, and I had to double check this, described his comments about Romanians as 'racism, pure and simple'. It makes you feel nostalgic for a bygone time. In reality, it barely constituted a bump in the road for Farage's bandwagon of bigotry. Later that week, he would lead UKIP to victory in the European elections and park his tanks on David Cameron's lawn. The Tory leader had already pledged in 2013 to hold a referendum on EU membership if he won the 2015 election. It was an unsuccessful bid to hold his own party together and UKIP's success in the 2014 European elections changed the game. In August, the Tory backbencher Douglas Carswell defected to UKIP and won the subsequent by-election in Clacton. In September, Mark Reckless, another backbench nonentity afforded momentary celebrity by Tory infighting, announced his defection to UKIP from the stage of the party's annual conference in Doncaster. He too won the subsequent by-election, in Rochester and Strood, although he lost his seat four months later at the general election that saw David Cameron prevail against Ed Miliband. It was a victory that rendered the referendum inevitable and, in his victory speech on 7 May 2015, Cameron confirmed that he would call a simple in/out ballot after 'negotiating a new settlement for Britain in the EU'. Cameron's pink-cheeked triumphalism on the night was nothing if not hubristic. He did not realise it at the time but two of the most fundamentally and flagrantly dishonest politicians in British history, Nigel Farage and Boris Johnson, already had his political balls in a vice.

It is a peculiar vagary of the British political system that claims made in washing powder adverts are subject to much more stringent scrutiny than claims made in political advertising. Consider, first, this syrupy voiceover from a campaign video made and distributed by Farage's Leave.EU campaign group in the run up to the 2016 referendum. It has high production values and a cast of smiling, almost exclusively white, characters enjoying life in a notional post-Brexit UK. The comparison with the post-Brexit reality of 2023 is, even for seasoned chroniclers of our self-inflicted decline, close to tear inducing. It is also a handy reminder why, for many years after the vote, I used my radio show to seed the notion that we should have 'contempt for the con men and compassion for the conned'. Watching this now, it is hard to fault anybody who fell for it. Funded by a £7 million donation loan from insurance tycoon Arron Banks, later apparently 'written off' by the businessman,[22] Farage finally had the financial backing to add a patina of professionalism to his spiv's patter.

You'll benefit from better care from the NHS thanks to the reallocation of funds from the EU budget. Controlled immigration will lead to reduced waiting times for you and your loved ones. The excess funding that would otherwise be sent to Brussels could also be directed to education, meaning better prospects for your children. Your wages will rise thanks to better controlled immigration which will lead to less competition for jobs. You weekly food shop will become cheaper. Food prices will no longer be inflated by agricultural policies controlled by the EU. You and your family will benefit from a resurgent economy led by new and flourishing small businesses following the removal of burdensome EU regulations and red tape. With less pressure on housing, younger generations will also find it easier to get on the housing ladder. Politicians, both local and national, will become more accountable, helping to strengthen your community and others. Especially those most damaged by EU policies like farming, fishing and industries like steel. A more prosperous and safer future awaits us outside the EU. A vote to leave is a vote for a brighter future for you, your family and your community.

Nobody will ever be held to account for this epic misrepresentation of what Brexit would deliver. Instead, its progenitors insist variously that 'everyone knew exactly what they were voting for', and that anyone pointing out the gulf between what was promised and what was delivered should 'move on', or that the mythical Brexit described above *could* have been delivered were it not for some enormous, unspecified betrayal. In other words, there *is* a brilliant Brexit. It just goes to a different school.

We are not concerned here with the full gamut of Farage's lies and deceptions. That would take a library. We are concerned, chiefly, with the creation of the media and political environment in which those lies and base bigotries could be first rejected by the 'mainstream', then tolerated and finally enthusiastically embraced. More than anyone else, he created the climate whereby the home secretary would boast about her dream of seeing front pages reporting the deportation of genuine refugees to a country where refugees are shot. He created the climate where an immigration minister would order cartoons at a processing centre for unaccompanied child asylum seekers be painted over. And here one episode stands above all others as evidence of just how low he was prepared to go, just how 'unspeakable' he was prepared to be and just how easily he would, by the time of the referendum, get away with behaviour that would have been 'unthinkable' just two years previously.

On 16 June 2016, exactly one week before the referendum vote, Leave.EU unveiled a poster. It showed a caravan of largely Syrian refugees crossing the border between Slovenia and Croatia on their way to a refugee camp. It featured the caption 'Breaking Point' below which appeared the words: 'The EU has failed us all'. Across the bottom of the billboard, in front of which Farage posed for press photographers, it said: 'Break free of the EU and take control of our borders'. It bore a marked resemblance to a particularly virulent example of Nazi propaganda, which deployed similarly framed footage with the captions: '... who flooded Europe's cities after the last war. Parasites, undermining their host countries and bringing with them crime, corruption and chaos.' Hours after the poster was unveiled, Jo Cox was shot dead by a white-supremacist terrorist. During his 'victory' speech a week later, Nigel Farage boasted that Brexit had been secured 'without a single bullet being fired'.

On 27 March 2017, Farage vowed that he would 'go and live abroad' if Brexit failed. On 15 May 2023, he told the BBC, where he still has a season ticket, that 'Brexit has failed'. Months later he was to be found publicly bemoaning the fact that Coutts, the so-called 'millionaire's bank', had downgraded him to an ordinary account with the NatWest high-street bank. Either because he was no longer sufficiently solvent or because they feared being tainted by association. Both grounds seem perfectly reasonable, particularly for 'free marketeers', but Andrew Neil, the *Daily Mail*, the *Telegraph*, the prime minister Rishi Sunak and the home secretary Suella Braverman all galloped to Farage's aid. He is yet to 'go and live abroad'. Nick Griffin, meanwhile, announced in 2017 that he wanted to emigrate to Hungary. Weeks later, the government of Viktor Orbán, who said in 2022 that 'We [Hungarians] are not a mixed race ... and we do not want to become a mixed race,' announced that Griffin was 'persona non grata' and barred him from entering the country.

Chapter 6
DAVID CAMERON

So what's happened to that twat David Cameron, who called
it on? How comes he can scuttle off? He called all this on.
He's in Europe, in Nice with his trotters up, yeah? Where is
the geezer? I think he should be held account for it. He should
be held account for it ... Twat.

Danny Dyer, *Good Evening Britain*, ITV, 28 June 2018

ON 15 JUNE 1988, the deputy director of the Conservative Research
Department received an unscheduled telephone call from Buckingham
Palace. It concerned an apparently unremarkable young man who had
found himself unexpectedly jobless. Recent Oxford graduate David
Cameron had, by his own admission, failed to secure a lucrative berth
in the City of London through the post-university 'milk round' of interviews with financial institutions and consultancies.[1] Among the many
unimpressed interviewers had been a young and highly regarded
management consultant at McKinsey called William Hague.[2] Cameron's
ambitions to enter journalism had, like his future friend and colleague
George Osborne's, also come to nought. Happily for him, although not
necessarily for anyone else, he had at least one admirer in high places.

'I understand that you are to see David Cameron,' said the
'distinctly grand' man from the Palace. 'I've tried everything I can to

dissuade him from wasting his time on politics, but I have failed. You are about to meet a truly remarkable young man.'[3]

History relates neither the grounds for this encomium nor the identity of its deliverer. Contenders included Sir Alastair Aird, then equerry to the Queen Mother and the husband of Cameron's godmother, and Sir Brian McGrath, a friend of his parents serving at the time as private secretary to Prince Philip. Another godparent, the Conservative MP Tim Rathbone, had provided young Cameron with employment at parliament during his 'gap year' between school and university. These links alone provide a snapshot of a class system so entrenched and unquestioned by its beneficiaries that when Cameron became prime minister of the United Kingdom just 12 years later, it seemed, to him at least, the most natural thing in the world. 'I felt exhausted, elated – but strangely at ease,' he wrote later of the moment he was 'clapped in' to Downing Street by staff after winning the 2010 election aged just 43 and with no serious frontline political experience. 'Not at ease in an entitled, born-to-rule sense. But because there is such a warmth from all the people in that building – and, for me, at least some familiarity.'[4]

Attacking inherited privilege can sometimes seem as bone-headed as defending it. Wealth and advantage do not necessarily prevent having empathy for those less privileged, or confer an inability to appreciate injustice. George Orwell, for example, is, like Cameron, an alumnus of Eton College. But so, at the time of Cameron's Downing Street installation, had been *20* other prime ministers. Every one of them Conservative. It is foolish not to recognise how this simple fact rubbishes any notion that Britain is a meritocracy, or how much it suggests that David Cameron would have got nowhere near Downing Street if he had attended what Alastair Campbell famously described as a 'bog standard comprehensive' school. Similarly, without understanding Cameron's ease and prominence in a social hierarchy forged to run the Empire and bake inequality into every stratum of society, we cannot hope to understand the patrician insouciance with which he would lead the United Kingdom over a cliff.

'He'll go down in history as the man who gambled everything on a referendum and lost, effectively blowing half a century of economic and diplomatic effort on the part of his predecessors,' Timothy Bale, professor of politics at Queen Mary University of London, told *USA Today* on 13 July 2016 in an interview marking Cameron's resignation. Subsequent events, of course, have shown that Professor Bale, always an acute observer of events, was rather understating the scale of Cameron's grim legacy, which is by no means confined to Brexit.

In modern times, there have always been at least two Conservative parties. One side, the Establishment vehicle of monarchy and aristocracy and, almost but not quite conversely the other side, the home for aspirational and ambitious people who believe the system has rewarded – or will soon reward – their own hard work and abilities with a perch on a higher rung. Electoral success always depends upon persuading enough of the electorate that those rewards are within reach for them if, and only if, the Tories are in power. The American author John Steinbeck encapsulated the conundrum in 1960, writing: 'Socialism never took root in America because the poor see themselves not as an exploited proletariat but as temporarily embarrassed millionaires.'[5]

Cameron's immediate Tory predecessors in Downing Street had been resolutely in the second category: the grammar-school boy Edward Heath, the grocer's daughter Margaret Thatcher and the former bus conductor John Major. Their successors while in opposition to the Blair/Brown governments had been born with similarly unsilvered spoons: the former political prodigy William Hague; the shapeshifting, CV-finagling Iain (Duncan) Smith; and the Romanian refugee's son Michael Howard. Nearly three decades in the background had not, however, extinguished the Conservative contingent that did indeed consider themselves 'born to rule'. They had merely been biding their time.

Cameron's family tree is peppered with politicians and baronets (one below an earl, if you care to know). Unlike the perspicacious actor and remorseful Leave voter quoted at the very top of this chapter, he did not need to go on genealogy TV to learn that he is descended from a king (William IV) and is a distant cousin to Queen Elizabeth II. His father-in-law, Sir Reginald Sheffield, is a multi-millionaire and, like his own maternal grandfather, an old Etonian baronet. In his autobiography, Cameron describes an idyllic childhood in rural Berkshire interrupted when he was, aged seven, sent to Heatherdown boarding school near Ascot, the alma mater of princes Andrew and Edward, alongside sundry aristocrats and the progeny of various plutocrats. As well, of course, as the children of aspirational middle-class professionals unblessed by inherited wealth or privilege. While successive Tory governments would leave many schools lucky to possess playing fields, Heatherdown had a miniature railway that chuffed around the grounds while visitors to the school sports day passed through one of three entrances: 'Ladies', 'Gentlemen' or 'Chauffeurs'.[6]

I received a similar, less gilded schooling, although my family circumstances were and remain markedly different from Cameron's. I have written at length about the emotional privations of such environments and the grisly consequences of having rulers raised in them.[7] Another old Etonian, Cyril Connolly, perhaps put it best when he wrote in his seminal 1938 memoir, *Enemies of Promise*:

Were I to deduce any system from my feelings on leaving Eton, it might be called The Theory of Permanent Adolescence. It is the theory that the experiences undergone by boys at the great public schools, their glories and disappointments, are so intense as to dominate their lives and to arrest their development. From these it results that the greater part of the ruling class remains adolescent, school-minded, self-conscious, cowardly, sentimental, and in the last analysis homosexual.

Twenty-first-century sensibilities render the final line ridiculous but another, better known one from the same source could have been written with Cameron in mind: 'Whom the Gods wish to destroy, they first call promising.'

In his own breezy and understandably defensive memoir, Cameron sounds like most boys who have been taught from an early age that a 'stiff upper lip' is more valuable than emotional literacy. Beatings, we learn, were commonplace at Heatherdown, naked communal bathing considered normal and maggots in the food a comical culinary hazard. You learn early not to 'care' about such things, because the alternative is to succumb to the casual cruelties and brutalisations typical of such schools until relatively recently. At the same time, admitting to mistakes or simply to being wrong about something is inconceivable. It would be a sign of weakness, and open chinks in the armour built simply to survive school and soon hardened into a second skin. What Cyril Connolly so presciently identified as 'Permanent Adolescence' is now a growing and compelling field of academic study known as 'Boarding School Syndrome'. In reference to this deliberate breaking of familial bonds, shown to shape a child for life, John Bowlby, a psychoanalyst renowned for his work on child and

HOW THEY BROKE BRITAIN

parent attachments, once said that he 'wouldn't send a dog away to boarding school aged seven'.[8]

After Heatherdown, Eton, where even more of the offspring of Britain's rich and powerful are educated. Princes William and Harry are alumni. A 16-year-old Boris Johnson wrote in the school magazine, the *Eton Chronicle*, that the education imbues its beneficiaries with 'the most important thing, a sense of his own importance'. Self-awareness, alas, proved rather harder to teach. School fees are currently around £50,000 per annum and students wear tailcoats and white ties to classes. It is, obviously, an absurd environment in which to place a child. Until, that is, you remember that it is an environment originally designed to make men of Empire, who never question their right to rule over any part of the world they choose.

Cameron has written of a 'strong academic pressure to be a success in the classroom, and powerful social pressure to be a success on the playing field'.[9] The pressure, however, was not sufficient to see him achieve either until the end of his schooldays, when, after disappointing O levels, his A-level results proved sufficient to secure a place at Oxford University.

In *One of Them*, a magnificent memoir of his own time at Eton, the author Musa Okwonga recalled: 'Visible effort is mocked at my school – the trick is to achieve without seeming to try.'[10] This obsession with *effortless* success is the bizarre bedfellow of permanent competition. 'Etonians have to compete for office within the school,' explains another old boy, Nick Fraser, in his book, *The Importance of Being Eton*. He in turn quotes the former Conservative minister Jonathan Aitken, whose own propensity to lie to win at all costs would see him end up in prison: 'It breeds a certain speciality of behaviour. You know how to get elected, you know how to please. You have to learn to oil. And at Eton you do learn.'[11] 'Oiling' is best understood as networking, based on an understanding that in the upper reaches of British society, connections and contacts have always mattered more than intelligence, talent or integrity.

The tragedy of David Cameron, and in many ways of modern Britain, is that the skills required to 'succeed' in these ridiculous citadels of entitlement and emotional illiteracy translate wholesale into the worlds of politics or business or, as we have seen, the popular media. And if at first you don't succeed then, like Cameron, try another path until you achieve the sort of status you believe to be your birthright. If you are particularly 'well-oiled' you might even enlist help from a Palace panjandrum. And when enough of the general public look at a Cameron or a Johnson or even a Jacob Rees-Mogg and judge them their 'betters', it becomes much easier to understand how, from 2010 onwards, the United Kingdom endured successive governments populated by politicians of unprecedented mediocrity.

I know better than most that attempting to secure sympathy for men who enjoyed unfair advantages is an often thankless task. And I won't essay it again here. But while these schools are bastions of privilege, and springboards to the highest echelons of society, they can leave their alumni emotionally crippled and so unable to acknowledge personal pain that they approach the world in a state of constant vigilance. Everything is a competition where winning is all that matters. Consider Cameron's response when his Eton contemporary Boris Johnson was hospitalised with coronavirus, an obviously lethal disease, and then moved to intensive care. 'Boris is a very tough, very resilient, very fit person,' he said. 'I know that from facing him on the tennis court and I'm sure he'll come through this.'[12] In short, this deadly virus – already responsible for the death of thousands of ordinary people – can somehow be countered with belligerence and sports skills! This daft but, in serious circumstances, deeply dangerous attitude lies at the heart of Cameron's unavoidably warped worldview and sowed the earliest political seeds of the catastrophes that would follow. In contrast to his more *ordinary* predecessors, Cameron was possessed of both epic entitlement *and* the emotionally stunted public schoolboy's deep, psychological need to 'win'. Consequently, he would usher in an era where truth would be subjugated by political expediency and national interest dwarfed by self-interest. For all his carefully contrived 'hug a hoodie' conviviality, we shall see that David Cameron's unnecessarily cruel policies, his political and personal carelessness, and profound cowardice in the face of epochal challenge set the scene for the depravity of Johnson's premiership, the madness of Liz Truss's and, under Rishi Sunak, the Faragification of his own party.

But first, Oxford. Haunted, according to his autobiography, by fears that he might turn out to be just another public-school mediocrity, Cameron applied himself to his studies and emerged with a first-class degree. And while his tutor recalls that Cameron 'didn't lose sleep over philosophical problems' and had a preference for instinct over introspection, it would be churlish not to recognise the scale of this achievement. Unlike many Conservative politicians who would flourish in the wake of Brexit, he is clearly not stupid. But his student days were also taken up with membership of the Bullingdon Club, commemorated in an infamous 1987 photograph that saw him and nine other men, Boris Johnson and George Osborne among them, apparently competing to appear the most arrogant and entitled. Johnson's journalist sister Rachel described it as 'elitist, arrogant, privileged and of an age that would have little resonance with people on low incomes who didn't go to Eton'.[13] When the picture's depiction of haughty condescension began to plague Cameron's attempts to portray himself as being in touch with 'ordinary people', its copyright holders withdrew permission for the image to be reproduced. It has never been established what strings were pulled or favours promised to achieve this but it was a largely futile exercise. Soon the BBC's *Newsnight* programme had even commissioned a portrait to circumvent the ban.

The late poet, polemicist and playwright Heathcote Williams, like George Orwell an avowedly iconoclastic old Etonian, made a study of the Bullingdon in his eviscerating 2016 volume, *Brexit Boris: From Mayor to Nightmare*. 'The Bullingdon Club,' he wrote, 'is for plutocratic undergraduates who think nothing of spending £3,500 on its royal blue tailcoats with ivory lapels and canary yellow waistcoats – a livery which prompted Evelyn Waugh in *Brideshead Revisited* to describe Bullingdon members as looking "like a lot of most disorderly footmen".'[14]

He recounts an episode which, had it featured two future Labour prime ministers, we would almost certainly have heard more about in the intervening years:

At one Club meal in 1987, attended by both Boris Johnson and David Cameron, someone – whose identity has never been properly established thanks to the Bullingdon rule of omertà – threw a large plant pot through the restaurant window. The burglar alarm was activated and Oxford's police force duly descended on the dining club's chosen venue with sniffer dogs in tow. Six of the group were apprehended and spent the night at Cowley police station. Cameron escaped but Johnson's attempt to evade the police by running off and crawling through a hedge in the Botanical Gardens failed and, by his own account, an overnight stay in a police cell reduced him to 'a gibbering namby-pamby'.

The tale tallies with the journalist Barney Ronay's memories of his Oxford contemporaries who joined the club. 'There's the air of lurking violence,' he wrote. 'And above all the sense that its members consider themselves above the law on such occasions.'[15]

Williams also reports that: 'Another stock-in-trade of the Bullingdon initiation rituals was for newly elected members to visit Bonn Square where Oxford's homeless congregate and to burn a £50 note in front of them by way of jeering at their misfortune.'

Cameron's retrospective contrition is unintentionally illustrative, as it demonstrates more regret over the damage the photograph did to his image than any of the violence or delinquency with which the club is associated. 'When I look now at the much-reproduced photograph taken of our group of appallingly over-self-confident "sons of privilege" I cringe,' he reveals in his autobiography. 'If I had known at the time the grief I would get for that picture, of course I would never have joined.'[16]

So Cameron left Oxford and, as we have established, failed to get a job in either the City of London or on Fleet Street that he felt would be deserving of his monumental talents. But, of course, the call from the Palace did its work and in 1988, the year after the Bullingdon photograph was taken, David Cameron arrived at the Conservative Research Department (CRD). He would stay there for five years. In 1991, just three years after graduating, he was tasked with briefing John Major for Prime Minister's Questions. Judged a success in the role, he was rewarded with the leadership of the political section of the CRD. During the 1992 general election campaign he was back at John Major's side, assuming responsibility for preparing the prime minister for press conferences. Following Major's widely unexpected victory, his star was in the ascendancy and he became special adviser to Norman Lamont, the chancellor of the exchequer. He arrived in the job just in time for 'Black Wednesday', the 1992 financial crisis that saw Major's government forced to withdraw sterling from the European Exchange Rate Mechanism (ERM) after failing to keep the exchange rate above the required level. Still just 27, and no doubt aware that Major was now highly unlikely to win another election, David Cameron temporarily quit politics in 1994 and determined that a 'proper' job in the private sector would burnish his political credentials. It was time for more 'oiling'.

In September 1994, he was appointed director of corporate affairs at the television company Carlton Communications, headed by the executive chairman Michael Green. 'The former special adviser had pulled strings to land the post,' explained the *Financial Times* in 2010. 'Annabel Astor, his future mother-in-law, persuaded Mr Green to take on a man with no corporate PR or investor relations experience.' Cameron was a qualified success in the role. Green was delighted, but journalists compelled to deal with him were less impressed, with the *FT* revealing: 'In a series of run-ins with financial journalists, Mr Cameron developed a reputation for arrogance, evasiveness and, in one case, alleged mendacity that dogged him during his attempt to become Tory leader in 2005 and may resurface during the imminent general election campaign.'[17]

In 1997, when he took leave from Carlton to fight what should have been a safe Tory seat, Stafford, he was not expecting to return. Boundary changes to the constituency and the scale of Tony Blair's landslide general election victory, however, dictated otherwise and Cameron was back at Carlton from where, it is fair to say, few suspected he would subsequently scale the political heights. 'I have to pinch myself when I think he could be prime minister,' a senior business journalist told the *Guardian* in 2010. 'I can still picture him wringing his hands behind Michael Green's back. It's like that saying from the US – they say "Anyone can become president" – and now I'm starting to believe it.'[18]

In the 2001 election, having been gifted an even safer seat to fight, David Cameron became the MP for Witney in Oxfordshire and began to rise almost without trace through the party ranks. It was, crucially, a party in dire political straits. William Hague's crushing defeat in 1997 had seen the party turn in desperation to a supremely unqualified candidate, Iain (Duncan) Smith. Beset by innate incompetence and, it quickly emerged, a distinctly casual attitude to the truth when it came to his own background and achievements, even the ravaged party realised that leaving him in post to fight a general election would be catastrophic. A vote of confidence in 2003 saw him become the first leader since Neville Chamberlain not to lead the party into a general election. (He has since been joined on that ignominious roster by Liz Truss.) The best available candidate to replace him proved to be Michael Howard, the shadow chancellor, who the Conservative Party elected as their leader, unopposed.

Like William Hague, but unlike Iain (Duncan) Smith, history will judge Michael Howard more kindly than contemporary commentators and colleagues. He led the party to its third consecutive defeat in 2015 but reduced Labour's majority from 167 to 66. Crucially, after determining to step down as leader, he set about preparing the party for the future by comprehensively reshuffling his front bench in May with at least one eye on the question of a potential successor. David Cameron was made shadow secretary of state for education and George Osborne became shadow chancellor. In yet another example of how intertwined opaquely funded think tanks are with the modern Conservative Party, Daniel (now Lord) Finkelstein, variously the chairman of Policy Exchange, director of the CRD, adviser to William Hague, and executive editor, associate editor and columnist on Rupert Murdoch's *Times*, recalled in 2010:

> Before the 2005 General Election, a small group of us (myself, David Cameron, George Osborne, Michael Gove, Nick Boles, Nick Herbert I think, once or twice) used to meet up in the offices of Policy Exchange, eat pizza, and consider the future of the Conservative Party. And we were stumped. It's not that we didn't understand what needed to be done. It is that we couldn't work out how to make it happen. All our theories about how to modernise the party just seemed impossible to deliver under any conceivable leader. That is because we hadn't properly considered that David himself could be leader.[19]

By September 2005, when the race to replace Howard began in earnest, Cameron was a contender but David Davis, the shadow home secretary, was the hot favourite. 'It was a big decision [to run] and I didn't do it lightly,' Cameron said later. 'I always thought there was a good prospect, a fair prospect of winning the competition to become leader … that may sound arrogant.'[20] If it was arrogant, it was well-placed. A speech delivered without notes (a speciality of public-school debating chambers) at the Conservative Party conference in October changed the game. 'Some say that we should move to the right,' he said. 'I say that will turn us into a fringe party, never able to challenge for government again. I don't want to let that happen to this party. Do you?' He continued: 'To the family trying to keep their heads above water to provide for their kids and to give them the time they need, we'll say:

"Yes, we believe in the family, because the most important thing in the world is that children are brought up in a stable, loving home.'"

Bolstered by Davis's lacklustre performance, he was snapping at the older man's heels in the first ballot of MPs. Daniel Finkelstein was also on hand to help, writing in his *Times* column: 'Some Conservatives whom I greatly respect gave Mr Davis their support on the ground that he might prove a modernising leader. This hypothesis has now been disproved. They should not feel bound to him any longer.'[21] By the second ballot, Cameron was streets ahead, securing 90 votes to Davis's 57. The margin of victory when the decision was put to the wider party membership was greater still. On 6 December 2005, David Cameron's election as leader of the Conservative Party was announced. On 13 July 2016, resigning as prime minister after setting in motion a chain of events that would scupper the country and see his own party lurch violently to the right, he told the House of Commons, accurately, that 'I was the future once.'

In his acceptance speech, he promised 'a more compassionate Conservatism, right for our times and right for our country'. But behind the platitudes, it was – and still remains – difficult to discern precisely what David Cameron stood for or believed in. In this, to be fair, he is not unique. After the 1997 defeat, the future universities minister, David Willetts, asked Denis Thatcher what he thought the party should do next. He replied: 'Get back to basic Conservative principles – but don't ask me what they are.'[22] Cameron, however, had become leader and would shortly become prime minister – not a prime minister's spouse – without ever providing much indication of why he wanted the job.

The former MP and New Labour communications guru, Peter Mandelson, shared a telling anecdote in his 2010 memoir:

He has a certain 'born to rule' thing about him. A sense of entitlement – somebody who thinks that he would be good at governing
and being Prime Minister. Indeed, I always remember the Editor
of *The Daily Telegraph* telling me, a year ago, when they had
Cameron to dinner, the first question they asked him was, 'Well,
why do you want to be prime minister?' And he said, 'Because I
think I'd be good at it.'[23]

The omens were not great. During the leadership campaign,
Cameron had made just one substantive policy promise to the party.
It concerned, perhaps inevitably, Europe, and it provides a helpful,
albeit harrowing, harbinger of what would follow. In the hope of
placating the right-wing headbangers of the 'Cornerstone' group
of MPs, Cameron pledged that he would lead Tory MEPs out of
the main centre-right grouping in the European Parliament, the
European People's Party (EPP). This was an immediate break from
cooperative union with like-minded centre-right European counterparts, and left the Tory party in bed with much more extreme
European right-wing parties. William Hague, probably the Tories'
most Eurosceptic leader to date, had not gone near the policy and
David Davis had declined to sign up to the withdrawal pledge during
the leadership contest. It marks the first example of David Cameron
eschewing cooperation and engagement with allies and equals in the
EU, and preferring to pander to the whims of his own party's luna-
tic fringe – Cornerstone, dubbed 'Tombstone' by critics, contained
political geniuses such as John Redwood, Nadine Dorries and future
'hardman of Brexit' Steve Baker.

This departure prompted Conservative MEP Caroline Jackson
to declare:

David Cameron's decision on the EPP is pathetic and will sow the seeds of endless trouble. It will leave David Cameron and [Shadow Foreign Secretary] William Hague very isolated because it will leave bad blood with Christian Democrat parties throughout Europe. It is a stupid, stupid policy ...

The Tories are doing this because the party is run by people whose ultimate agenda is to pull Britain out of the EU. I have been a member of the Conservative party since 1963 and started working for the Conservative Research Department in 1973. This is one of the most dotty escapades the Conservative party had ever embarked on.[24]

The shadow business secretary, Kenneth Clarke, had described the pledge as 'rather dangerous' in 2006 but revealed in 2009 that the party leadership had assured him that Tory MEPs would not be sitting with 'neo-fascists or cranks or anything of this kind'.[25]

In the event, the 26 Tory MEPs elected in 2009 became the largest contingent in the newly formed European Conservatives and Reformists group. Poland's opposition Law and Justice party, some of whose members had expressed homophobic and anti-German views, had the second largest number of MEPs in the new group. Latvia's For Fatherland and Freedom/LNNK party was also part of the new coalition. Some of its members celebrated the Latvian Legion, the Latvian units of the Waffen SS. Their MEPs would, perhaps, have fitted in at Andrew Neil's *Spectator* summer parties but made a strange bedfellow for British Tories in 2009.

At the time, most future Remainers failed to note the significance of Cameron's weakness in this case but the words of Ed Davey, then the Liberal Democrats' foreign affairs spokesman and now the party's leader, have proved prescient: 'The Conservatives have opted to throw away influence in Europe in favour of ideological isolationism. Conservative political leaders in Paris, Berlin and Rome must be shaking their heads in disbelief, while President [Barack] Obama will be shocked that a party that hopes to be the government of Britain would associate with a range of fringe parties, most of which have minimal influence in their home countries.'[26] By contrast, Mark Francois, the shadow Europe minister who would go on to become one of the most reliably ridiculous 'Brexiteers', insisted that they were 'very excited about this important new development' in European politics.[27] It may not have been clear at the time, but the headbangers were now calling the tune. And Cameron was already dancing to it.

On 18 December 2005, Cameron gave his first newspaper interview as party leader. That he chose the *Observer* was evidence of his determination to appeal beyond traditional Tory territories. Reading it now, three things stand out. The first, once again, is the hideous transformation his party has undergone in the 18 years since. In 2023, as we have seen, senior Tories compete over who can be most deliberately cruel and callous towards refugees and asylum seekers. In 2005, their shiny-faced young leader stated: 'I'm passionately committed to giving people who are being tortured and persecuted asylum, and that means not just letting them in, but taking them to our hearts, and feeding and clothing and schooling them.' Second, the blasé acknowledgement of what would prove to be a serious flaw: 'I'm not a deeply ideological person – I'm a practical person, and pragmatic. I know where I want to get to, but I'm not ideologically attached to one particular method.' And third, between the lines, the *reason* why not believing in anything much or seeming to care particularly deeply about politics didn't set off more alarm bells at the time. The 2008 financial crisis was barely a speck on the horizon, economic stability had been taken for granted for years, 'austerity' belonged to a different age, the prospect of war in Europe was an almost unthinkable idea and few people knew precisely what constituted a pandemic. There was, in other words, no obvious danger in having a prospective prime minister so removed from the implications of his policies that he would boast the following year that 'I probably have more hinterland than front-end. For me family, friends and home are the most important thing in my life. If politics interfered with that too much I'd call it a day.'[28]

The Greeks, as ever, have a word for it. *Hamartia* is the fatal flaw that will bring down even the most highly favoured hero. Cameron's was a combination of ambition for ambition's sake, self-importance and complacency. Ed Miliband, whom he would defeat in the 2015 general election, once observed that Cameron did not really want to *be* prime minister, he just wanted to *have been* prime minister.[29] From a rather different political perspective, Rupert Murdoch told the *New Yorker* that Cameron was 'charming, he's very bright and he behaves as if he doesn't believe in anything other than trying to construct what he believes will be the right public image. He's a PR guy.'[30]

The opposite, in other words, of his opponent in the 2010 election, Gordon Brown. Dour, detail-obsessed, irascible and, perhaps crucially, unpolished enough to be accidentally recorded describing Gillian Duffy, a voter who had button-holed him with tabloid-fresh immigration scare stories during the campaign, as 'that bigoted woman'. Whether through personal flaws, widespread media enmity or a combination of both, during the May 2010 election Brown failed to capitalise on his genuinely world-leading response to the 2008 financial crisis.

In October of that year, Brown and his chancellor, Alistair Darling, persuaded sceptical G7 and EU leaders that recapitalisation of banks was the only way to avert catastrophe. The scale of this achievement is all the more impressive as Brown hadn't originally been invited to the definitive meeting of Eurozone leaders in France but, having received a late invitation from the French president, Nicolas Sarkozy, ended up persuading everyone present to follow the British model. On the evening of 14 October, at 8.30 Paris time, Sarkozy stepped out of the Élysée to tell the assembled media that those present had agreed, in broad principle, to follow Gordon Brown's recapitalisation schemes. Back in London after an overnight flight from Washington where he had secured similar success, Alistair Darling imposed stringent 'bail out' conditions on British banks that had teetered on the brink of collapse just two days earlier on 'Black Friday'. He prevailed. It was, by any standards, a remarkable display of economic acumen and international statesmanship by Brown and Darling, who would later admit that he believed 'we faced a situation where the banking system right across the world, never mind Britain, could have collapsed'.[31]

Yet, David Cameron, his colleagues and their client media would shamelessly lie about what had happened that weekend and what had caused the crisis for the duration of the 2010 election campaign and seemingly, at the time of writing, for the rest of their lives.

It is impossible to exaggerate the egregiousness of the lie that propelled Cameron into Downing Street, in coalition with Nick Clegg's Liberal Democrats, and formed the foundation stone of his ruinous programme of 'austerity'. *Thirteen years later*, in 2023, the party chairman Greg Hands was still desperately referring on Twitter (or X) almost daily to a valedictory line written by Liam Byrne, chief secretary of the Treasury, addressed to his successor, that said: 'I'm afraid there is no money.'

The grossly fallacious idea that the 2008 economic meltdown was due to Labour's public sector spending, as opposed to a banking crisis born largely from the American subprime mortgage scandal, was absolutely crucial to Cameron and, even more so, his chancellor, George Osborne. 'How,' asked the former Labour MP Chris Mullin in 2015, 'did the party of bankers, hedge funders and light-touch regulation manage to turn what was by any measure a crisis of capitalism into a crisis for the public sector?'[32] The answer is now depressingly familiar: blatant lies, media complicity and an absence of accountability and integrity at the heart of government.

All the talk of 'Gordon Brown's debt', 'the mess that Labour left us' and 'the chaos we inherited' not only justified austerity and defied reality – in fact, Cameron's government inherited a growth rate of 1.9 per cent that would not be exceeded until 2014 – but also provided cover for their own fiscal failures. In the absence of proper journalism, *everything* undesirable or sub-optimal could be blamed on 'Labour's legacy'. Ironically, Cameron would eventually be undone by the fact that the same would soon be said of 'the EU' or 'Brussels' or, even, 'immigration'. It is easy to trace both the casual misrepresentations by Vote Leave and the delinquency with which they were treated by the Fourth Estate to the lies and nonsenses of 'Gordon Brown's debt'. One wonders just how emboldened Cameron's cabinet colleagues-turned-referendum opponents were by witnessing just how easy it was to escape the blame.

'Lives lost, earnings lost, years lost,' wrote the *Financial Times*'s chief data reporter, John Burn-Murdoch, at the end of 2022. 'Unlike Trussonomics, austerity is a slow and silent killer. For the best part of twelve years, the Conservatives sowed the seeds. This year they're reaping the harvest.' He explained:

If you're lucky, you can get away with cutting investment for a few years. Everything gets a bit more fragile, but as long as there are no nasty external shocks, you might be able to avoid disaster. The effects of slashing public services are a little harder to hide, but you might get away with gradual deterioration. The problem is, when you're hit by a pandemic, an energy crisis and an act of gross economic self-sabotage in short order, your now brittle and exhausted public services will buckle where a healthy system would have taken the strain.[33]

Burn-Murdoch's crunching of OECD numbers paints a grim picture, particularly when graphs are adjusted to show the precise point at which Cameron came to power. Underpinning an almost unprecedented period of national decline are the swingeing cuts to public spending and, crucially, the effective cessation of investment in public sector infrastructure. Cameron and Osborne's cuts went further and faster than comparable 'peer' countries. Even healthcare, supposedly ring-fenced from 'austerity', went into steady decline from May 2010 because our ageing, ailing population needed *more* spending not the stagnation that Osborne deployed. Worse, and in contrast to those 'peer' countries, as a share of GDP, public spending actually went down. Consequently, for example, by the end of 2022 the 'real term' pay of nurses was a full 12 per cent below where it stood before the 2010 election.

The failure to invest in NHS infrastructure and technology – long before Boris Johnson started boasting about building fantasy hospitals – created a huge shortage of both beds and the equipment required to get patients quickly out of hospital. While Tories boasted about record numbers of doctors and record levels of funding, they entirely neglected the fact that their policies were making it measurably harder for those doctors to do their jobs. After years of falling under Labour, NHS waiting lists began to lengthen almost from the moment David Cameron walked in to Downing Street. Other measures, such as being seen at A&E within four hours of arriving, reflect similar deterioration. The figures for 'avoidable deaths', or deaths that would simply not occur if the patient had been treated quickly and effectively, began climbing after years of coming down, while life expectancy slowed more quickly than in comparable populations. In October 2015, the independent health think tank, the King's Fund, found that under the Cameron–Osborne regime, the NHS had suffered its lowest annual average spending increase in real terms since it was founded in 1948 at 'around a quarter of the long-run average increase in funding since 1951'.[34]

Soon there were unprecedented ambulance delays, and the first ambulance driver and nurse strikes for 30 years. Then came the junior doctors. Then the consultants. In July 2023, prime minister Rishi Sunak argued in the House of Commons that striking NHS staff were to blame for the total number of people on NHS waiting lists rising during the nine months of his premiership.

Despite the frequent insistence that 'We are all in this together,' Cameron and Osborne, who cut the top tax rate for the country's highest earners in 2012, ushered in an era of almost unimaginable harm. The gap between rich and poor has widened; the young are now worse off than their parents were at the same age; and home ownership has declined steeply. After years of 'pay freezes', strikes are now so frequent that even the right-wing media no longer routinely reports them. People across the UK are dying younger. British children who grew up during 'austerity' are measurably shorter than both previous generations and their European counterparts. In 2023, GPs in poorer areas of the country reported a resurgence of Victorian diseases such as rickets and scurvy.

Nowhere was the cost of Cameron's brutal denigration of public services more evident than in the country's response to the COVID-19 outbreak. On 16 June 2023, Michael Marmot, professor of epidemiology and public health at University College London, told the independent COVID-19 inquiry that 'The UK entered the pandemic with its public services depleted, health improvement stalled, health inequalities increased and health among the poorest people in a state of decline ...' Typically, and deliberately, with 'austerity' policies, the poorest areas of the country were the most affected. Marmot added: 'The greater the deprivation of the area, the steeper the cuts in social care spend. In the most deprived 20 per cent of areas, it went down by 32 per cent. In the least deprived, it went down by 3 per cent.'

The contribution that 'austerity' made to the Brexit vote can feel almost trivial in comparison to its impact on healthcare and the COVID-19 response. It isn't. The squeeze on incomes of ordinary people was a major contributory factor in support for Brexit-supporting political parties. Between 2010 and 2016, just as their social capital was being deliberately eroded, the people of Britain saw zero-hours contracts and food banks proliferate. Burn-Murdoch shows that, even in 2022: 'Real wages are below where they were 18 years ago. There has not been a single year since austerity began when the average wage has matched the peak under the last Labour government.'[35] In September 2017, the Institute for Labor Economics, an international non-profit research institute comprising around 2,000 scholars from more than 60 countries, published research that found 'unhappy feelings contributed to Brexit. However, contrary to commonly heard views, the key channel of influence was not through general dissatisfaction with life. It was through a person's narrow feelings about his or her own financial situation.'[36]

In August 2019, Thiemo Fetzer, a professor in economics at the University of Warwick, went further:

> I gathered data from all electoral contests that took place in the UK since 2000, and assembled a detailed individual-level panel data set covering almost 40,000 households since 2009. Through these data, I studied to what extent an individual's or region's exposure to welfare cuts since 2010 was associated with increased political support for UKIP in the run up to the Brexit referendum in 2016. The analysis suggests that this association was so strong that the 2016 EU referendum would have resulted in a clear victory for Remain (or the referendum might never have happened) had it not been for austerity measures such as extensive cuts to public spending.[37]

In other words, David Cameron and George Osborne *created* the dissatisfaction and distress that would prompt many people to vote for Brexit. Into this space sashayed the deliberate and deceitful demonisation of workers from other EU countries, perpetrated by Nigel Farage and co., and the unkeepable promises about prosperity punted by the likes of Boris Johnson and Jacob Rees-Mogg, drawing on erroneous economic modelling. On 3 November 2015, Patrick Minford, the lonely pro-Brexit economist who would later inspire Emily Maitlis's 'Minford paradigm', told the Foreign Affairs Select Committee: 'We have done a simulation of leaving the EU. The first thing that comes out is an 8 per cent drop in the cost of living on day one … Now that is really worth having.' The previous April, launching a report by his Economists for Brexit Group, Minford had said that his modelling also showed 'output would be 2 per cent higher by the end of the decade, Britain would be 5 per cent more competitive on global markets and real wages would be 1.5 per cent higher than if the UK remained in the EU'.

When David Cameron announced his attention to hold a referendum on EU membership on 23 January 2013, it is highly likely that he believed he would never be called upon to deliver it. Up until polling day in 2015, his best chance of staying in government involved a second coalition with the Liberal Democrats, who could be relied upon to veto the proposal. His words that day – 'I am in favour of a referendum. I believe in confronting this issue – shaping it, leading the debate. Not simply hoping a difficult situation will go away' – did not reflect any particular clamour from the country. In the month prior to the 2015 election, EU membership had come tenth in the pollster Ipsos's monthly monitor of voter concerns.[38] Significantly, the same polling showed Labour enjoying a four-point lead over the Tories on voters' confidence in their ability to handle 'asylum and immigration'. Rather, Cameron was trying to appease both his party's Eurosceptic fringe and more moderate Tory MPs fearful of the growing threat to their own seats posed by UKIP. Even George Osborne was opposed to the idea but Cameron rolled the dice regardless, apparently too arrogant to realise that, with Murdoch, Dacre and the *Telegraph* all determined to leave the EU, they were loaded. Nevertheless, when he won the election and was compelled to deliver on the referendum it was still eminently winnable.

In retrospect, it is a miracle that the losing Remain campaign did so well. Cameron's leadership was catastrophic, his campaign a catalogue of missteps and miscalculations. The first and the biggest was the failure to understand, never mind communicate, the strength of the 'deal' that we already had. As head of the Foreign Office in 1991 John (now Lord) Kerr had secured opt outs on both the euro currency and the Social Chapter. From a Eurosceptic perspective, we had the best deal going. (Poignantly, Kerr also drafted what would become Article 50 in order to allow a 'dictatorial regime' to 'storm out' of the EU and said, when Theresa May triggered it: 'I don't feel guilty about inventing the mechanism. I feel very sad about the UK using it. I didn't think that the United Kingdom would use it.'[39]) Kerr's colleague in those negotiations, the former Europe minister Tristan (now Lord) Garel-Jones, said something in 2009 that perhaps explains why Cameron's own colleagues failed to appreciate the scale of the risk he was taking. After Cameron's withdrawal from the EPP signalled his first capitulation to cranks and crackpots, Garel-Jones observed: 'It is now a tradition in Britain that all the major parties in Britain behave badly on Europe in opposition and they all behave fairly sensibly when they get into government. Cameron is a sensible, clever, thoughtful young man. If he becomes prime minister he will behave in a sensible, clever and thoughtful way and in the best interests of Britain.'[40]

In the event, he did no such thing. Whether through his assumption of British exceptionalism or arrogance, or both, the idea that he would be able to extract more 'concessions' from the EU was doomed from the start. At every stage of Brexit, both before and after the referendum, the idea that we merited special treatment was as daft as it was damaging. Whether it was David Davis insisting that the German car industry would allow us to retain all of our trading heft despite quitting the trading bloc, or countless commentators intoning that 'they need us more than we need them', there was an almost psychological inability to accept that, as a member of a 'club', we would be expected to abide by the rules and requirements of membership. Cameron's attempted 'renegotiation' was effectively an early iteration of the same delusion.

But if Cameron's arrogance in calling a referendum was unsurprising, his inability not to foresee the epic disloyalty of his fellow Eton alumnus, Boris Johnson, may be more of a shock. We will see that Johnson's decision, at the eleventh hour, to move against Cameron was motivated entirely by self-interest. But while the rest of the country was not yet fully familiar with Johnson's epic ego and deep dishonesty, Cameron as a former schoolfriend and fellow member of the Bullingdon Club had no excuse. Similarly, Michael Gove. If David Cameron could not navigate the Brexit sensibilities of his closest friends and colleagues, then what chance did he have of steering the country to safety? Gove, a Murdoch lifer married at the time to a *Mail* columnist who is godmother to Cameron's youngest daughter, was almost the embodiment of media enmity to EU membership and yet Cameron was completely blindsided by his 'betrayal'. If he hadn't suspended collective cabinet responsibility, it is also possible that neither Gove nor Johnson would have risked the careers they had in pursuit of the ones they wanted.

The appointment of Craig Oliver and Will Straw to run 'Britain Stronger in Europe', the clumsily named official Remain campaign, looked lightweight and complacent in light of the heavyweight ogres they were lined up against. Oliver was an uninspiring BBC man turned Tory communications director, while Straw was the affable son of former Labour foreign secretary Jack. And putting the almost invisible Stuart (now Lord) Rose, a former CEO of Marks and Spencer, in charge of the whole campaign looks, in retrospect, like an act of deliberate sabotage. 'I should have said no,' he admitted in

2021. 'Instinctively, I didn't think it was for me. I felt strongly about remaining in Europe but I didn't think I was the sort of person who should lead that campaign. But sadly, nobody else would volunteer and I was lent on and persuaded and I weakened and I took it.'[41] Again, hardly a ringing endorsement of the man making these decisions: David Cameron.

Cameron can't be blamed for the uselessness of Jeremy Corbyn, who not only refused to share platforms with Conservatives but also gave the (later confirmed) impression of being a 'Leaver' in all but name, but it was his job to accommodate it. He can categorically be blamed for the circumstances that left him unable to counter the immigration lies and exaggerations of both the official Vote Leave campaign and the Faragist Leave.EU. When they very deliberately portrayed Polish builders or Romanian neighbours as the cause of British voters' financial discomfort, Cameron and his colleagues could hardly turn around and explain that the real source of their difficulties was the Conservative 'austerity' policies pursued with Victorian vigour since 2010. Worse, countless regretful 'Leave' voters have told me on the radio since the referendum that they voted both in expectation of ending up on the losing side and, crucially, of punching David Cameron on the nose. Perhaps most importantly, a man who had spent years rubbishing Gordon Brown's economic forecasts and predictions was unable to counter the media insistence that any economic forecasts or predictions of Brexit problems, almost all subsequently realised by reality, were just 'Project Fear' scaremongering.

Tim Bale of Queen Mary University of London, quoted early in this chapter, identifies another reason for Cameron's failure: 'Hoping and believing that Remain would win, Cameron was so anxious about putting the Conservative Party back together again after the campaign that he pulled his punches when it came to criticising Tories on the Leave side, refusing again and again to fight fire with fire.[42] Indeed, it often appeared that Cameron, so capable of casual cruelty at PMQs, turned up for a knife fight with a pair of battered boxing gloves and a dog-eared copy of the Queensberry rules.

Apart from the personal and largely short-lived career advancements of a few key players, I still don't know what 'Leavers' think they won. By the second decade of the twenty-first century, any talk of increased prosperity and imminent improvements to the cost of living, of 'sunlit uplands' and enormous injections of cash for the NHS, of cheaper food, cheaper energy and amazing new trade deals with unspecified new lands, had largely disappeared. Instead, they now insist that blue passports and vague notions of improved 'sovereignty' were the real prizes all along. Either that, or the unhappiness of people who opposed the madness from the start. Or, increasingly, they argue that Brexit could and would have been brilliant were it not for the failures of the people charged with delivering it. Such bilge is sustained and remains largely unchallenged due to a combination of lies, media complicity and a deliberate detachment from the truth from those at the very heart of government. It is ironic that a Remainer, through incompetence, arrogance and patrician complacency, did more than any 'Leaver' politician to break Britain.

'Trouble started brewing for me in my third year [at Eton],' recalled David Cameron in his autobiography. 'Due to my growing sense of being slightly mediocre, a mild obsession about being trapped in my big brother's shadow, and a weakness for going with the crowd, even when the crowd was going in the wrong direction.'[43] Tragically for the rest of us, by the time David Cameron elected to go into politics, he believed he had changed.

Chapter 7
JEREMY CORBYN

In general, his intellectual CV gives an impression
of slow-minded rigidity; and he seems essentially
incurious about anything beyond his immediate sphere.
Martin Amis[1]

Everyone likes him, even people who thought he was
a left-wing loony.
Jon Lansman[2]

ON 22 FEBRUARY 2012, a Conservative MP called Stuart Andrew retired to the Strangers' Bar at the House of Commons for a nightcap. He had lunched earlier with Prime Minister David Cameron and expected to pass a convivial but uneventful evening with fellow Tory MPs Alec Shelbrooke, Guto Bebb and Andrew Percy. Instead, he would shortly find himself bleeding from the nose after being head-butted by a fellow parliamentarian. This contretemps inadvertently helped to set in motion a chain of events that would see the Labour Party led through an era of unprecedented political importance by a man spectacularly ill-equipped for the job. To understand how that could happen, and how the leader of the main opposition party would end up waving through Brexit and oiling Boris Johnson's passage to a historic majority, is to understand how Jeremy Corbyn got there in the first place.

It is not clear precisely what prompted Eric Joyce, then the Labour MP for Falkirk, but drink had been taken and his frenzied attack on Andrew and three others was preceded by a bellowed complaint that the bar 'was full of fucking Tories'. What followed was, even by the standards of an occasionally rowdy drinking hole, a shameful display. 'I was having a lovely evening chatting and relaxing,' recalled Stuart Andrew. 'Andrew [Percy] came back to the table and said, "Excuse me, can I just get to my seat?" but Joyce would not let him. He said, "There are too many Tories" and pushed him against the wall. I stood up and said, "You can't do that."'[3] A police officer restrained Joyce briefly but, having been released, he head-butted Andrew in the face. 'The police held him but let him go for a minute,' Andrew added. 'He just went for me and head-butted me on the nose. My nose was bleeding heavily. I kept holding it and grabbed a tissue from somewhere.' Joyce also attacked Tory councillors Luke Mackenzie and Ben Maney before turning on the Labour assistant whip, Phil Wilson, who was trying to calm him down.

The following month, Joyce pleaded guilty to assaulting the four men. He was banned from pubs and restaurants for three months, subjected to a weekend curfew and ordered by magistrates to pay a total of £4,400. The former soldier, who was suspended by the Labour Party immediately after the incident, had already announced his intention not to seek re-election in 2015. The competition to replace him as the Labour candidate in Falkirk prompted the changes to party rules that ultimately allowed Jeremy Corbyn to become leader against the express wishes of the vast majority of the Parliamentary Labour Party. Given that his leadership would veer between the appalling and the absurd, it seems grimly apt that its origins lie in an episode of appalling absurdity.

Shortly after Joyce's resignation, the chairman of Unite the Union in Scotland, a former shop steward called Stephen Deans, became chairman of the Falkirk West Constituency Labour Party (CLP). He began recruiting fellow Unite members to join the CLP and, entirely legitimately, the union started paying their membership fees. By February 2013, the total membership had soared from fewer than 100 to more than double that number. Under Labour Party rules at the time, every member was eligible to vote in the process to select the new candidate. The union's choice was a former nurse called Karie Murphy, a Unite activist who at the time worked in the office of the Labour MP Tom Watson, himself a former flatmate of Unite general secretary Len McCluskey. Allegations that the union was trying unfairly to finesse her passage to the candidacy were denied by Unite, but a leaked December 2012 document contained a self-congratulatory account of contests the union claimed to have directly influenced. It described its work in Falkirk as 'exemplary', stating: 'we have recruited well over 100 Unite members to the party in a constituency with less than 200 members. 57 came from responses to a text message alone (followed up face to face). A collective effort locally, but led and inspired by the potential candidate'.[4]

In a typical example of recondite Labour Party procedure, the selection process was referred to the Labour Party's National Executive Committee (NEC), which in turn recommended that it be scrutinised by the Labour Party organisation sub-committee. As a result of the NEC investigation, Murphy withdrew her name from the selection process and, along with Deans, was briefly suspended by the party in June. In July, Labour leader Ed Miliband called in the police to 'investigate whether criminal activity had taken place'.[5] Police Scotland shortly concluded that it hadn't. Deans and Murphy were reinstated but Miliband's grip on his party looked perilously weak. Tom Watson resigned as Labour's election coordinator and even Eric Joyce, whose drunken violence had set the whole process in motion, stuck his oar in, saying: 'It is a nonsense and I am afraid the way it has been handled by the Labour Party headquarters is nothing short of disgraceful. The Labour leadership have shot themselves in the foot and created this media storm over what is a genuinely irrelevant issue to ordinary workers. We believe they have handled it absolutely amateurishly and they have played into the Prime Minister's and the coalition's hands. They must be rubbing their hands at this.'[6]

They certainly were. Prime Minister David Cameron immediately availed himself of the opportunity to resurrect claims of Labour politicians being puppets whose strings were pulled by union barons. The rhetoric may not have carried the same heft with voters as it had done in the seventies and eighties but right-wing newspapers could still be relied upon to demonise trade unions and exaggerate their influence. Similarly, Tory politicians had never tired of pointing out that the unions accounted for around 80 per cent of Labour's funding or that they controlled half of the votes at party conference. Cameron used the old accusation to particular effect at PMQs on 3 July 2013, saying: 'His questions are written by Len McCluskey', and branding Miliband 'too weak to run Labour and certainly too weak to run the country'.

Bruised by Falkirk and in the hope of fending off future accusations of being in the pocket of union barons, Ed Miliband proposed a major change to the relationship between unions and the party. At constituency level, unions would no longer be able to stack a local deck by paying the CLP subs of members. The changes at national level were to prove more significant. Previously, individual trade unionists were automatically affiliated to the Labour Party. They could opt out if they didn't want to be, but the default position was that union membership entailed party affiliation, and the attendant voting rights, unless it had been formally rejected. Miliband himself had relied upon union support to beat his brother, David, in the 2010 Labour leadership contest. His most fundamental change to the existing system essentially replaced the opt-out with an opt-in. For just £3 *anybody* could effectively join the Labour Party as a 'supporter'. On the one hand, this watered-down version of one member/one vote (OMOV) seemed close to a distillation of democracy itself; on the other, it would reduce Labour MPs with decades of parliamentary experience or trade unionists with activism in their blood to the same level of importance as a newly minted, £3-paying supporter when it came to, for example, electing the next party leader.

On 1 March 2014, at a special conference in London, delegates backed the reforms by 86 per cent to 14 per cent. Despite delivering critical speeches and warning against further dilution of union–party links, Labour's three most powerful union leaders, Unison's Dave Prentis, Unite's Len McCluskey and the GMB's Paul Kenny all backed the plans. It was an impressive victory for Miliband. 'He is not always the most inspiring leader,' wrote the *Guardian*'s political correspondent, Andrew Sparrow. 'But, at party management, he is proving superb.'[7] It was also a shining example of the wisdom of the warning to be careful what you wish for.

Just over a year later, Miliband was defeated by David Cameron in the 2015 general election. Crucially, Cameron defied the polls to win an overall majority and was newly unencumbered by Liberal Democrat coalition partners. To look at it another way, he was now hostage to his headbanger-appeasing promise to hold a referendum on EU membership and about to be embarrassed by his ludicrous pledge to secure unspecified 'improvements' to our membership, already the best available from a 'Eurosceptic' perspective. Following Miliband's decision to step down, the election of a new Labour leader would determine who would be fighting alongside, or at the very least in cooperation with, the Conservatives campaigning to 'Remain'. Or so pretty much everybody presumed.

The story of what happened next begins, for our purposes, in 1983. Having campaigned on a manifesto that shadow cabinet member Gerald Kaufman would later describe as 'the longest suicide note in history', the donnish, 'hard' left Labour leader Michael Foot was routed at the ballot box by Margaret Thatcher. Among the new intake of Labour MPs were three young unknowns: Tony Blair, Gordon Brown and Jeremy Corbyn. At least as relevant to the events of 2015, however, was Tony Benn's experience in Bristol East. The veteran left-winger's Bristol South East constituency had been abolished by boundary changes and, having lost the contest to stand in the winnable new seat of Bristol South, he fought Bristol East instead and lost to the Conservative candidate. This meant that the iconoclastic stand-ard bearer for the Labour left, who had come within a percentage point of beating Denis Healey to the deputy leadership just two years previously, was in the political wilderness until he could secure a new seat. Crucially, it left him ineligible to stand in the leadership contests prompted by the post-election resignations of Healey and Foot.

So it was that when Neil Kinnock and Roy Hattersley launched their leadership bid from the party's centre ground, the 'left' found itself without an obvious champion. For a young Jeremy Corbyn, as recalled in Benn's seminal diaries, this was no accident: 'Kinnock lost the deputy leadership for Tony in 1981 deliberately and specifically and he was busy preparing himself for the leadership campaign during the general election. There must be a left candidate.'[8] Some may detect familiar strains of bitterness, victimhood and an affinity for conspiracy theory here, others no doubt see an analysis of unimpeachable ideological purity. Benn's diaries, incidentally, are remarkable and frequently delightful. Of Ralph Miliband's funeral at Golders Green Crematorium in 1994, he records: 'Anyone on the real left of any significance was there. Jeremy Corbyn couldn't make it.'[9]

The left now found itself in the Labour Party wilderness for over three decades. Crucial to understanding what happened after they unexpectedly and almost accidentally gained control of the party in 2015 is the fact that key players like Corbyn, John McDonnell and future Momentum founder Jon Lansman (still arguing in 2018 that Benn 'would have squeezed Kinnock out'[10] if he'd been in the 1983 leadership contest) did not dedicate themselves to licking their wounds during this period. They kept the wounds open, waiting – often, it seemed, with absurd optimism – for another opportunity to present itself. This seems to me to be crucial for understanding the view of party politics held by Corbyn and his closest associates: the enemy within demands just as much attention and energy as the enemy without. If not more. This led almost inexorably to a cultish Corbyn following that concentrated their fire at 'centrists' and 'Blairites' in their own party, to the extent that campaigning for Remain or opposing Tory governments of unprecedented awfulness seemed to be regarded as merely an unwelcome distraction.

The key Corbyn adviser Lansman, previously a 'chief fixer' for Tony Benn, is a particularly pertinent case study here. Indeed, in many ways he is the central figure of the whole saga (which is explored in depth in David Kogan's richly detailed *Protest and Power: The Battle for the Labour Party*). For while Corbyn remained peripheral to both the national and the party picture until the moment of his arrival on the leadership ballot, Lansman sometimes seemed to be lurking behind every pillar waiting for an opportunity to grab the reins of power. An ardent Bennite who also worked for Michael Meacher (the doomed candidate the left finally turned to in 1983), it was Lansman who persuaded a reluctant Corbyn to run in 2015 and Lansman who managed to secure the requisite nominations from Labour MPs with, legend has it, seconds to spare.

A pivotal figure here was Byron Taylor, a Labour councillor in Basildon with a trade union background and connections to both the Socialist Campaign Group and the Trade Union and Labour Party Liaison Organisation. Jon Lansman and others were pessimistic about the prospects of identifying a 'hard' left candidate who might get on to a ballot featuring favourites Yvette Cooper and Andy Burnham. After all, John McDonnell, who would become Corbyn's shadow chancellor, had withdrawn from the 2010 contest after failing to secure the requisite number of nominations. Taylor, however, had something of a revelation while recalling that Jeremy Corbyn had been the only MP happy to help a lost-cause candidate in his constituency during the general election campaign. 'I thought, it's got to be Jeremy. Jeremy's got to win. He's the man ... I mean it was desperate stuff, but Burnham was in the City talking to business and making clear he was going down exactly the same route as New Labour and Ed Miliband had done.'[11] Lansman, crucially, was convinced:

Byron said Jeremy Corbyn ... Jeremy's got no enemies ... he will get on the ballot paper ... and I thought I've never taken Jeremy even remotely seriously. Byron was not a rabid left-winger. He was a trade union bureaucrat who had been a party bureaucrat under New Labour, and he was saying Jeremy Corbyn would get on the ballot paper, and it just made me think, actually. I mean he hasn't got enemies. Everyone likes him, even people who thought he was a left-wing loony.[12]

When Lansman succeeded in securing Corbyn a place on the leadership ballot at the eleventh hour, this harmless 'loony' reputation would prove to be the most powerful weapon in his arsenal. As director of the Labour Party's Constitution Unit, Declan McHugh worked on the reforms that had been passed so spectacularly at that special conference in March 2014. He wrote later:

> Ironically, the system was intended to stop a candidate who could not command the Parliamentary Labour Party (PLP) reaching the ballot. In response to the dissolution of Electoral College, including the MPs' selection, the nomination threshold to enter the contest was raised to 15 per cent of Labour MPs. Consideration was initially given to a higher threshold of 20 per cent or 25 per cent. But that was rejected on the grounds that it would narrow the field too much; members from both the Blairite and Campaign Group wings of the party favoured a lower number. Nonetheless, 15 per cent was judged to be a safe barrier to any outsider – especially someone from the hard left. That judgement proved to be mistaken.[13]

It most certainly did. Keen to convey at least the impression of a broad church of candidates, Labour MPs who had absolutely no desire to see Corbyn become their leader added their names to his list of nominees.

Three London mayoral contenders, David Lammy, Sadiq Khan and Gareth Thomas, signed up at the last minute because, with one eye on their own election prospects, they wanted to see Corbyn's simplistic strand of anti-austerity politics represented in the contest. Before Corbyn had even secured his famous victory against Andy Burnham, Yvette Cooper and Liz Kendall, John McTernan, a former adviser to Tony Blair, suggested that 'The moronic MPs who nominated Jeremy Corbyn to "have a debate" need to have their heads felt.' He added: 'They should be ashamed of themselves. They're morons.'[14] Former foreign secretary Margaret Beckett, one of those nominators, agreed that she had been a 'moron' for backing him. 'We were being urged as MPs to have a field of candidates,' she explained. 'At no point did I intend to vote for Jeremy myself, nor advise anyone else to do it.'[15]

In addition to what we might call the 'moron factor', there are three key components to the Parliamentary Labour Party's epic miscalculation. First, the popularity of the £3-a-vote supporter scheme. By the time of the ballot, nearly 200,000 people had signed up for it and Corbyn was the only candidate with a link to it on his campaign website. Second, the quality of competition. Corbyn may have been widely perceived *inside* the PLP as a largely well-meaning crackpot (little of his more questionable conduct and associations was known at this point) but nobody on the ballot held particular appeal for people *outside* it. Bigger beasts like Alan Johnson and Harriet Harman had ruled themselves out of the running early while Ed Balls, for example, had managed to lose his seat. Andy Burnham and Yvette Cooper had been in Gordon Brown's final cabinet while Liz Kendall was an avowed 'Blairite'. These previous affiliations would prove crucial to the third factor: Corbyn, or at least Lansman's deft packaging of him, was nakedly populist and so able to capitalise on the contrast between himself and more 'normal' politicians.

The more disillusioned people are with a status quo, the more political capital can be accrued by promising to change it. And because Corbyn had spent his entire career quite sincerely seeing Labour colleagues as the enemy of his politics, he was uniquely placed to trash the legacies of Blair and Brown while promising nothing more substantive than 'difference'. It was, perhaps, the first political cult of personality to be led by a man who had little discernible personality.

It was, nevertheless, an extraordinarily effective leadership campaign, capturing the imagination of increasingly dispossessed young voters and their increasingly disillusioned older counterparts. It caught Corbyn's rival candidates, most of the media and the whole 'New' Labour movement completely by surprise. I wonder now whether the fact that Labour had recently been in power had bred complacency; figures at the centre of the party expected their more middle-of-the-road policies to have enough appeal to lead them back to power before long, and this blinded them to the intoxicating nature of promises to upend the status quo. The attraction of a radical alternative would have been greater in the context of 'austerity' policies, seen by many as deliberately and unnecessarily cruel. Parallels with Donald Trump are surprisingly apposite here. For the avoidance of doubt, at a personal level Corbyn is obviously nothing like the secret-stealing, sex-offending election fraudster. But at a purely political level, any candidate who embodies a rejection of the entrenched political system *and* promises immeasurably to improve the lives of 'ordinary' people can be unstoppable in the right circumstances. And the more desperate a certain type of voter is for unspecified but glorious 'change', the less likely they are to dig too deeply into its plausibility.

As a career-long 'outsider', Corbyn could be cast in complete contrast to the managerial politicians who had dominated the party for years. The ludicrously Tory-leaning media ecosystem described in earlier chapters had long spawned a sort of subconscious self-censorship among ambitious Labour politicians. Just as Miliband was desperate to defuse the perception of the party dancing to the unions' tune, so the popular and wholly inaccurate refrain that Labour governments were profligate perhaps prevented him and his colleagues from mounting the stinging attacks on 'austerity' that much of the country, and almost all potential or past Labour voters, wanted to see. For many, this surfeit of caution has reached an apotheosis in Sir Keir Starmer and it remains a key indicator of the difference between what is needed to win control of the party and what is needed to win control of the country. Lansman (and later Seumas Milne, the *Guardian* journalist who became Corbyn's executive director of strategy and communications) understood that Corbyn's platitudinal idealism worked well online or in front of adoring crowds, but not under robust scrutiny. So they studiously steered him clear of broadcast studios and ensured that his campaigning (and later his 'leading') was confined almost exclusively to contexts where he was comfortable and unchallenged.

And it worked beautifully. 'All over the country we are getting these huge gatherings of people,' Corbyn told a standing-room-only crowd in Euston, north London in early August 2015. 'The young, the old, black and white and many people that haven't been involved in politics before.' A clearly gobsmacked BBC reporter in attendance that night wrote: 'On this Monday evening so many people have turned up, some supporters are left standing in the street scouting for spare tickets. It feels more like the build-up to an album launch than a political meeting. For those unable to pack into the hall Corbyn ends up speaking from the roof of a waiting fire engine.'[16]

In order to understand the cultishness that followed, it is important to imagine the euphoria that those present must have felt. Here, it seemed to them, was a man entirely at odds with traditional perceptions of politicians, saying exactly the same things about wars, wealth distribution and the NHS that they said to each other in their online chatrooms, CLP meetings and festival tents. That he was, in many ways, a walking cliché at his happiest operating the office photocopier and putting leaflets through constituency letterboxes would not have occurred to them. Like all populists, he secured a core following of people who tied their identity so tightly to their perception of him that no criticism was permitted and no self-reflection indulged.

By now, the Labour establishment was comprehensively spooked. A week after the supposedly dark-horse candidate hopped off that fire engine, Gordon Brown became the latest senior Labour figure to warn against the dangers of a Corbyn victory. On 16 August he gave a 50-minute speech to party members and invited journalists at the Royal Festival Hall in London. While he did not mention any candidate by name, there was no doubt who he was talking about. Labour, he argued, must be 'credible, radical, sustainable and electable to help people out of poverty' and yet there was one candidate, he explained, whose own supporters did not believe their man would win the next election, meaning everything would be 'even worse if we leave ourselves powerless to do anything about it'. The problem was that Brown could be simultaneously right *and* damaging to his own cause. For Corbyn's growing base, every attack from the centre enhanced their man's reputation, up to and including critiques of his deeply dubious past associations, by now emerging almost daily. 'Don't tell me that we can do much for the poor of the world if the alliances we favour most are with Hezbollah, Hamas, Chávez's successor in Venezuela and Putin's totalitarian Russia,' thundered Brown, preaching powerfully but largely to the choir.

A few days previously, in what would become a recurring theme of Corbyn's imminent leadership, the *Jewish Chronicle* had accused him of associating with 'Holocaust deniers, terrorists and some outright anti-Semites'. In an unprecedented front-page editorial, the oldest Jewish newspaper in Britain claimed to speak for the vast majority of British Jews in 'expressing deep foreboding at the prospect of Mr Corbyn's election as Labour leader'. It continued: 'If Mr Corbyn is not to be regarded from the day of his election as an enemy of Britain's Jewish community, he has a number of questions which he must answer in full and immediately. The JC asked him earlier this week to respond. No response has been forthcoming.'[17]

In 2023, eight years after the leadership battle and four years after his resignation, Corbyn's most committed rump of support continues to pop up periodically on social media to insist that all reports and criticisms of his well-documented proximity to anti-Semitism were part of 'a scam' and that the (often 'Jewish-controlled') 'media' conspired to misrepresent him. It is not the first delusional narrative of bogus victimhood that we have encountered in these pages but it is the first to come from the 'left' of British politics. It is relevant here only in so far as it illustrates three key components of Corbyn's contribution to the national catastrophe.

First, the cultish refusal of his core support to countenance *any* criticism of their clay-footed hero enabled the Labour leader to fail to turn up for the Brexit referendum and ensured that the Labour Party would approach the catastrophic 2019 election in a state of utter disarray. Ultimately, this created a parallel universe in which lifelong Labour voters, clear that Corbyn had no chance of winning because he had so effectively alienated their friends, colleagues and family members, would be portrayed as the *reason* for his defeat while Corbyn himself somehow remained blameless. It was the political equivalent of weather forecasters being blamed for the weather when their forecasts proved correct.

Second, the mealy-mouthed and unconvincing way in which Corbyn and his team sought to counter criticism helped to ensure that the single biggest factor prompting former Labour supporters to vote for Boris Johnson in 2019 was, according to all available data, Jeremy Corbyn.

And third, both cohorts – leadership and core support – persisted in portraying a deeply hostile and biased media as an excuse for failure as opposed to an obstacle to be negotiated or even an enemy to be vanquished.

This last remains, for me, the most remarkable element of the whole Corbyn episode. Suggesting that the media, which as we have seen thinks nothing of maligning Ed Miliband's dead father, reserved special vitriol for Jeremy Corbyn entailed either epic dishonesty or complete ignorance of the extant media/political ecosystem. I think the latter description applied to many of his supporters. As he said himself in Euston that night, he was attracting people who hadn't 'been involved in politics before'. Somebody who had never previously encountered the oeuvre of Paul Dacre, for example, could quite conceivably come away from the *Mail*'s reporting of Corbyn convinced that it had unleashed the furies for the very first time. And that, of course, added to the myth that the 'Establishment' was so terrified of Corbyn's transformative powers that it was making things up to harm him. Anybody even half-versed in the reality of right-wing media, however, would know differently. Including everybody in the leadership team. They weren't playing to win, they were playing to whine.

Consider the 'alliances' with Hezbollah and Hamas referenced in Brown's speech. Asked on *Channel 4 News* on 13 July 2015 why he had referred to the terrorist organisations as his 'friends', Corbyn showed immediately why Lansman and later Milne were so keen to keep him out of studios. Not only did he lose his temper with the scrupulously equable Krishnan Guru-Murthy almost immediately, he also embarked on an intellectually bereft, barely coherent defence, claiming: 'I'm saying that people I talk to, I use it in a collective way, saying our friends are prepared to talk. Does it mean I agree with Hamas and what it does? No. Does it mean I agree with Hezbollah and what they do? No. What it means is that I think to bring about a peace process, you have to talk to people with whom you may profoundly disagree. There is not going to be a peace process unless there is talks involving Israel, Hezbollah and Hamas and I think everyone knows that.'

Unfortunately for Corbyn, Hamas certainly didn't know that. Its charter states: 'Initiatives, and so-called peaceful solutions and international conferences, are in contradiction to the principles of the Islamic Resistance Movement ... There is no solution for the Palestinian question except through jihad.' And if that were too nuanced for Corbyn and his 'it was a scam' acolytes to comprehend, the charter goes further: 'The prophet, prayer and peace be upon him, said: "The time will not come until Muslims will fight the Jews (and kill them); until the Jews hide behind rocks and trees, which will cry: O Muslim! there is a Jew hiding behind me, come on and kill him!"' It is also worth wondering what role an obscure backbench MP with a long history of defying his own party's whip might have envisioned for himself in any putative Middle East peace process. Not that his core supporters would ever do that. They soon claimed, with characteristic contempt for readily available facts, that he had played a key role in the Northern Ireland peace process.

By the time of his leadership candidacy, he had also taken tea on the House of Commons terrace with Raed Salah, sentenced to eight months in prison in Jerusalem in 2008 for inciting anti-Jewish racism and violence. Described by Corbyn as 'a very honoured citizen', Salah was also found by a British judge to have used the 'blood libel', a medieval anti-Semitic trope that claims Jews use the blood of gentiles for religious rituals. In a speech at an East Jerusalem protest in 2007, he said: 'Whoever wants a more thorough explanation, let him ask what used to happen to some children in Europe, whose blood was mixed in with the dough of the [Jewish] holy bread.'[18] Four years later, Corbyn wrote of Salah in the *Morning Star* newspaper: 'The sadness is that his is a voice of Palestinian people that needs to be heard. It's time that Western governments stood up to the Zionist lobby which seems to conflate criticism of Israel with antisemitism.'[19] In February 2020, Salah was jailed again for inciting violence.

In February 2015, a Church of England priest, Stephen Sizer, was banned for six months by Church authorities after linking to an article on social media entitled '9/11: Israel Did It' and asking his followers: 'Is this antisemitic?' The Bishop of Guildford, the Right Reverend Andrew Watson, was pretty clear, concluding that Sizer's campaigning on the Middle East was 'no longer compatible with his ministry as a parish priest'.[20] Corbyn begged to differ, writing to Church authorities to claim that Sizer had been unfairly targeted because he 'dared to speak out against Zionism'.[21] Listing these and still more examples of Corbyn's judgement on issues of anti-Semitism, the journalist James Bloodworth, himself a former member of a Trotskyist group, wrote very presciently in the *Guardian* on 13 August 2015, 'I believe it shows that the Labour party – and the left more generally – no longer takes antisemitism seriously.'

The evidence of Jeremy Corbyn's unsuitability for office was as varied as it was considerable. For example, in 1984, he invited convicted IRA volunteers Linda Quigley and Gerry MacLochlainn to the House of Commons two weeks after an IRA bomb killed five at the Tory Party conference in 1984. Thirty years later, he could be heard claiming that the USA was launching 'a proxy war' against Russia after the latter had invaded Crimea. More evidence of his unsuitability would continue to emerge throughout his leadership.

In 2018, it was reported that, six years previously, Corbyn had publicly supported Los Angeles-based street artist Mear One when his mural, featuring several apparently Jewish bankers playing a game of Monopoly with their table resting on the bent backs of several workers, was due to be removed. Mear One wrote on Facebook: 'Tomorrow they want to buff my mural Freedom of Expression. London Calling, Public art.' Corbyn replied: 'Why? You are in good company. Rockerfeller [*sic*] destroyed Diego Viera's [*sic*] mural because it includes a picture of Lenin.' Leaving aside the fact that he could neither spell Rockefeller nor the name of the muralist Diego Rivera, and all the attendant pseudo-intellectualism, the official party response was typical of 'Corbynism': incompetent, unconvincing and begrudging. First, they tried to obfuscate and diminish: 'In 2012, Jeremy was responding to concerns about the removal of public art on the grounds of freedom of speech,' said a party statement. 'However, the mural was offensive, used antisemitic imagery, which has no place in our society, and it is right that it was removed.' Then, when this failed to placate Labour MPs like Luciana Berger, Corbyn claimed he hadn't properly looked at the artwork he was defending, saying: 'I sincerely regret that

I did not look more closely at the image I was commenting on, the contents of which are deeply disturbing and antisemitic.'

Even if you approved of every meeting and association, every misstep and mealy-mouthed apology, you could not conceivably believe that the more widely known they became, the more electable he would become. Rehashing the record any further is pointless. His remaining supporters will be unpersuaded and his well-evidenced detractors have moved on. Because it is crucial to understanding his broader failure, I have sought to establish here that any suggestion that the case against him was invented is ridiculous and that his defences of his own behaviour are routinely shrouded in disingenuousness and petulance. And they remained so until the bitter end. In October 2020, after a lengthy investigation, the Equality and Human Rights Commission (EHRC) published its report into allegations of anti-Semitism within the party. Its analysis 'points to a culture within the party which, at best, did not do enough to prevent anti-Semitism and, at worst, could be seen to accept it'.

The EHRC also found that Labour under Corbyn had committed three breaches of the Equality Act: political interference in anti-Semitism complaints; failure to provide adequate training to those handling complaints and harassment, including the use of anti-Semitic tropes; and suggesting that complaints of anti-Semitism were fake or smears. In relation to the first type of breach, the investigation found evidence of the 'inappropriate involvement' of Mr Corbyn's office 23 times in the 70 files it looked at. Corbyn's response was at least consistent with previous conduct. Half an hour after the report was published, he issued a statement claiming that 'The scale of the problem was also dramatically overstated for political reasons by our opponents inside and outside the party, as well as by much of the media.' He was suspended from the Labour Party and later banned from standing as a Labour candidate.

It was an inglorious, if inevitable, end to one of the oddest episodes of party leadership in the history of British politics. Had it occurred during almost any other peacetime period it would probably have been little more than a footnote, like Iain (Duncan) Smith's leadership of the Conservatives or Michael Foot and eighties Labour. But while Jeremy Corbyn was aspiring to run the country, despite proving himself signally incapable of running his own party, Brexit was being sold to the British people under egregiously false pretences and Boris Johnson was manoeuvring to become the most dissolute prime minister of the modern age. Counterfactuals are generally unhelpful and it would be unfair to contend that *any* other leader might have somehow steered Brexit into the realms of reality or stopped the Johnson juggernaut. But no examination of how low Britain has been brought can be complete without explaining the role of the man who, more than any other, was supposed to be opposing the dismal direction of traffic.

There used to be two ways for non-Conservative politicians to negotiate the UK's hideously right-wing media: either you appeased them in the hope of avoiding their nastiest attacks or you took the fight straight to them and relied on sympathetic or impartial outlets to get your message out there. Corbyn and his closest advisers invented a third: completely fail to engage; alienate and demonise almost all journalists; claim constant victimhood; and offer up pathetic excuses when confronted with evidence of your own poor judgement.

For some observers, Tony Blair and Alastair Campbell adopted too much of the first approach prior to the 1997 election. In 2011, it emerged that Blair was even godfather to one of Murdoch's children. 'It's a fair point and it's a criticism I often think about,' Blair told me in 2019 in response to a question about whether their decision not to pick more of a fight with the likes of Murdoch and Dacre had helped to create the environment in which Brexit could happen. 'We'd lost four elections in a row and were very conscious of the power of the right-wing media,' he explained. 'I mean, I think you've got to reflect on that but it's easy to say when you're not fighting a battle. And, you know, look: although there were certain concessions you might say we made to that wing, there was never any doubt where the country stood on Europe.'[22]

To date, no Labour leader has tried the second approach. Keir Starmer's determination to pursue 'non-dom' taxpayers suggests that he is happy to earn the enmity at least of the *Daily Mail*'s owner but his broader approach, as we have seen, entails seeking to defuse traditional criticisms by explicitly refusing to align himself with, for example, striking nurses or environmental protesters.

Had Jeremy Corbyn possessed the intellectual capacity and personal skills to carry his convictions to TV and radio studios and defend them with force and charm, he could perhaps have changed the game. Instead, when he found himself under constant attack from right-wing newspapers he somehow contrived to add broadcasters such as the BBC and Channel 4 to his list of enemies. Seumas Milne would rarely allow him to be interviewed and, when he was, his inability to defend his record or contradict his critics left him looking petulant and often quite stupid.

This combination of stubbornness and self-sabotage, sustained by delusional support, was best described by Matt Seaton in the *New York Review of Books* in August 2018. He was directly addressing Corbyn's abject failure to handle the anti-Semitism crisis by now engulfing his party but the analysis holds true for the fatal flaws in his entire approach to getting elected. The article begins with a helpful reminder of exactly how the party appeared to everybody outside the bunker: 'Earlier this week, I got a direct message from a US columnist I've worked with in the past. It read: "Has Labour lost its mind? Was the party always this anti-Semitic or is it just blind fealty to Corbyn? Everything about his support within the party is bewildering to me."' The article goes on to pinpoint not just why Corbyn wouldn't handle the matter better but why he *couldn't*: 'It is necessary to understand … that his mishandling of the anti-Semitism crisis is not a display of incompetence; it comes from his being unwilling and, in fact, unable to disavow one iota of the hard-left ideology, including reflexive solidarity with any group describing itself as a national liberation movement, to which he has adhered all his adult life.'[23]

Having spectacularly won the leadership, the first major battle into which Jeremy Corbyn was required to lead his party was the referendum on EU membership. Speaking to Stuart McGurk for a *GQ* magazine profile and interview with Corbyn in February 2018, a source from Britain Stronger in Europe, the official cross-party Remain campaign group, revealed that they had first sought a meeting with him a month before he won the Labour leadership in September 2015. 'Just to say, you know, who knows what's going to happen with the leadership contest?' explained McGurk's source. 'We'd love to brief you on the campaign. And we didn't hear anything.'[24] It would be the following March, a full eight months after contact was made, before any meeting took place. And even then it was not with Corbyn but with a single member of his staff. 'Whereas with the broader Labour In team, we were speaking to them every day', the source added. Incredibly, the first meeting between the Labour leader's team and the key cross-party Remain campaign group would also be the last.

Corbyn, who routinely voted against closer political and economic ties with the EU as a backbench MP, immediately refused to share any pro-Remain platform with David Cameron, because they were 'not on the same side of the argument'.[25] In 2017, Gordon Brown revealed in his memoirs that Corbyn had even blocked plans for a pro-EU rally to be attended by all living Labour leaders because he did not want to appear with Labour's most electorally successful leader, Tony Blair. In the *GQ* interview, Stuart McGurk draws Corbyn's attention to a claim made by Alan Johnson, chair of Labour's In For Britain campaign, in Tim Shipman's masterful account of the whole Brexit saga, *All Out War.*[26] Johnson told Shipman: 'We kept trying to get [Corbyn] to say, "That's why I am campaigning to Remain in the EU." It's a simple sentence. It kept going into speeches, and it kept coming out.' McGurk asks Corbyn whether the line was routinely removed. His response is typically disingenuous and obtuse: 'I don't know what he says was taken out.'

McGurk: 'That's why I am campaigning to Remain in the EU ...'

Corbyn: I don't know what he's talking about. I stood alongside him in St Pancras Station and said exactly that about why I'm campaigning to remain in the EU.

McGurk: So Milne wouldn't have taken that line out?

Corbyn: Well, I said it, so it can't have been taken out. I think it's extremely unhelpful and unfair for him [Johnson] to have said that.

'After the interview,' writes McGurk. 'I struggle to find the event where Corbyn told me he said the line. I check in with his office and they send me a link. It was 22 June – the day before the referendum.' Until then, in other words, Seumas Milne had apparently succeeded in having the line excised.

As is often the case with Corbyn's most committed supporters, those rejecting the obvious criticism that his support for Remain had been at best half-hearted, at worst downright detrimental, ended up being embarrassed by their own allies. 'Jeremy in his heart of hearts is a Brexiter,' said his former shadow foreign secretary, Diane Abbott, in February 2023. 'Remember in the 80s, when both of us were starting out in the party, Tony Benn, who was a huge hero to all of us, and a hero to the Labour Party grassroots, he was anti-EU. He saw it as a conspiracy of business people and so on. So, that was the common view on the left in the 80s. And I think it's the view that Jeremy still held.' Asked if Corbyn voted to Leave, as many suspect, Abbott hesitated before saying: 'Oh, he would have voted Remain because that was the policy of the party.'[27] But not, evidently, the policy of the man.

Bizarrely, Brexit would account for both Corbyn's biggest setback as leader and his greatest 'success'. On 26 June 2016, three days after the referendum result, Corbyn sacked his shadow foreign secretary, Hilary Benn, after reports that he had been organising a mass resignation of fellow shadow ministers to compel Corbyn to stand down. 'There is no confidence to win the next election if Jeremy continues as leader,' Benn explained. 'In a phone call to Jeremy I told him I had lost confidence in his ability to lead the party and he dismissed me.'[28] There followed what was then the biggest mass resignation in British political history. Twelve more shadow cabinet members followed Benn out of the door the following day. By the end of the week, 65 members of his government-in-waiting had quit, with most citing his handling of the EU referendum as a key reason. On 28 June he lost a vote of confidence by Labour Party MPs by 172 votes to 40.

It is worth pausing to consider the scale of opposition to his leadership from people who would have had to campaign to make him prime minister. Privately, according to Tim Shipman and others, Corbyn was 'a broken man', being prevented from resigning by Seumas Milne and other aides. Publicly, a statement was issued denying the 'constitutional legitimacy' of the vote and asserting Corbyn's intention to continue as leader.

There was an air of Groundhog Day to the ensuing leadership challenge. And once again, despite enjoying so little support among his parliamentary colleagues, Corbyn romped home when the question was put to the broader membership, securing 313,209 votes to challenger Owen Smith's 193,229. In normal circumstances, the chaos would surely have been unsustainable. Even Barack Obama, asked whether he feared a politician like Bernie Sanders might bring about a 'Corbynisation' of the US Democratic Party after Donald Trump's victory, was critical, saying: 'I don't worry about that, partly because I think that the Democratic Party has stayed pretty grounded in fact and reality ... I think people like the passion that Bernie brought, but Bernie Sanders is a pretty centrist politician relative to ... Corbyn or relative to some of the Republicans.'[29]

But what was clear to Obama remained resolutely invisible to many British voters. The gulf between the reality of Corbyn the man and public perception was still being masterfully navigated by Milne and co. while the wisdom of keeping him out of studios as much as possible would shortly be rewarded in unexpected fashion. Put simply, the less people saw of him the more his 'folk hero' status grew on the back of vague promises of a 'kinder, gentler politics' and undergraduate ideal-ism. Most crucially, though, these were not 'normal circumstances'. Theresa May's fool's errand of trying to deliver a Brexit that would satisfy a significant swathe of the people that voted for it was, inevi-tably, starting to come apart at the seams. The country was plunged into a ridiculous purgatory where the absence of any settlement meant that the liars and charlatans could continue to promise the earth while the millions of Remainers, already seeing much of 'Project Fear' come true, had nowhere to turn. Except, incredibly, to Jeremy Corbyn.

On 8 June 2017, Theresa May went to the country in the hope of extending her working majority of 17 seats. After a decent set of local election results, the calculation was not as daft as it would later appear. Her advisers, including the ludicrous Nick Timothy, were overlooking one crucial factor. The vote would mark the first opportunity since 2016 for 'Remain' voters to vote against a candidate dedicated to delivering Brexit. Consider the irony. May, a Remain voter and one of the few politicians to display a pre-referendum understanding of the danger posed by Brexit to the Good Friday Agreement, was the Brexit candidate while Corbyn, a lifelong Leaver, was the only real option available to Remainers. This anomaly, mixed with Corbyn's appeal to cohorts routinely dubbed 'dreamers' and 'students', threw opinion polls and predictions into complete disarray and ultimately saw the Conservatives return 317 MPs – 13 fewer than in 2015 – while Labour gained 30 seats, taking their total to 262. In percentage terms, May won 42.4 per cent of the vote (the Conservative's highest share since 1983) and Corbyn 40 per cent (Labour's highest share since 2001). Inevitably, the political scientist John Curtice, doyen of psephologists, found that many of Labour's most successful results occurred in seats that had voted Remain by a large margin. 'It seems to be the case,' he wrote, 'that Mrs May's brand of Brexit may have helped to squeeze the UKIP vote, but that at the same time it put off some Remain voters.'[30]

The result would leave both Theresa May's premiership and the Labour Party's hopes of winning the next election completely doomed. The former because she was vulnerable to attacks from an opportunistic charlatan prepared to lie egregiously about Brexit, the latter because the numbers gave Corbyn and his crew more than enough room to claim, absurdly, that Labour's third general election loss in a row was, somehow, a victory. Accordingly, he would not be resigning. When Gordon Brown trailed David Cameron's Tories by 48 seats after the 2010 election, Jeremy Corbyn wrote in the *Morning Star* that the result was 'disastrous for New Labour'.[31] When he found himself 55 seats behind Theresa May seven years later, he said: 'I think it's pretty clear who won this election.'[32] He was, incredibly, talking about himself.

Just two and a half years later, he would lead Labour to its worst general election defeat since 1935, securing less than a third of votes cast and returning just 202 MPs. Pollster Opinium found that among 2017 Labour voters who switched allegiance to another party, 37 per cent of them cited Corbyn's leadership as their main reason.[33] Despite this dismal figure almost doubling the percentage who cited Brexit, he claimed that the election 'was taken over by Brexit', an extraordinary excuse given his own abject and repeated failure to make a compelling case for EU membership. Among Labour voters who switched allegiances to the Tories, 45 per cent cited Corbyn's leadership as the main issue with 29 per cent of defectors from the Liberal Democrats saying the same. Of all the people polled who said they did not vote for the Labour Party, 43 per cent said their main reason was the leadership, with 17 per cent blaming Brexit and 12 per cent Labour's economic policies. Another survey of 10,000 people, conducted by the Brexiter peer Lord Ashcroft, found that 53 per cent of those who deserted Labour between 2017 and 2019 did so because they 'did not want Jeremy Corbyn as prime minister'.[34]

For some, as ever, this was nothing to do with Jeremy Corbyn. An internal report conducted by his own election coordinators, Ian Lavery and Andrew Gwynne, found that 'four years of unrelenting attacks on the character of the party leader, an assault without precedent in modern politics, had a degree of negative impact.'[35] For others, a man who had voted against his own party leadership in the House of Commons on more than 400 occasions was a victim of unconscionable disloyalty.

By now permanently 'high on his own supply', Corbyn would claim this time that: 'I am proud that on austerity, on corporate power, on inequality and on the climate emergency we have won the arguments and rewritten the terms of political debate.'[36] It is a statement of almost unbelievable arrogance and delusion, nouns that perfectly distil both the post-2017 period of his leadership and his remaining cheerleaders. As support drained away, so the purblind certainties of his remaining cultists increased. The pitiful performance of a general despised by his most senior troops and derided by opponents and reluctant supporters alike would remain, for evermore, the fault of somebody, anybody, everybody but him. Unfortunately for the country he had sought to govern, the full reality of what had actually been helped to power by Jeremy Corbyn's querulousness, stubbornness and incompetence was about to become horribly clear. Even to Dominic Cummings.

(Parts of this chapter originally appeared in the author's *Times Literary Supplement* review of *Protest and Power: The Battle for the Labour Party* by David Kogan.)

Chapter 8
DOMINIC CUMMINGS

A basic problem for people in politics is that approximately none have the hard skills necessary to distinguish great people from charlatans.

Dominic Cummings[1]

ON 9 JUNE 2017, the former director of 'Vote Leave', Dominic Cummings, shambled on to the stage at 'Nudgestock', an annual festival that bills itself as the UK's largest gathering of behavioural sciences experts. He was there to deliver a speech entitled 'Why Leave Won the Referendum'. Listening to it now, it is easy to understand why a rare, in-person, public speech from a man widely credited with 'masterminding' the 'Vote Leave' operation garnered so little attention at the time. Cummings appears deliberately obtuse, and most of the print media was still reeling from the shock of the referendum result, with the BBC particularly hidebound by instructions from on high to focus on the result itself, rather than asking questions about its validity or the methods behind it. *Channel 4 News* did its best to reflect its significance but it was ploughing a lonely furrow. It was during this period that Robbie Gibb, the BBC's director of live political programmes who became Theresa May's director of communications a month later, instructed the Corporation's editor Rob Burley not to interrogate the infamous claim on the side of a bus that leaving the European Union would somehow enable £350 million a week to be spent on the NHS.

'Summer 2015, I was sitting at home, happily unemployed, in the garden, having a beer, reading,' Cummings told the audience. 'And I started to get phone calls. The election had just happened a couple of days earlier. Cameron had unexpectedly won and I started to get phone calls from a few MPs and some campaigners and a few Tory Party donor billionaires, saying, essentially, "Well this referendum is now going to happen but no one's actually prepared anything for it, no one's built anything, there's no campaign. What are you doing? Can you come and help? Can you create something that could actually fight it?'

Leave aside, for now, the irony of billionaire donors trying to enlist an unelected bureaucrat for a campaign that would profess to be 'anti-Establishment' and effectively cast people in both categories as enemies of their 'Brexit'. Instead, consider both why Cummings was unemployed and why *his* phone started trilling on that May evening. For many outside Westminster, Cummings was largely unknown before he accepted those invitations to set up a leave campaign. Inside Westminster, however, he was seen as a formidable, unstable, force who could sway voters and deliver the results billionaire donors desired. But why they put their faith in him is as fascinating as it is unknown. Indeed, for all his carefully contrived attempts to appear an 'outsider' or a 'maverick', the Cummings backstory could hardly tick more *How They Broke Britain* boxes: mysterious Russian connections, hard-right think tanks, roles in the Tory high command and a pronounced cosiness with right-wing media. His father-in-law is, like David Cameron's, a baronet, and his wife, Mary Wakefield, an editor at Andrew Neil's *Spectator*.

After graduating from Oxford in 1994, Cummings moved to Russia to work for a group hoping to set up an airline. These past activities came to new light in November 2019, when Cummings was Prime Minister Boris Johnson's most senior adviser. The *Sunday Times* reported that a 'whistleblower has approached senior Labour politicians to raise questions about the "relationships" that Boris Johnson's chief of staff – Cummings – may have developed with people involved in "politics, intelligence and security" when he worked in Russia between 1994 and 1997'.[2] The shadow foreign secretary, Emily Thornberry, wrote to her opposite number, Dominic Raab, to ask whether Cummings's past raised 'concerns' about him being granted 'access to the highest levels of classified material, or given such high levels of influence over UK government policy'. Her message copied in the cabinet secretary and national security adviser as well as the heads of MI5 and MI6. As far as I'm aware, Cummings has never responded to these claims.

Thornberry's concerns coincided with widespread worries that the so-called 'Russia report', the Intelligence and Security Committee's (ISC) investigation into allegations of Russian interference in British politics, would not be published before the general election scheduled for 12 December 2019. The committee had completed the report in March and, after undergoing redaction by security and intelligence agencies, it was delivered to Johnson on 17 October, but he refused to then make it public. On the failure to publish, the Conservative chair of the ISC, Dominic Grieve MP, said: 'What has absolutely astonished me is the mendacity of the response from the No. 10 press office, which I do take to be linked to Cummings. They have come up with a series of utterly bogus explanations why it can't be published now, and they really are whopping lies.'[3] These are remarkably strong words for a former attorney general – a role that historically had been reserved for parliamentarians with impressive legal backgrounds, although this precedent would be abandoned when Boris Johnson appointed Suella Braverman to the position in February 2020.

Grieve's reservations proved well-founded. Johnson cleared the report for publication the day after securing an 80-seat majority in the December 2019 election. It was finally published in July 2020 and was, by any account, damning. Vladimir Putin's administration had been engaged in 'hostile foreign interference' and Russia was identified as 'significant threat ... on a number of fronts – from espionage to interference in democratic process, and to serious crime'. In a distinct echo of the Brexit purdah imposed at the BBC and the police failure to investigate 'Vote Leave', the report criticised the 'illogical' approach by MI5 not to fully investigate how much Moscow had tried to influence the referendum due to 'extreme caution' about being seen to interfere in 'democratic processes'. Committee member Stewart Hosie MP told a news conference that ministers 'did not want to know' and 'actively avoided looking for evidence'. The government's official response – 'We have seen no evidence of successful interference in the EU referendum' – rather ignored the fact that they had, apparently quite deliberately, not looked for any. As Dominic Grieve would tell the BBC, 'When the committee came to ask the question – can you tell us there wasn't interference? – we really weren't able to get an answer.'[4] Once again, we can only wonder what the UK media would have done with both of these stories if the individuals under suspicion had been perceived as unsympathetic to their shared cause.

But to return our focus back to Cummings in the mid-1990s, after the Russian airline plan proved 'spectacularly unsuccessful',[5] Cummings returned to the UK in 1997. Two years later, he started publicly cutting his Eurosceptic teeth as 'campaign director' of Business for Britain. Its mission to oppose the UK changing its currency to the euro was rendered redundant after Gordon Brown prevailed over Tony Blair and ruled it out completely. Cummings, who often insists that he is not a Conservative, then went to work as 'director of strategy' for the Conservative leader Iain (Duncan) Smith. He lasted eight months and, in what would become a familiar refrain throughout his subsequent career, quit in protest at his colleagues' perceived failings, describing Smith as 'incompetent' and potentially 'a worse prime minister than Tony Blair'.[6]

Next, in a move echoed by much of the cast of this book, it was time for a senior role in a 'free-market' think tank. Cummings had sufficient connections – despite professing to be anti-Establishment – that he merited one all of his own. In December 2003, he became the founding 'director' of the New Frontiers Foundation. His 'campaign director' at NFF was James Frayne, formerly of the TaxPayers' Alliance, now 'director of policy and strategy' at the Policy Exchange 'think tank'. The chairman was Lord Salisbury, a former Tory leader in the Lords. Given what transpired long after their initial association, it is interesting to see how Salisbury regarded Cummings's referendum tactics, when writing to Theresa May in April 2019 to complain about her Brexit negotiations and inform her that his stately home, Hatfield House, would no longer be made available for Conservative Party functions. 'I am not naive enough to believe that leaving would not be painful,' he wrote. 'It clearly would be and I thought the Leave campaign was most unwise not to say so.'[7]

The New Frontiers Foundation barely lasted a year and I have been unable to establish who funded it, but its 'advisory council' contained some interesting names. Stuart Wheeler is the Eton-educated spread-betting magnate and former Tory donor who would become treasurer of UKIP in 2011. Stanley (now Baron) Kalms, the head of the electrical retailer, Currys, had just stepped down as treasurer of the Tory party and spent ten years from 1991 as director of the Centre for Policy Studies. Another member, Nile Gardiner, is today a director of the Margaret Thatcher Center for Freedom at The Heritage Foundation 'think tank' in Washington, DC, a regular contributor to Fox News and the *Daily Telegraph*'s go-to correspondent for hatchet jobs on Joe Biden. Recent highlights include: 'Here comes Biden, the world's worst diplomat' (8 July 2023); 'Joe Biden helped cause this global downturn. He's in no position to lecture Truss' (18 October 2022) and, in an all too rare foray into British political analysis, 'Liz Truss can be a powerful leader of the free world' (28 August 2022).

At least one element of the short-lived New Frontiers Foundation's lean output seems significant. In 2004, it described the BBC as the 'mortal enemy' of the Conservative Party and called for the 'end of the BBC in its current form'. Given that the NFF only boasted two staff members and that Cummings would later become a prolific 'blogger', it seems fair to assume that he was at the very least partly responsible for encouraging the 'development of the web networks scrutinising the BBC and providing information to commercial rivals with an interest in undermining the BBC's credibility'. Furthermore, the NFF argued that the Conservatives 'can only prosper in the long-term by undermining the BBC's reputation for impartiality in the way CBS's reputation is being undermined now, and by changing the law on political advertising'.

In September 2004, another blog post stated: 'There are three structural things that the right needs to happen in terms of communications ... 1) the undermining of the BBC's credibility; 2) the creation of a Fox News equivalent / talk radio shows / bloggers etc to shift the centre of gravity; 3) the end of the ban on TV political advertising.' It was also suggested that government ministers should avoid appearing on BBC Radio 4's *Today* programme, as indeed they did after Cummings entered Downing Street.

It is clear already that, far from being the genius outlier of his own mythology, Dominic Cummings is every bit as embedded in the ecosystem of cronyism and manipulation as anyone else in this book. The only, almost endearing, difference is that he seems to despise almost everybody else in it. Nevertheless, as we shall shortly see, his feelings didn't prevent him from going to work for Andrew Neil or his most abiding contribution to national politics from being achieved in partnership with Matthew Elliott. First, though, I want to tilt at the 'genius' element of his self-styled reputation as opposed to the 'maverick', with compelling evidence that some of the strategies he deployed when running 'Vote Leave' were simply reheated manipulations.

In 2004, shortly before the failure of the New Frontiers Foundation, Cummings popped up in his native north-east as a 'strategic adviser' to Nesno (the North East Says No campaign against regional devolution). It is largely forgotten now, but Deputy Prime Minister John Prescott's plans for regional assemblies were initially very popular. In many ways, his dream of shifting the balance of power in the UK away from Westminster should have found favour with the sort of people that Cummings specialises in manipulating. In the event, the north-east England devolution referendum turned out to be a dry run for the Brexit referendum because rather than merely demonising out-of-touch London-based politicians, Cummings and his colleagues framed their cause as 'anti-politics' itself.

'The messaging was all about being the cheeky upstarts,' recalls Graham Robb, the campaign's chief spokesman. 'We were the insurgents, it was the anti-politics approach. It was the first time that approach had been taken.'[8] In addition to attacking politicians in general, three more elements of the campaign stand out: an eye-catching gimmick, nonsensical claims about NHS funding and relentless, unapologetically vicious attacks on the opposition. 'We did not need a positive message,' wrote William Norton, Nesno's referendum agent. 'We were the no campaign. That's a negative act.'[9]

An enormous, inflatable white elephant proved the most memorable contributor to the referendum campaigns. Emblazoned with the slogan 'VOTE NO TO A REGIONAL ASSEMBLY – IT'S A WHITE ELEPHANT', it captured the 'anti-politics' sentiment perfectly and, alongside the Cummings-coined catchphrase 'Politicians talk, we pay', it helped to deliver a stunning turnaround at the ballot box, with 78 per cent voting 'No'. It also marked the first time that Cummings had been part of a campaign that owed its success to telling fibs about NHS funding. It would not be the last.

'The regional assembly would create more politicians, so as you would expect it means the regional assembly will come with huge extra cost,' intoned Graham Robb in a film that was broadcast on regional television in the north-east during the run up to the vote. 'The bill for the north-east would be a staggering £1m per week.' Crucially, the caption, 'More doctors, not politicians,' appeared on the screen.

The difficulty of debunking seductive disinformation, of fighting feelings and falsehoods with facts, would prove all too familiar to Remain campaigners 12 years later. But at the time of this devolution referendum, it was articulated particularly well by Julie Elliott, Sunderland Central MP and a prominent 'Yes' campaigner. 'It was ludicrous to suggest that any additional money spent on a regional assembly could instead have been used to fund more doctors,' she said. 'Local governments do not have extensive responsibility for medical services. But the problem was that once that disinformation was out there, it was impossible to extinguish it in many voters' minds.'[10] Prescott insisted that regional government would actually cost '£12m less to the people in the north-east'.[11] But it didn't matter. People voted to reject the 'political establishment' and to secure more money for the NHS. And where the inflatable elephant led, a bus would one day follow. As Cummings blogged in March 2019: 'It was a training exercise that turned out surprisingly well. SW1 100% ignored it, thankfully.'[12]

I would like to make a small personal confession at this point. Of all the characters featured in this book, Cummings is the one I find most interesting and even, much to my own surprise, often the one to whom I am most sympathetic. He is clearly as mad as a box of frogs but I think he is driven by demons rather than defined by them. And although he carries a considerable sense of entitlement, it is at least based upon his largely justified opinion of his own intelligence relative to most of the people around him, rather than any form of birthright. Profilers make much of an unlikely period spent working at his uncle's notorious Durham nightclub, Klute, and he certainly has never shown himself to be motivated by measurable personal advancement. This last point alone makes him almost unique in public life today, never mind in the circles he seems to have moved in since returning from Russia. Perhaps the most interesting element of his CV concerns the period immediately after the Nesno referendum when he 'proceeded to spend two and a half years in a bunker he and his father built for him on their farm in Durham, reading science and history and trying to understand the world'.[13]

Make no mistake, Cummings's contribution to the breaking of Britain is immense. As if the reality of Brexit were not bad enough, he also steered Boris Johnson to the 80-seat majority that he would use to smash up the last vestiges of parliamentary democracy and political integrity. Tragically, as nobody appreciates more than Cummings, it also meant that Johnson was in charge when COVID-19 came calling. And the Barnard Castle affair surely did untold damage to lockdown observance and what remained of the government's authority. But unlike the rest of the key architects of our national malaise, I think Cummings acted throughout with something close to good intentions. Researching this chapter, I have been reminded repeatedly of a cross-country runner: solitary, preternaturally committed, clear-eyed, contemptuous of distraction and competition alike but, ultimately, unable ever to stop and wonder whether he might be running in the wrong direction entirely.

I reserve the right to regret these words but Dominic Cummings, however deluded or deranged he may have become in trying to deliver them, seems to have always acted in pursuit of what *he* genuinely believed to be the best interests of the country. It makes him the polar opposite of a Boris Johnson or a Nigel Farage, and of no use whatsoever to a Dacre or a Murdoch. An oddly solipsistic ideologue, there were times during the Brexit campaign when he seemed to hold some of the people on his own side in even lower regard than his opponents. His personal manifesto, for want of a better word, required existing structures, from the civil service to ministerial government, to be razed so that something superior could be built in its place. Understand this and his willingness to break rules, laws and untold conventions in pursuit of victory becomes understandable if no less unforgivable.

Neither would he be of much use to an Andrew Neil – as it turned out. In 2006, Cummings emerged from his bunker to take a job running the *Spectator*'s embryonic website. It was a short-lived adventure. In early February, he uploaded a controversial cartoon of the Muslim prophet Muhammad with a bomb, fuse ignited, in his turban.

The *Guardian* reported that 'the magazine's acting editor, Stuart Reid, said he had not been responsible for uploading the picture' but 'after a call from *Spectator* publisher Andrew Neil, he gave instructions for the image to be taken down ... He said the website did not have an editor but "the guy who has overall responsibility" was Dominic Cummings.'[14] The text accompanying the cartoon, originally published in Danish newspaper *Jyllands-Posten*, rather makes one wonder where Cummings would have ended up if he had not found an outlet for his energies in Westminster:

> European newspapers reprint Muhammad 'Bomb turban' cartoon, but as European populations die and Muslim populations grow, and as more and more European students are taught Foucault and 'literary critical theory', the balance of power shifts every day; meanwhile Britain's comic political class cannot even control Islamic terrorists when they finally lock a few up in prison ...

After the *Spectator* incident, Cummings began a seven-year stint as an adviser to Michael Gove, beginning in 2007 and spent in both opposition and government, where he ignited many more workplace fireworks and attracted decidedly mixed reviews from media and colleagues. Apart from cementing his deep loathing of the civil service and most politicians, the period is only tangentially pertinent to the broader project here. There was a brief hiccup to his progress when Andy Coulson, for reasons unknown, sought to keep him out of government but, once there, he made no secret of his loathing for the deputy prime minister, Nick Clegg. David Cameron was widely presumed to be describing Cummings when he mentioned a 'career psychopath' in a speech to a Policy Exchange garden party in 2014 and Clegg himself is on the record as calling him 'some loopy individual who used to be a sort of back-room adviser'.[15]

'Some thoughts on education and political priorities',[16] a very long 'essay' (it runs to 237 pages) written in 2013, provides a helpful insight into how Cummings found himself 'happily unemployed' in summer 2015. As special adviser to the secretary of state of education, the scale of his ambition for British school leaders was immense. 'We need leaders with an understanding of Thucydides and statistical modelling,' he wrote. 'Who have read *The Brothers Karamazov* and *The Quark and the Jaguar*, who can feel Kipling's Kim and succeed in Tetlock's Good Judgment Project.' But even in Michael Gove's Department of Education, the ambition of delivering 'an "Odyssean" education so that a substantial fraction of teenagers, students and adults might understand something of our biggest intellectual and practical problems, and be trained to take effective action' was surely unrealistic.

This disconnect between his ambitions and the reality of what is possible is significant for three reasons: it signals the first depiction of the civil service as 'the Blob', resisting reform and allergic to change; it enforces his belief that meaningful improvement necessitates the destruction of the status quo; and it puts him intriguingly at odds with his professed political hero, Otto von Bismarck, who maintained that 'Politics is the art of the possible, the attainable – the art of the next best.' It is hard to think of an attitude more diametrically opposed to the one that Cummings, who quit the department in early 2014, would take to 'Vote Leave'.

There are, then, three key constituents to the Cummings conundrum. First, his contempt for pretty much everybody. This is obvious and born of a belief that his prescription is the only cure for any given ill. In the context of short term, 'achievable goals' like referendums, this is more strength than weakness. In the context of long, incremental missions such as rewriting education policy or even governing, it is a monumental flaw. Realising his dreams in Downing Street, for example, would have involved being able to control Boris Johnson for *years*. Johnson, as anybody with any experience of his personal, professional and political activities had known for decades, is at best a capricious egotist, at worst a sociopathic narcissist. It is, in retrospect, almost impossible to understand how Cummings thought he might exercise Rasputin-like influence over a man interested exclusively in his own immediate gratification. As he would tell the joint hearing of the Science and Technology Committee and Health and Social Care Committee of the House of Commons in May 2021: 'It doesn't matter if you've got great people doing communications if the PM changes his mind ten times a day and then calls up the media and contradicts his own policy day after day after day. You're going to have a communications disaster-zone.' Adding: 'Nobody could find a way around the problem of the prime minister [who was] just like a shopping trolley smashing from one side of the aisle to the other.'

Second, his conviction that *anything* is acceptable in pursuit of victory – that the end justified any means. This is defined by his belief in the unquestionable importance of that victory and therefore leaves him conveniently immune to any moral or ethical qualms. Again, this seems more suited to snappy, single-issue movements than to drawn-out projects where scrutiny and accountability, however unappealing, are unavoidable.

Finally, and most remarkably, he is not interested in personal enrichment, advancement or status. This is why he finds it so easy to walk away from the fray and, I think, why he so often seems almost detached from humanity itself. If *everything* is a model or part of a wider ideological project, then *everybody* is a spot on a graph or an algorithmic input. People are reduced to mere data, their lives important only in so far as they indicate voting intentions and susceptibility to manipulation. And again, you can get people to do what you want in the short term by deploying this approach but it is less helpful answering the question of what happens after. This is why his seniority in Downing Street at the start of the COVID-19 outbreak would prove so problematic – something that, as we shall see, he seemed eventually to acknowledge himself.

On 20 April 2016, an appearance before the Treasury Committee saw these 'attributes' on startling display. Cummings was there to account for some of the claims being made by 'Vote Leave'. The chair, Conservative Andrew Tyrie, is by turns bewildered and enraged by his testimony. In retrospect, it feels like a much more significant moment than was acknowledged at the time. It is essentially a clash of political culture, with Tyrie and most of his colleagues clinging to the notion that you can't simply make stuff up to suit your aims and Cummings condescendingly certain that you absolutely can. Nowhere is this clash, or Tyrie's incredulity, more evident than in an early exchange over the relevance of the actual *numbers* used by Cummings in campaign literature. In this case, the claim that EU 'regulation' costs the UK £33.3 billion per year.

> **Tyrie:** What you are saying is that there are a range of numbers. We should not take any particular number that you are using as a headline number – and you are using the £600 million per week and £33.3 billion per annum cost of regulation all the time in your literature – and you are now telling us in evidence that we should set that at a heavy discount and not worry about it or its accuracy

too much because it is just one of a range of numbers that may be taken into consideration. Is that summary of your evidence right?

Cummings: Roughly speaking, what you are saying is a reasonable perspective. As I said, campaigns on both sides and the Government produce these economic studies that have various numbers. It is crazy for anyone to take decimal points seriously in these things.

Tyrie: This is a decimal point that is moving along quite a long way, is it not? We are talking about a decimal point that has shifted quite a bit from £33 billion to £13 billion at the stroke.

The contents may be a little turgid, but this reveals much about how Cummings thinks and operates. Another exchange, in which Cummings seeks to somehow negate the £6 billion rebate Margaret Thatcher negotiated on the UK's annual contribution to the EU budget, begins in remarkable fashion.

Tyrie: Do you know how much the rebate is?

Cummings: The rebate is £3 billion or £4 billion.

Tyrie: It is £6 billion. Are you aware of what happens to the rebate physically?

Cummings: Yes.

Tyrie: Perhaps you would like to describe that to the Committee.

Cummings: The interesting thing about the rebate is …

Tyrie's point is to demonstrate that after the agreed rebate, the UK's annual contribution to the EU stands at £13 billion per annum and not the £19 billion figure used for all Vote Leave's 'calculations', including the £350 million on the side of the infamous bus. Not only that, but the same money has apparently been earmarked for sundry other destinations. It reminds me of a young child asking, in all seriousness, to spend their birthday money 'again'.

Tyrie: I am just asking you why you are suggesting in some of your literature that you might allocate all of that to extra spending on hospitals. As an organisation you are proposing that.

Cummings: As an organisation we are saying that once we stop the £19.1 billion debit then we will have roughly £350 million per week to spend on our priorities, like the NHS. The NHS is the country's top priority and is a fairly obvious target for where a lot of these savings would be spent.

Tyrie: I am asking you the same question a third time. You have made it clear that there are a number of other priorities that you personally may want to spend money on, such as science, and you have agreed that a number of other groups are going to get financial protection. Why have you nonetheless persisted with the idea that this same pot can be raided and used exclusively for the NHS? That is what I am asking you.

Cummings: We are not.

Tyrie: I have here one of your posters, which is available and you are encouraging your supporters to download. It gives a clear enough message, to any reasonable persons, that is telling you that we should give the whole of this £350 million per week to the NHS, does it not?

And finally, in the section that follows, note the supreme casualness with which Cummings approaches the question of precisely what 'information' his organisation is putting in the hands of public, and how. His only colleague at that short-lived think tank, Tufton Street veteran James Frayne, wrote in 2013 that: 'Messages that touch people on an emotional level cause a physical reaction in the brain that makes such messages more likely to be stored in our long-term memory, and therefore more likely to affect our political outlook.'[17] By 2016, Cummings seemed not to care how you get those messages there, or indeed whether or not they are even true.

Tyrie: … I just want to touch on one more point. You are saying in your literature, in hospitals, that we can give a lot more money to hospitals, are you not? You are distributing literature to that effect. You are doing that, are you not?

Cummings: No, we are not. We have not distributed any literature whatsoever to hospitals.

Tyrie: I have a piece of literature here with your logo. Is this a pirated piece of literature? It says, 'Vote Leave. Take control.' It is badged as your literature. It says, 'Help protect your local hospital.' It has here at the bottom, 'Vote Leave. Take control.org.' Is that not your organisation?

Cummings: It looks like it is one of our leaflets, yes.

Tyrie: So you are distributing these things to hospitals. This was picked up from Guy's Hospital.

Cummings: I saw that story, I think, on a website.

Tyrie: I have one of the leaflets here, yes.

Cummings: Yes. I saw that story on the website last week. We do not have a clue where that has come from. It certainly was not done by us.

Tyrie: So is this pirated?

Cummings: No. Well, I have no idea. I very much doubt it.

Tyrie: I just want clarity.

Cummings: I am giving you clarity.

Tyrie: You have not yet on many of the points that I have been asking. Let me go through some very simple questions. Did your organisation print this leaflet?

Cummings: It looks likely that we did, but I cannot tell about any individual leaflet.

Tyrie: You do not know which leaflets might be printed by your organisation. You are running a campaign and do not know …

Cummings: You are misunderstanding what I am saying.

Tyrie: I do not think you are understanding the question. I am asking a straightforward and simple question. We are getting down to very simple questions. Is this a leaflet of your organisation?

Cummings: Do you mean that design of leaflet, or that individual leaflet?

Tyrie: I am asking you if this leaflet is one of your organisation's leaflets.

Cummings: Yes, it is.

Tyrie: Good. We have answered question 1. Now let us try question 2. Is it reasonable that somebody might misconstrue this leaflet at first glance as a leaflet produced by the NHS, since it has an NHS logo in the top right-hand corner?

Cummings: No. It says, 'Vote Leave. Take control' at the bottom, with our logo.

Tyrie: What do you make of that NHS logo there?

Cummings: What do you mean, 'What do I make of it?'

Tyrie: Does it look like the logo of the NHS?

Cummings: It looks roughly like it from here.

Tyrie: It looks roughly like it from almost any distance. Here is an NHS document encouraging you to eat better food and you will see that the logo is strikingly similar. They are in fact almost identical. It takes an expert eye to tell that the one is not the other. One of them is slightly italicised; the other is not. Now that you have had a chance to consider whether you did in fact produce this leaflet and you have agreed that it does look like an NHS leaflet at any reasonable distance, do you think it might be a good idea to think twice about putting out literature as misleading as this?

Cummings: No, I certainly do not and you are confused about what my answer was before. I thought you were asking me if the leaflet you were holding in your hand had been put into a hospital and had come from us, and I was saying, 'No, it has not come from us' – as in we did not distribute leaflets to the hospital. We are as baffled as everybody else about the story that appeared on the website. That has not happened because of us or at my direction; nobody in the office knows why it has happened. That is what I was saying. If you are saying you have one of the leaflets from that hospital and you are holding it up in front of me asking, 'Is this yours?' my answer is, 'It looks like something that we have printed, but it is certainly not something that we have put into Guy's Hospital.'

It doesn't matter now, of course, but the fact that it didn't even matter *then* is another mark of how deeply the discourse had been corrupted to allow these levels of disingenuousness and deceit to go unchecked. Incidentally, there were two Tory Brexiters on the committee, Jacob Rees-Mogg and 'hard man of Brexit' Steve Baker. One sketch writer encapsulated their contributions: 'They did their best to tee their man up with a few easy questions, much like members of a parole board trying to find some good in a prisoner who has managed for the first time to get through an entire group therapy session without assaulting anyone, but Cummings was much too far gone.'[18]

. . .

With Brexit, two of the three key Cummings characteristics – the unshakeable beliefs that his prescription is the *only* cure and that the end justifies *any* means – would collide in catastrophic fashion. We have explored, at length, why by 2016 the UK media was utterly ill-equipped to report the facts of the referendum with even a modicum of objectivity or accuracy. False equivalence, epic proprietorial and editorial biases, a cowed BBC, emotional appeals to nativist bigotries and the weaponised populist ignorance of many pro-Leave politicians saw to that. Factor in the insipid Remain campaign and the pathetic contributions of Cameron and Corbyn – the first accidentally, the second deliberately – and you have an almost perfect recipe for the disaster that has followed.

The final, essential ingredient, however, was not added in public. It was added in the privacy of their computers and smartphones. For all the talk of the 'will of the people' and the 17.4 million leave voters, Cummings implicitly understood what was needed to tilt the scales. He defined it as 'about 600,000 people – just over 1% of registered voters'.[19] To fully understand their significance and how completely they were misinformed, we must go back to his appearance at Nudgestock that opened this chapter.

The speech was delivered the day after Theresa May's embarrassment in the 2017 general election. Assured by advisers like Nick Timothy, her joint chief of staff, that she would enhance her fragile majority by going to the polls, she ended up losing that majority and was forced in to a 'supply and demand' arrangement with the Democratic Unionist Party (DUP). She would be toast within two years, while Timothy would inevitably end up writing hysterical columns for the *Daily Telegraph*, including 'Britain's passive surrender to a woke minority risks everything we cherish' (9 July 2023) and 'A crisis of masculinity imperils the foundations of the West' (30 April 2023). At the end of July 2023, he was selected to fight Matt Hancock's old seat at the next general election. It is hard to think of a finer example of Conservative Party members being forced to reward failure in order to continue denying they have helped usher in disaster.

At Nudgestock, Cummings, comfortable on stage and wearing a shirt that looked almost ironed, could not resist a quick dig. 'I think what's happened in the last 24 hours with the election and the Tory party campaign,' he said, 'is another good example of how hard it has been for the bubble in SW1 to actually get to grips with what the effects of the financial crisis in 2008 were.' Listing the key concerns underpinning a Brexit vote he also cited immigration, obviously, and, somewhat less convincingly, the euro. He claimed that seeing Greece 'literally on fire on TV screens' had hardened anti-EU sentiment despite the fact that there was, by 2016, no appetite anywhere for the UK to join the single currency.

The speech gets really interesting about 13 minutes in, although his language is so opaque that the audience could be forgiven for not noticing. I am conscious of repeating myself when stressing that there is no point trying to relitigate Brexit today, however decisive the polls demonstrating leave voters' regret or a desire to rejoin may be. Yet to understand how lies, prejudices and delusions could, in various combinations, come *completely* to dominate the governments of Johnson,

Truss and Sunak, it is absolutely essential to understand how they were used to deliver the Brexit that started the wrecking ball rolling.

'We had to take risks and we had to do things in a slightly new way,' said Cummings. 'One of the basic things that I did was I brought in a team of physicists who essentially looked at campaigning from complete first principles.' Sounds reasonable, right? Even clever. Physicists deal in scientific facts, after all. In fact, these 'physicists' were data scientists working for AggregateIQ (AIQ), the obscure Canadian web analytics company, based above a shop in Victoria, British Columbia, which featured in Shahmir Sanni's disclosures about BeLeave's finances covered in Chapter 4. The indefatigable and supremely courageous *Observer* journalist Carole Cadwalladr unravelled the web in which AIQ sits almost single-handedly from 2017 onwards. For this and her wider work exposing what would become known as the Facebook–Cambridge Analytica data scandal, she has won enough awards to fill several mantelpieces. In the corrupted British ecosystem under scrutiny here, however, she is a regular target of the right-wing media: from the salaried trolls at the 'Guido Fawkes' blog to Andrew Neil, who, despite being supposedly bound by BBC impartiality requirements, called her 'Karol Kodswallop' and a 'mad cat woman' during one of his late-night Twitter rants in November 2018. He has never apologised.

Carole's broader mission to expose the links between AIQ and Cambridge Analytica, Steve Bannon, Donald Trump, Nigel Farage and (another) secretive hedge-fund manager called Robert Mercer remain riveting, deeply troubling and criminally under-reported. I urge you to read further in to Carole's quest but, for our purposes here, it is Dominic Cummings's AIQ 'physicists' who merit most attention.

Cummings continued in his speech: 'They [the physicists] also constructed models to help direct resources for the ground campaign

... and the digital campaign ... Essentially you had streams of data coming in from all sorts of different ways: the website, email, on the ground, canvassing, er, social media blah blah blah ... All of this stuff coming in and you had the data science people sitting at the heart of the operation and essentially taking our core messages and just running experimentally a whole bunch of things on Facebook and elsewhere and figuring out what things work and what things don't work.'

Cummings is, in fact, describing 'data mining'. In the USA in December 2022, Facebook's owner, Meta Platforms, Inc., agreed to pay $725 million to resolve a class-action lawsuit accusing them of allowing third parties, including Cambridge Analytica, to access users' personal information. Reuters reported that: 'The proposed settlement ... would resolve a long-running lawsuit prompted by revelations in 2018 that Facebook had allowed the British political consulting firm Cambridge Analytica to access data of as many as 87 million users.'[20] In the light of what Dominic Cummings said next at Nudgestock about how his campaign identified Facebook users most likely to respond to its advertising, it remains remarkable that no similar investigation has been conducted in the UK.

'You can define the demographics that you interrogate yourself,' he said, 'and what we did was we basically used the exact same categories ... for demographics that Facebook uses for its digital advertising platform. So we sucked in data on the precise same basis that Facebook marketing allows and then we had therefore large sub-samples of the overall polling samples that you could actually rely on. And then you could take that data and plug it straight back in to Facebook. So you could say, for example, that we would target women between 35 and 45 who live in these particular geographical entities who don't have a degree ...'

'Finding "persuadable" voters is key for any campaign,' wrote Carole Cadwalladr in 2017, 'and with its treasure trove of data, Cambridge Analytica could target people high in neuroticism, for example, with images of immigrants "swamping" the country. The key is finding emotional triggers for each individual voter.'[21]

Cummings continued: 'We basically dumped our entire budget in the last ten days, and really in the last three or four days. And we aimed it at, I can't remember exactly, but roughly about 7 million people saw something like one and a half billion digital ads over a relatively short period of time.' In total, Vote Leave spent £3.9 million, more than half its official £7 million campaign budget, with AggregateIQ. Three other affiliated Leave campaigns: BeLeave, Veterans for Britain and the Democratic Unionist Party, spent a further £757,750.[22]

So what was in the carefully targeted advertisements on which Dominic Cummings spent most of Vote Leave's budget and remains convinced were absolutely crucial to its referendum success? It would be over a year before anyone except their recipients would know. On 19 July 2018, Rebecca Stimson, Facebook's UK head of policy, wrote to Damian Collins, the chair of the Digital, Culture, Media and Sport Committee:

Your original question was: Can we see copies of adverts from AIQ? Who were these adverts shown to? Who paid for them? We have previously answered the third part of this question, as to who paid for these ads, and we explained that we were in the process of identifying and compiling these ads. We have now completed that process and enclose a copy of the ads run for the following Facebook pages by AIQ: Vote Leave; BeLeave/Brexit Central; DUP Vote To Leave.

There are, literally, pages of them but a few stand out. 'TURKEY HAS A 511 MILE BORDER WITH SYRIA TURKEY IS JOINING THE EU GOOD NEWS???' Facebook users are invited to click on YES or NO. The same invitation accompanies another ad: 'TURKEY HAS A POPULATION OF 76 MILLION TURKEY IS JOINING THE EU GOOD IDEA?' Another features a photograph of a mother holding her newborn baby and smiling at the camera. A large, shop door-style 'CLOSED' sign dominates half of the page. The text reads: 'IMAGINE IF WE COULD KEEP OUR MATERNITY UNITS OPEN BECAUSE WE WEREN'T SENDING £350 MILLION A WEEK TO THE EU.' Again, recipients are invited to click on the page. In this case on a bright red 'SAVE MATERNITY UNITS' button. Another bizarrely insists that 'THE EUROPEAN UNION WANTS TO KILL OUR CUPPA' and features a clenched fist in the colours of the EU flag heading towards a cup of tea adorned with British iconography including a Routemaster bus, a red phone box and Big Ben. Another oddity insists that 'The EU blocks our ability to speak out and PROTECT polar bears!' It features a cute photograph of an adult polar shielding two cubs.

It is not hard to imagine the effect that a veritable avalanche of these ads might have upon a Facebook user, already identified by the algorithm as susceptible to the messaging. 'We need an immigration system that ensures British young people more jobs'; 'Albania, Macedonia, Montenegro, Serbia and Turkey are joining the EU'; 'MIND YOUR OWN BUSINESS, OBAMA'. Leaving the EU would ensure that 'we' had better flood defences, that fluffy sheep (pictured) would have better lives, that the UK steel industry would be supported (remember Cummings's relish for geographical targeting), and that the shipping of whale meat 'through our ports' would be stopped.

On 27 March 2019, Dominic Cummings was ruled to be in contempt of parliament after refusing to appear before MPs investigating 'fake news'. The case had been referred to the House of Commons Committee of Privileges the previous June after Cummings failed to respond to an order of the House requiring him to give an undertaking to appear before the DCMS Committee. Its report concluded that Cummings committed a contempt 'both by his initial refusal to obey the DCMS committee's order to attend and by his subsequent refusal to obey the house's order of 7 June'. Committee chair, the Conservative Damian Collins, said Cummings had shown a 'total disregard' for the authority of parliament and called for statutory powers to 'reassert the authority that is missing'. He added: 'The Dominic Cummings case highlights the need for parliament to define in law what its powers should be to require witnesses to attend hearings, and what sanctions should apply if they do not.'

Significantly, many of the adverts scaremongering about the almost non-existent prospect of Turkey or Serbia joining the EU featured photographs of doctors or nurses looking glum, presumably at the prospect of having to treat their citizens. Indeed, it is almost impossible to separate the NHS messaging from the immigration provocations. This can't be a coincidence but, in another hint at the internal conflict he feels at winning 'dirty', Cummings was desperate with the Nudgestock speech to see the two issues separately. 'So why did this happen?' he asks. 'Was it just immigration? No, it wasn't just immigration. If it wasn't for the £350 million and turning the campaign, giving people a chance to vote *for* the NHS as well as voting against the EU. Without that, then the economic scares of the Establishment would have been too powerful and we would have lost. Could we have won without immigration? Absolutely not.'

I found the next bit of the speech quite disturbing. It took me a moment to realise that he was referring to the assassination of Jo Cox by a white-supremacist terrorist, just as the anti-immigrant rhetoric of both leave campaigns reached fever pitch. There may be another explanation but it seems fair to presume that his apparent inability to say her name came from the same place as Paul Dacre's decision to report the sentencing of her murderer on page 30 of his newspaper: namely, shame.

Referring to the 'Establishment', he explains: 'They lived in the bubble and you could see that in the last ten days. After the terrible murder, they ditched their whole campaign, stopped talking about economic risks and tuned the whole thing in to "well, we're the good people and you're the bad people". Because that was the self-reinforcing culture that you heard in London ... and Cameron and Osborne were psyched out by that whereas, in fact, as soon as you went outside the M25 and did the market research, the rest of the country had a totally different reaction to the murder than better-educated, richer people living in London did. And our campaign took advantage of it.'

The loudest (indeed, only) cheer of the afternoon came when an audience member asked Cummings whether he ever felt 'guilty about what you've done?' His answer is fascinating as much for its insight into his epic fallibility as his thinking. 'No, not in the slightest ...' he said. 'The single most important reason for why I wanted to get out of the EU is it will drain the poison out of a lot of political debates. I predicted that if we get out UKIP and Nigel Farage would be finished. That's an early gain for Vote Leave. As you can see, that's happened. That whole side of British politics will go. Once there's democratic control of immigration policy, immigration will go back to being a second or third order issue and that will be a positive and healthy thing for the country.'

Bless him. Two years later, Farage's rebranded 'Brexit Party' not only won the European elections but also struck a general election pact with Boris Johnson (senior adviser: D. Cummings) and stood down 317 candidates in constituencies where a split vote would have aided Labour. Nevertheless, two years after that Cummings was still celebrating. 'Obviously I think Brexit was a good thing ...' he told (who else?) the BBC's Laura Kuenssberg, 'I think that the way in which the world has worked out since 2016 vindicates the arguments that Vote Leave made in all sorts of ways. I think it's good that, that Brexit happened.'[23] And two years after *that*, as we have seen, the Conservative government's attitude to immigration and refugees bore more resemblance to 1930s Germany than the post-Brexit United Kingdom of Cummings's fond imaginings. That, at least, was the expressed opinion of the Holocaust survivor Joan Salter when she begged Suella Braverman, promoted far beyond her limited capabilities by Boris Johnson, to moderate her language.

Cummings has had wobbles, most obviously in a 2017 Twitter exchange with David Allen Green. Green, a brilliant legal commentator who once worked alongside Daniel Hannan in the office of veteran Eurosceptic Bill Cash, asked Cummings: 'Is there anything which could now happen (or not happen) which would make you now wish leave had not won the referendum result?' Cummings replied: 'Lots! I said before REF was dumb idea, other things shdve been tried 1st. In some possible branches of the future leaving will be an error.'

We do not know whether Dominic Cummings considers the current situation to represent one of the 'branches of the future' in which leaving the EU has been rendered an 'error'. Certainly, his predictions of what it would entail have come to nought and his main reason for wanting it has not been realised. But the satisfaction of getting one over on the 'Establishment' of which he insists that he – senior adviser to not one but two Tory leaders, *Spectator* employee, 'think-tank' founder, airline entrepreneur and son-in-law of a baronet – is most definitely *not* a part will probably sustain him well into old age. We do know, however, that his second greatest contribution to the breaking of Britain, the installation of Boris Johnson in Downing Street, will haunt him to his dying day. And so it should.

On 26 May 2021, a joint hearing of the Science and Technology Committee and Health and Social Care Committee was investigating the government's response to the COVID-19 crisis. A cowed Cummings, who had departed Downing Street in acrimony the previous November, told them: 'The truth is that senior ministers, senior officials, senior advisers like me fell disastrously short of the standards that the public has a right to expect of its government in a crisis like this. When the public needed us most, the government failed. I would like to say to all the families of those who died unnecessarily how sorry I am for the mistakes that were made and for my own mistakes at that.'

Dominic Cummings was finally telling the truth.

Chapter 9
BORIS JOHNSON

I have a hunch that Johnson will come to regret securing the prize for which he has struggled so long, because the experience of the premiership will lay bare his absolute unfitness for it.
Former boss Max Hastings

Tens of thousands of people died who didn't need to die.
Former senior adviser Dominic Cummings

ON 26 MAY 2021, Dominic Cummings appeared before the joint Science and Technology Committee and Health and Social Care Committee inquiry in the House of Commons. The air of wide-eyed mania remained but gone was the arrogant disdain of his previous, Brexit-related testimonies. Instead, the man who had always displayed unleavened contempt for MPs daring to interrogate him appeared contrite, reflective and even, in perhaps the least convincing element of the often surreal session, almost modest.

'It is completely crazy that I should have been in such a senior position in my personal opinion,' he said of his role at Boris Johnson's side when the COVID-19 crisis began. 'I'm not smart. I've not built great things in the world. It's just completely crackers that someone like me should have been in there, just the same as it's crackers that Boris

Johnson was in there.' Leaving aside the obvious fact that nobody had forced the self-confessed inadequate to take the job, the speed with which scales had apparently fallen from eyes was notable. Five years after the referendum divorced British politics from observable reality for at least a generation and, we learned, just one year after that result had helped Johnson to a historic majority, the person who had perhaps done more than any other to secure *both* dismal outcomes was suddenly, bitterly regretful.

This public self-flagellation must be taken with a cellar full of salt. Cummings had essentially been thrown out of No. 10 in November 2020 after losing a power struggle with the prime minister's then fiancée, Carrie Symonds. He was photographed carrying a cardboard box out of the Downing Street door in the week when the official COVID-19 death toll passed the 50,000 milestone and yet office vendettas and fights for Johnson's ear were still, apparently, paramount concerns inside.

In front of the inquiry, Cummings threw around apologies like confetti and portrayed Johnson's leadership until that point as a picture of almost criminal negligence, yet he was silent about his own part in such pettiness. Indeed, it was hard, throughout his eight hours of testimony, to separate the boundless bitterness from the professed desire to set the record straight. Symonds and her husband were not the only people with whom he appeared desperate to settle old scores. The hapless health secretary Matt Hancock came in for frequent, well-deserved kickings. Most of the Downing Street staff, cabinet members, fellow COBRA meeting attendees and even Dilyn, the Johnsons' dog, were in the firing line too.

The castigation of Boris Johnson, however, remains by far the most significant element of his evidence. This partly, for obvious reasons, because of the urgency of all inquiries into the government's handling of COVID-19 but especially, for our purposes, because Cummings became an unwitting exemplar that day of *all* the people who had laboured under the lethal illusion that the depravity of Boris Johnson should be allowed anywhere near Downing Street. That the electorate could end up letting him was due to the work of every other chapter dedicatee in this book (except, perhaps, Jeremy Corbyn, who simply failed to oppose him), most of the rest of the British media and, by the end of 2019, almost the entire Conservative Party.

Johnson will 'star' in many stories, some already written. In this one, he is relevant for just two reasons. First, he is living, lying proof of just what can rise to the top when the subversion of the media/political ecosystem described here has come close to critical mass. He has shown us all exactly what can happen when newspaper editors and proprietors abnegate any responsibility to hold politicians to account. He has shown us what will rise when the BBC is compromised by political appointments, cowed by negative outside coverage and reserves its richest rewards for journalists committed to cultivating the likes of Cummings (who revealed to that select committee that the 'main' journalist he briefed in the early weeks of COVID-19 was Laura Kuenssberg), Matthew Elliott and Boris Johnson. And he has shown us what will prosper when a favoured politician's previously honourable colleagues sacrifice their integrity on the altar of personal ambition. To understand what Johnson was known to be long *before* he became prime minister is to understand the rotted core of a country in which such a calamity could come to pass.

Second, a catalogue of the catastrophe and moral corruption he brought into government and then proceeded to inflict upon the country will highlight how completely the checks and balances of parliament and the fourth estate were rendered redundant by complicity and contempt. When someone truly believes themselves to be above the petty requirements of decency and honesty, they will triumph only if other people condone, collude or look the other way. It is well-documented that Johnson's (house)master at Eton identified precisely this personality defect early in his life. 'I think he honestly believes that it is churlish of us not to regard him as an exception,' wrote Martin Hammond to Johnson's father Stanley in April 1982. 'One who should be free of the network of obligation that binds everyone else.'

Less well-known is a letter written by another former Eton teacher and published in *The Times* on 13 June 2023, John Claughton, master from 1984 to 2001, wrote:

> Whatever wider attitude Eton adopts the school itself will continue to educate the global elite. Perhaps its most important mission will be to ensure that its pupils are saved from the sense of privilege, entitlement and omniscience that can produce alumni such as Boris Johnson, Jacob Rees-Mogg, Kwasi Kwarteng and [former Tory chairman, appointed by Johnson] Ben Elliot and thereby damage a country's very fabric. Sadly, I failed in that purpose.

It is important to record not only how Johnson and his accomplices damaged the 'country's very fabric', but also how he could ever have ended up in a position where he could do so. He illustrates, almost perfectly, both what had happened to Britain to allow him to become prime minister and what could happen as a consequence of promoting such an irredeemable charlatan.

My (probably naive) hope here is simply to collate a mound of publicly available evidence in the hope that people will wonder how on earth they could ever have tolerated, never mind supported, Boris

Johnson. Peter Oborne has already undertaken the task in much greater detail in his 2021 volume, *The Assault on Truth*. The entire book, which should be required reading for any political journalist or, for that matter, voter, is dedicated to Johnson's lies and their corrosive effect on society. Here, the serial mendacity and moral turpitude are just one crucial piece of a larger jigsaw. And while I may be throwing stones, I am not without sin. My own scales-from-eyes moment came shortly after I foolishly voted for him in the 2008 London mayoral election, partly due to his raising the prospect of an amnesty for foreign-born people working here illegally. It quickly became clear that, contrary to a specific election pledge, he would soon be presiding over the closure of fire stations and cuts to the fire service. My awakening was rude. In 2013, the Labour leader on the London assembly, Andrew Dismore, would ask the then mayor about his plans: 'How can cutting fire stations, cutting fire engines and cutting firefighters posts not be a reduction in fire cover? ... You've lied to the people of London.' Johnson's reply was as brief, arrogant and obnoxious as his future term as prime minister. 'Get stuffed,' he barked.

After Eton, Oxford. The public mythology is well-documented. President of the Union, Bullingdon Club member, tireless self-promoter, student journalist and betrothal to Allegra Mostyn-Owen, a landowner's daughter who had already graced the cover of *Tatler* magazine. Johnson, 'hilariously', turned up with neither trousers nor shoes. By the time of their divorce six years later, Johnson's mistress and future second wife, Marina Wheeler, was already pregnant with their first child.

In December 2019, a writer and healthcare worker called Damian Furniss wrote a Facebook post recalling his time at Oxford when Johnson and David Cameron were also students.[1] He is warm about the latter, not least because 'Even when I sabotaged his college beagle pack he took it in good humour.' But his memories of Johnson are of an entirely different flavour:

> I have different memories of Alexander Boris de Pfeffel Johnson who was the first Oxford student I met when I was at Balliol College for interview in 1984. I was a rural working class kid with a stammer from a state school which hadn't prepared me for the experience, but I was bright and well read, with more interest in and knowledge of my subjects of Philosophy, Politics and Economics than most of my public school rivals could muster. My session with the dons was scheduled for first thing after breakfast, meaning I was staying the night and had an evening to kill in the college bar Johnson was propping up with his coterie of acolytes whose only apparent role in life was to laugh at his jokes. Three years older than me, and half way through the second class degree in Classics he coasted through with the diligence he later applied to journalism and red box briefings, you'd have expected him to play the ambassador role, welcoming an aspiring member of his college. Instead, his piss-taking was brutal. In the course of the pint I felt obliged to finish he mocked my speech impediment, my accent, my school, my dress sense, my haircut, my background, my father's work as farm worker and garage proprietor, and my prospects in the scholarship interview I was there for. His only motivation was to amuse his posh boy mates.

That second-class degree caused Johnson, forever caught in the competitive cycle of Cyril Connolly's 'permanent adolescence', particular irritation. Years later, when reminded that his rival Cameron and brother Joe had both achieved first-class degrees, he would describe them, with characteristically casual misogyny, as 'Girly swots who wasted their time at university'.[2] In 2019, by now prime minister, he would repeat the insult about Cameron in a cabinet paper.[3]

Furniss's conclusion was both brutal and prescient: 'In short, he demonstrated all of the character flaws that make him unfit to be our Prime Minister. Nothing I see today suggests he has changed. He's not Falstaff, he's Faust. If you are an ordinary working person and think he has your interests at heart, think again.'

Decades before his ascent to the highest office in the land, his unsuitability was evident to teachers and fellow students alike. It would soon become evident to employers and colleagues too.

In May 1988, having secured a prized graduate traineeship on *The Times*, he wrote a front-page story about the archaeological discovery of Edward II's long-lost 'Rosary' Palace. 'According to Dr Colin Lucas of Balliol College, Oxford,' wrote Johnson, 'this is where the king enjoyed a reign of dissolution with his catamite, Piers Gaveston ...' Conveniently for Johnson, Dr Lucas, a future vice-chancellor of Oxford University, was his godfather. Somewhat less felicitously, he had said no such thing. Given that Gaveston had been beheaded some 13 years before the Palace was built, it would have been remarkable if he had. In an early display of his preternatural lack of conscience, Johnson wrote another, entirely manufactured, story claiming that the date of the palace's construction was now being disputed. When the full scale of his deceptions became known, not least because of the protestations of his own godfather, *Times* editor Charles Wilson summarily sacked him.

His later account of the incident is revealing if you are interested in the inner workings of Johnson's mind: 'It was a complete nightmare of a disaster, and to make it even worse, that very week Colin was trying to become master of Balliol College. He later succeeded – but not that time. Of all the mistakes I've made, I think that takes the biscuit.'[4]

History does not relate whether the editor of the *Daily Telegraph*, Max Hastings, was aware of the grounds for Johnson's dismissal from *The Times* but it is hard to imagine that he would not be. Nonetheless, he gave him a berth on the newspaper's leader desk. It was here that he developed his distinctive and, for many readers, winning style. Most notable, perhaps, was a habit of referring to readers as 'my friends' that would later inform his political speechmaking. It was his next posting, secured partly as a consequence of his peculiar knack for indulging the concerns of the *Telegraph*'s older, distinctly 'Middle England' readership, that would change the course of his career and, incredibly for a young journalist, in many ways the country.

At the beginning of 1989, Hastings sent Johnson to Brussels to report on the European Commission. Previously a pretty dry patch, he quickly discovered that largely mythical tales of overbearing bureaucracy and ridiculous rules were breakfast catnip to *Telegraph* readers. During this five-year period, Johnson essentially popularised a genre of journalism that would come to define 25 years of EU coverage across most of the UK media and so indubitably influence the 2016 referendum result. David Usborne, the *Independent*'s EU correspondent at the time, later explained: 'He compromised his intellectual integrity to get on,' adding that Johnson was well aware that he was 'writing out of his ass'.[5] Peter Guilford, in Brussels for *The Times*, has spoken of the midnight phone calls he would receive from London when Johnson's inventions landed on editors' desks. 'We are under pressure to follow it up,' he said. 'So there was this sort of Eurosceptic-generating machine that we were all part of, and Boris was driving harder than anyone else.'[6]

I'm not sure the significance of this cynical but enormously success-ful opportunism can be exaggerated. Political enmity towards the EU had previously been a largely Bennite project of the left while more populist 'Eurosceptic' journalism, such as it was, had been typified by the vulgar, xenophobic posturings of Murdoch lieutenants such as Kelvin MacKenzie. His infamous 'Up Yours, Delors' *Sun* front page, for example, appeared in November 1990. Johnson's sub-Wodehousian flights of fancy were a lot more palatable and the misrepresentations of what EU membership entailed much subtler. Their impact, however, was considerable, as he explained himself in 2005: 'I was just chucking these rocks over the garden wall, and I'd listen to this amazing crash from the greenhouse, next door, over ... over in England, as every-thing I wrote from Brussels was having this amazing, explosive effect on the Tory party, and it really gave me this, I suppose, rather weird sense of ... of power.'[7]

The 'rocks' appear ridiculous now but then so does almost every-thing about Boris Johnson. At the time, they were incredibly effective. 'They read like a collection of April Fools' Day hoaxes, but their consequences were far from funny,' wrote Martin Fletcher, a former foreign editor of *The Times*, in 2019:

> They helped ignite the simmering euroscepticism of the Conser-vative right. They also set the tone for much of the rest of British journalism, which found Johnson's cartoon caricature of Brussels much more appealing than the real thing. I know this because I later became the Brussels correspondent for a rival paper, and it had become almost impossible to write serious stories about the EU even for my more discerning readers.[8]

In May 1991, Fletcher recalls, under the headline 'Italy fails to measure up on condoms', Johnson wrote that 'Brussels bureaucrats have shown their legendary attention to detail by rejecting new specifications for condom dimensions', claiming that the Italian rubber industry had sought a smaller minimum width because of the dimensions of Italian penises. He quoted an official spokesperson, Willy Hélin, as stating: 'this is a very serious business'.[9] Thirty years later, Hélin told the *Observer* Johnson had written a 'load of bullshit', explaining, 'We were not interested by sizes. We had had requests from medical institutions across Europe to check on the safety of condoms. That has nothing to do with the size of dicks. All the journalists went on about comparing the size of penises in Germany and France. It's about safety, because so many doctors were interested to know about the risks for Aids patients,' he said, before describing Johnson, 'He was the paramount of exaggeration and distortion and lies. He was a clown – a successful clown.'[10]

In March 1992, there was more bullshit. This time, literally. Under the headline 'Brussels recruits sniffers to ensure that Euro-manure smells the same', he claimed that 'A smelly farmyard could become an offence under Brussels plans to quantify "maximum permissible odours" from manure heaps.'[11] Two months later, the headline was 'Delors plan to rule Europe' and the story: 'European foreign ministers were stunned yesterday to learn of a plan by Jacques Delors to transform the Brussels Commission into a "European government" with himself, or his successor, becoming a fully-fledged "President of the European Community".'[12]

A few days after this piece was published, in a perfect illustration of the serious consequences Johnson's silliness would have almost 25 years later, Denmark voted against the Maastricht Treaty with a majority of just 50.7 per cent. Johnson later claimed his story, picked up extensively by Danish media, had helped to swing the result. He was probably not exaggerating. 'It definitely had an impact,' said Uffe Ellemann-Jensen, Denmark's then foreign minister. 'The story was that once the Danes had voted yes then we would have much more Europe, much more union and all that stuff. When I said it was nonsense, I was called a bloody liar.'[13] Sonia Purnell, Johnson's deputy in Brussels and one of his first former colleagues to warn against the dangers of his political ambitions, explains in her excellent 2012 biography, *Just Boris*, that this cavalcade of calumnies inspired and informed the growth of UKIP, the platform from which Nigel Farage would later launch his own toxic misrepresentations of the EU.

Among countless other nonsenses and shameless exaggerations, Johnson reported that 'the pinkness of the British breakfast sausage' was 'imperilled',[14] there would a 'directive on a standardised Euro-coffin',[15] and 'The Berlaymont building – Brussels headquarters of the European Community, is to be blown up ... the 13-storey building which is to be replaced because of the danger from asbestos used in its construction.'[16] The building, needless to say, is still standing. A particularly pungent example from November 1993, shortly before he was recalled to London, perfectly illustrates the patrician suspicion of Johnny Foreigner that Johnson did not personally feel but would always prove more than happy to indulge. Under the headline, 'Coming soon ... the day Herr Speaker rules Westminster', he wrote: 'Achtung! British domestic politicians! Your lives are set to change: your wards, town halls, your seats are targets for the Maastricht Euro-carpetbaggers. The Treaty's new electoral law could even allow Germans, French, Italians and other EEC nationals to stand as Westminster MPs or, indeed, to be raised to the peerage'. This too never came to pass, although the Labour MP who chaired the Vote Leave campaign committee, Gisela

Stuart, was born and raised in West Germany. Boris Johnson would later put her in the House of Lords.

He also, of course, ennobled Charles Moore, who was editor of the *Sunday Telegraph* for the last two years of Johnson's Brussels posting. He makes for an interesting comparison today with Max Hastings, his counterpart at the daily title who has subsequently repented of his role in promoting, platforming and amplifying Johnson. 'I have known Johnson since the 1980s, when I edited the *Daily Telegraph* and he was our flamboyant Brussels correspondent,' Hastings wrote in 2019 under the headline 'I was Boris Johnson's boss: he is utterly unfit to be prime minister', 'I have argued for a decade that, while he is a brilliant entertainer who made a popular maître d' for London as its mayor, he is unfit for national office, because it seems he cares for no interest save his own fame and gratification.'[17]

Moore, as we have seen, remained a fully paid-up member of the Johnson fan club. In August 2023, Ivo Dawnay, Johnson's brother-in-law and foreign editor of the *Sunday Telegraph* under Moore, provided a helpful answer to the lingering question of how Johnson's lies and exaggerations could possibly have been printed by supposedly respectable individuals and once respectable organs. 'I objected only mildly when his fanciful (not to say purely fictitious) copy landed,' he wrote. '"Oh but it's so well written," the then *Sunday Telegraph* editor Charles Moore used to say as I hovered, eyebrow raised, in his office doorway. "Bung it in."'[18] This, of course, is the journalistic approach to truth and accuracy that continues to grace Andrew Neil's *Spectator* and the *Telegraph* comment pages. Johnson sought to bring it to the chairmanship of the BBC.

By the time he left Brussels in March 1994, the nature of reporting from there for British newspapers had changed forever. It appears, for example, that he wasn't personally responsible for one of the most enduring media-manufactured EU myths of all. By the time the tale of the 'bendy banana' saw the light of day, Johnson had been ensconced in his new *Telegraph* berth as chief political columnist and assistant editor for six months. In September 1994, under the headline 'Now they've really gone bananas', the *Sun* reported that the EU was 'outlawing curved bananas'. The story was immediately followed up by the *Mirror*, *Mail* and *Express*. *Twenty-two years later*, while campaigning for Brexit, Johnson would complain that it was 'absolutely crazy that the EU is telling us what shape our bananas have got to be, and all that kind of thing'.[19] By then, it was far too late for anyone to set the record straight. The following year, an audience member told BBC *Question Time* that she had revised her intention to vote 'Remain' after encountering a 'straight' banana in her local supermarket.

The next stage of Johnson's career saw him accumulating the celebrity that would revivify political ambitions that briefly stalled when his 1994 attempt to become a Conservative MEP (yes, really) foundered on his failure to find a constituency. As ever with Johnson, the difference between fame and infamy was often blurred. In June 1995, a recording emerged of a 1990 telephone conversation between Johnson and a schoolfriend and Bullingdon alumnus, Darius Guppy. In it, Guppy, later jailed for faking a jewellery heist and claiming £1.8 million from insurers, pleaded for the home address of a *News of the World* journalist, Stuart Collier, who was looking into his affairs. It was, as the transcript attests, another potentially career-ending episode.

Guppy: … I am telling you something, Boris. This guy has got my blood up, all right? And there is nothing which I won't do to get my revenge. It's as simple as that.

Johnson: How badly are you going to hurt this guy?

Guppy: Not badly at all.

Johnson: I really, I want to know …

Guppy: Look, let me explain to you …

Johnson: If this guy [see/sues?] me I will be fucking furious.

Guppy: I guarantee you he will not be seriously hurt.

Johnson: How badly will he …

Guppy: He will not have a broken limb or broken arm, he will not be put into intensive care or anything like that. He will probably get a couple of black eyes and a … a cracked rib or something.

Johnson: Cracked rib?

Guppy: Nothing which you didn't suffer at rugby, OK? But he'll get scared and that's what I want … I want him to get scared, I want him to have no idea who's behind it, OK?

Eventually, Johnson agrees: 'OK Darrie, I said I'll do it and I'll do it. Don't worry.'

Asked in 2019 what message he would like to pass on to Johnson, by now all but guaranteed to be the next prime minister, Collier replied: 'I just don't think you're fit to be prime minister. At the very least, come clean on all your skeletons in the closet. I'm sure this is just one of them.'[20]

Max Hastings who, as we have seen, had long held the same opinion about Johnson's fitness for office, was less forthright in 1995. He apparently disciplined his star columnist but did not sack him. Instead, his career went from strength to strength.

A column in the *Spectator* (not chaired by Andrew Neil at this point) and a particularly cushy number reviewing cars for *GQ* magazine were the next additions to the already bulging portfolio. The editor who commissioned the latter would later reveal that his correspondent hadn't driven many of the cars dispatched for review. 'I once worked out that in the decade he worked for *GQ*, Boris had cost us about £4,000 in parking tickets,' wrote Dylan Jones in 2022.

> Interestingly, Boris never got any speeding tickets and I've got a pretty good idea why. When the cars were delivered to his house in Islington, the car company always made a note of the mileage, something that is standard practice. The mileage would also be noted when they came to pick them up again. And on more than one occasion – OK, on many, many, many occasions – the mileage was precisely the same. So I leave you to draw your own conclusions.[21]

One cannot help wondering whether Johnson became even more emboldened every time an editor failed to find the gumption displayed by Charles Wilson at the beginning of his career. He seemed to hold the view that he could do whatever he wanted without any consequences. It was an attitude he would shortly carry into politics, but not before a succession of other scandals.

The sex stuff, lurid and voluminous though it may be, is only relevant here for one reason so we will spare ourselves the salacious detail of his multiple betrayals, affairs and children born outside marriage. What is important to understanding the ecosystem is the way in which these serial infidelities were excused, accommodated and ignored by people and institutions that had long sat in moral judgement on almost anybody else. The hypocrisy of Paul Dacre, Charles Moore, Tony Gallagher or any Conservative MP demonising 'single mothers' while cheering a politician who made a hobby of creating them is clear. More importantly, it highlights how Johnson was turning his old headmaster's warning into a prophecy. If these self-appointed guardians of public decency could turn a blind eye to Johnson's sexual incontinence, they could turn a blind eye to anything. In other words, it was no longer problematic for him to believe that he 'should be free of the network of obligation that binds everyone else'. Instead, thanks to an epic dereliction of duty from many of the most powerful right-wing figures in the UK media, it was fast becoming a superpower.

In 2004, he was sacked for lying for the second time, on this occasion from the Conservative front bench. Five years previously, he had been offered the editorship of the *Spectator* by the Canadian owner, Conrad Black, on condition that he abandon his political ambitions. Johnson accepted the job, and the precondition, then successfully applied to fight for the safe Conservative seat of Henley-on-Thames at the 2001 election. Contrasting him with his predecessor in the constituency, the statesmanlike and widely respected former deputy prime minister Michael (now Lord) Heseltine, provides a snapshot of the journey undertaken by the Conservative Party in the twenty-first century. In June 2023, as Johnson's house of cards finally collapsed, Heseltine would provide a neat distillation of his Henley successor's success, perfectly capturing the conflation of gift and grift: 'Words are designed to make his audience believe whatever they want to believe. There is no anchor to any discernible truth or sense of integrity.'[22]

Partly as a consequence of his burgeoning celebrity, bolstered enormously by multiple appearances on the BBC panel show *Have I Got News for You?*, Tory leader Michael Howard had appointed Johnson, already vice-chair of the party, shadow minister for the arts in May 2004. By October, Howard was despatching him to Liverpool to apologise to an entire city after the *Spectator* published an editorial believed to have been written by Simon Heffer (another permanently furious columnist whose career was spent shuttling between the *Mail* and the *Telegraph*) and extensively amended by Johnson.[23] The article accused Liverpudlians of wallowing in their 'victim status' and over-reacting to the murder of Ken Bigley, a 62-year-old engineer who had been kidnapped and murdered by Islamist extremists in Iraq. Apparently 'an excessive predilection for welfarism' had 'created a peculiar, and deeply unattractive psyche among many Liverpudlians. They see themselves whenever possible as victims, and resent their victim status; yet at the same time they wallow in it'. The editorial even regurgitated lies about Hillsborough, describing 'Liverpool's failure to acknowledge, even to this day, the part played in the disaster by drunken fans at the back of the crowd who mindlessly tried to fight their way into the ground that Saturday afternoon'.

The new position also brought a higher level of scrutiny of his personal affairs and it was reported in November that he had been conducting a four-year-long extra-marital affair with a *Spectator* colleague, Petronella Wyatt. His denials to both media and the party's director of communications were characteristically bombastic. The story, he insisted, was 'complete balderdash' and 'an inverted pyramid of piffle'. But they fell apart somewhat when Wyatt's mother claimed that her daughter had become pregnant by Johnson and had an abortion the previous month.[24]

Howard offered Johnson the opportunity to resign but Johnson refused. This, often overlooked, element of the episode is fascinating and instructive. Johnson's modus operandi when confronted with evidence of his own lies is to bluster, distract and then deny everything that cannot be definitively proved, and this is an early, classic, example. Like Billy Bunter insisting he has not eaten a cake despite being covered in cake crumbs, Johnson *always* backs himself against his accusers' inability to prove beyond all doubt that he is guilty. The system, such as it is, is not equipped to accommodate such blatant, unapologetic dishonesty and so, like Trump, he often prevails. Sean O'Grady put it rather well in the *Independent* in July 2022:

> The lines he pumps out of Downing Street about virtually everything just keep changing. His web of lies is poorly constructed – lazily and carelessly thrown together. It requires constant repair. Facts are 'clarified', adjectives added and subtracted, euphemisms honed and then corrected, inquiries and investigations instigated to buy time, in the hope problems will just go away or get forgotten. The fresh distortions are added, or new revelations, and it never ends.[25]

Even after the mother of his alleged paramour had given the game away in this case, Johnson was presumably confident that Petronella Wyatt herself would not and so he could continue to claim innocence. Ergo the refusal to resign and so avoid admitting a lie. Way back at the beginning of his career, remember, when he lied about what his godfather had said to him and then lied about the established history of a palace built in 1325, he only ever admitted to a 'mistake'. When, years later, his various lies about 'Partygate' were unravelling in public, his entire defence consisted of stressing the impossibility of anybody else knowing exactly what was in his *mind* when he said apparently dishonest *words*. As with Bunter's cake, unless you could somehow cut him open and examine the evidence, it would be impossible to prove him wrong, however certain you may have been that he was. Johnson would stake everything on this tactic until the very last, when he lied about his knowledge of Chris Pincher's previous sexual misconduct but insisted that he had not. Nonetheless, back in 2004, Howard 'relieved him of his duties'. The recurring theme of Johnson surviving scandals that would likely have curtailed other careers was unintentionally captured by the *Observer*'s Gaby Hinsliff, who wrote in that year: 'The episode brings an end to an unlikely but uniquely engaging political career.'[26] In the case of anyone else, of course, it would have done.

But on he ploughed. When Cameron, three years his junior at Eton, became Tory leader in 2005, Johnson's own ambitions in that direction were effectively put on ice. Already relieved of his duties at the *Spectator* by Andrew Neil, he was too distracted by the trappings of celebrity and other lucrative jobs to make much of a mark as a junior education minister and so when, in 2007, the opportunity arose to run for mayor of London he jumped at it. It was, in many ways, perfect for him. High profile and replete with almost daily photo opportunities, it also offered fewer opportunities for catastrophic mistakes or egregious lies. Allegations around his extra-marital activities surfaced sporadically but it was during this period that his capacity for being forgiven for any transgressions within 'normal' politics expanded most rapidly from media owners and editors to the broader electorate.

It would be churlish to pretend that he was not popular and moderately effective, his inevitable howlers mostly more silly than sinister. He squandered £43 million of public money on a ludicrous 'garden bridge' vanity project and £300,000 on water cannon that were illegal under UK law but, largely because most of the media was eating out of his hand, neither did him lasting harm.

It was during this period that I first encountered him and, at risk of mitigating the case against other people in the dock here, I think I can explain some of his appeal. Because he doesn't care about *anything* (except his own immediate gratification) he creates an environment in which *nothing* is taken seriously. It is as if his carelessness is contagious and people who really should know better get caught up in it. Most obviously, this imparts an air of impunity even when he is being interrogated about misrepresentations and the like – interviewers often end up laughing with him at his 'antics' – but, crucially, it also creates the idea in the minds of viewers, listeners and voters that he is a jester in *their* court.

Accordingly, they will forgive him anything and by the time his true nature emerges it is too late for them to turn back. I suspect that this is as true for employers and colleagues as it is for voters and interviewers. Even Max Hastings took several years to see the light, while Peter Oborne was appointed to the political editorship of the *Spectator* by Johnson. When Eddie Mair, one of the finest journalists of his generation and a personal hero of mine, gave Johnson a grilling on the BBC on 24 March 2013, it was notable for two reasons: highlighting how rarely interviewers had properly held his feet to the fire and the way it saw *Mair* come in for widespread criticism from Johnson's support staff in the media and beyond. The BBC received 600 complaints about the interview.[27] For myself, when, for example, he hailed me with a 'Hello comrade!' from a bicycle on Charing Cross Road – and the friend I was with was mightily impressed – I had a tiny taste of why so many people turn off their normal standards in his presence. Happily, I did not suffer from this condition for long but I think it explains why all the nonsense about 'witch-hunts' and 'kangaroo courts' and 'getting all the big calls right' and the rest would later go so unchecked by so many for so long.

Inevitably, after insisting that he had no intention of seeking a return to the Commons before the end of his second term as mayor of London,[28] Johnson did exactly that. In September 2014, he was selected as the Conservative candidate for the safe seat of Uxbridge and South Ruislip in the 2015 general election. Though few realised it at the time, the political landscape was about to become a hotbed of xenophobia, misinformation and propaganda. Lies would be indulged and incompetents promoted on a scale never imagined during the postwar period of British politics. Cometh the hour, cometh the man. With Dominic Cummings by his side, Nigel Farage playing the role of electoral fertiliser and right-wing newspapers fawning over his every cock-up and calumny, Boris Johnson would flourish as never before.

In his crowdfunded online magnum opus, boris-johnson-lies.com, Oborne attempted to chronicle the 'Lies, Falsehoods and Misrepresentations' of his former editor, but 'documenting Boris Johnson's lies and false statements is like painting the Forth Bridge', he wrote in the mission statement. 'The task can never be completed because he and his ministers are constantly producing more examples.' Even with Johnson gone from Downing Street and, it must be hoped, politics, the task remains impossible. Never is the power of Steve Bannon's instruction to 'flood the zone with shit' more evident than in approaching the Augean stables of Johnson's career and we have already sifted through much of it. Shortly, we will focus here on just five examples of how, back in the Commons, the cabinet and shortly the prime minister's office, he would take a wrecking ball to what John Claughton called 'the country's very fabric': his betrayal of a British citizen abducted by a rogue regime; his mysterious assignations with a former KGB spy; his Brexit lies about Northern Ireland; the corruption of parliamentary democracy; and his lethal handling of COVID-19. A proper understanding of all these moments renders the subsequent 'Partygate' scandal as predictable as it was shameful. In every case, of course, the complicity of client journalists is a given. For many, the true scale of how completely he set about trashing the most fundamental checks and balances on the exercise of power remains unappreciated. And it remains so because his media cheerleaders and corrupted colleagues are still, even now, under his cultish spell.

His last-minute decision to back Leave was, as with every other decision in his life, famously motivated entirely by cynicism and self-interest. When Remain's expected victory was delivered, he would have the votes of Eurosceptic MPs and party members in his back pocket for the subsequent battle with George Osborne to succeed David Cameron. The fact that he had written two columns, one in favour of leaving, one against, only added to the sense that he was a politician like no other – a rare point of agreement for defenders and detractors alike. His campaigning was effective and often dishonest. He embraced Cummings's indulgence of xenophobic fears and, as with his years in Brussels, made amusing but baseless claims about the EU's role in British governance. Again, not caring about *anything* and believing in nothing liberated him to refresh parts that other politicians could not reach. Farage delivered the racists, Cummings delivered the wobblers and Johnson delivered the brighter, more cautious exceptionalists who just needed persuading that the experts were being unduly pessimistic. It was a coalition of snake-oil salesmen and it found a lot of customers.

After they won and Cameron resigned, his leadership campaign imploded after Michael Gove concluded that he was not capable of uniting party or country. 'It had to fall to someone else …' Gove explained 'selflessly', 'I felt it had to fall to me.'[29] It didn't, of course, but although Theresa May would lift the poisoned chalice, that abortive leadership contest marked the beginning of an era of disastrous prominence for MPs too blinkered or too stupid to understand the scale of the task before them. Nadine Dorries, later to become a poster girl for the promotion of the supremely unqualified, visibly wept as Johnson announced his own withdrawal from the contest. Andrea Leadsom, the politician invited by the BBC to tell the former WTO director general that her understanding of the WTO was superior to his, briefly looked as if she might become prime minister. Even Jacob Rees-Mogg, a penny-farthing in human form best known for taking his childhood nanny on the campaign trail, was now being treated as a qualified contributor to public discourse.

The first of Johnson's assaults on all that was decent about our democracy occurred after Theresa May's desperate and doomed attempt to buy his loyalty by making him foreign secretary. An early, potentially deadly blunder involved a November 2017 appearance before the Foreign Affairs Select Committee where he addressed the plight of Nazanin Zaghari-Ratcliffe, a British-Iranian woman serving a five-year sentence in Iran. 'When I look at what Nazanin Zaghari-Ratcliffe was doing, she was simply teaching people journalism, as I understand it,' said Johnson. 'Neither Nazanin Zaghari-Ratcliffe nor her family has been informed about what crime she has actually committed. And that I find extraordinary, incredible.' What was both extraordinary and incredible was the level of ignorance required to make this comment.

Tehran's prosecutor general had said in October that Zaghari-Ratcliffe had been arrested because she ran 'a BBC Persian online journalism course which was aimed at recruiting and training people to spread propaganda against Iran'. Her family and her employer, Thomson Reuters Foundation, had repeatedly insisted that she was *not* working in the country but was there to introduce her parents to their granddaughter. Just three days after Johnson's statement, it was cited at a specially convened court in Tehran as proof that she was engaged in 'propaganda against the regime'. The British foreign secretary's job would traditionally involve working to secure the release of British citizens imprisoned by rogue regimes on trumped-up charges. This one, through his innate carelessness and utter disregard for others, had made Nazanin's situation measurably worse.

'Nazanin was on holiday in Iran with Gabriella when she was abducted,' her husband Richard explained at the time. 'We demand a clear statement from the foreign secretary to correct his mistake – in parliament and in Tehran at the earliest opportunity.' There would be no statement. Neither, after her eventual release four years later, would there be any apology from Johnson when she explained in person the 'massive impact' of his comments and revealed that Iranian authorities had cited his words again during interrogation before her release. 'I have to say the Prime Minister looked quite shocked, I think, when she said that,' said Tulip Siddiq, the Zaghari-Ratcliffes' MP, who accompanied them to the meeting with Johnson in May 2022. 'But I was really proud she did say that because she wanted to make it clear to him that she's happy now, she's grateful, she appreciates the fact that she is home now, but there was a time when the words had a big impact.'[30]

If his conduct on duty was contemptible, his conduct off duty could be worse. In April 2018, Johnson attended a NATO summit in Brussels where a nerve agent attack in the Wiltshire town of Salisbury the previous month was on the agenda. The intended targets were Sergei Skripal, a former Russian officer and double agent for the British intelligence agencies, and his daughter, Yulia. They survived the attack after spending several weeks in hospital but a local woman, Dawn Sturgess, died after spraying herself with nerve agent contained in a discarded perfume bottle. At the NATO meeting, world leaders agreed it was 'highly likely' that Russia was behind the attack. In September, British authorities would identify two Russian nationals suspected of it.

Johnson, incredibly, made his way directly from the NATO summit to the Italian home of Evgeny Lebedev. It was at least his fifth visit. En route, he apparently jettisoned the 24/7 security detail that would ordinarily accompany a foreign secretary. In attendance was Evgeny's father, Alexander, a former lieutenant-colonel in the KGB who had been stationed in the Russian embassy in London in the 1980s and served alongside one Vladimir Putin. The former foreign office minister Rory Stewart revealed in March 2022 that he had declined a similar invitation, saying, 'the idea that the foreign secretary would think this is a respectable thing to do with his weekend is staggering. The Profumo guy lost his job for a lot less than that.'[31] In July 2019, photographs emerged of Johnson making the journey home from San Francesco d'Assisi airport in Perugia. Improbably, he appeared even more dishevelled than usual. 'It was a surprise to see him. There was nobody with him and he didn't appear to have any luggage,' a fellow passenger told journalists. 'He was such a mess. He was quite dishevelled and his trousers were twisted and creased. He looked like he had slept in his clothes.'[32]

'We still don't know what was said at that meeting,' wrote Carole Cadwalladr, one of the few journalists to cover the story from the start, in 2022 after Johnson was compelled to confirm the meeting to the Commons Liaison Committee. 'We don't know if there are any official records of it. We don't know who else was there. We don't know what documents Johnson had in his possession. We don't know if he betrayed secrets – either deliberately or inadvertently – about Nato's strategy.'[33]

We do know that, on the day after his election victory in December 2019, Johnson and Carrie Symonds attended a Christmas party hosted by the Lebedevs. We do know that, the following year, Lebedev junior was gifted a seat in the House of Lords by Johnson despite reported unease among security services. We do know that, in May 2022, Lebedev senior was sanctioned by the Canadian government as one of 14 people who had 'directly enabled Vladimir Putin's senseless war in Ukraine and bear responsibility for the pain and suffering of the people of Ukraine'. We do know that, in June 2023, Ukraine also sanctioned him over the Russian invasion. We do know that neither Johnson nor Rishi Sunak have followed suit (Liz Truss, to be fair, barely had time). And we do know that, in July 2023, Channel 4 reported that Italian intelligence services had been monitoring the Lebedev palazzo at the time of Johnson's visit. The makers of the documentary, *Boris, the Lord and the Russian Spy*, were shown a report by Italy's foreign intelligence agency that described Lebedev senior as continuing to enjoy the 'favour and friendship' of Vladimir Putin. Consider, for a moment, the shameless cynicism required for Johnson to cast himself as the great ally of Ukraine in the final months of his premiership.

Selecting his most egregious lie about Brexit is, given the size of the choice, surprisingly easy. Largely because it is unique to him and involved doing precisely the thing that he claimed he could not tolerate when summoning a photographer to record his resignation from Theresa May's cabinet in July 2018. Speaking at the DUP conference earlier that year, he said: 'We would be damaging the fabric of the union with regulatory checks and even customs controls between Great Britain and Northern Ireland on top of those extra regulatory checks down the Irish Sea that are already envisaged in the withdrawal agreement.' As prime minister, he reiterated the pledge to the *Irish News* on 14 August 2020, stating: 'There will be no border down the Irish Sea – over my dead body.' When he 'got Brexit done' there was, as everybody honest understood there would have to be, a 'border down the Irish Sea'. By the time it came to pass, diehard Brexiters were well used to pretending that they had never actually wanted what they had been promised and were, rather, delighted with whatever they got instead.

On 3 September 2019, Boris Johnson (and Dominic Cummings) withdrew the whip from 21 MPs who had supported a cross-party bill to prevent a 'no-deal' Brexit that would have left the United Kingdom without *any* free trade agreements. Among the dispossessed were two former chancellors, Philip Hammond and Ken Clarke. By now, the Brexit mess and attendant denialism had become so all-encompassing that politicians and public alike apparently believed that a 'no-deal' outcome was in any way desirable. It was obviously no such thing but he was now hostage to the radical English nationalist fringe of his party and understood that electoral success depended, as Brexit itself had done, on the support of the foreigner-hating Faragists. Accordingly, as he sought to reassemble the 2016 snake-oil salesmen coalition, he would describe the legislation as a 'surrender bill' and so portray an attempt to defend democratic norms as collusion with an enemy. Similarly, he would describe pro-European politicians as 'collaborators'.

Parliament would continue to lay bare the deceits and dangers of all his Brexit promises unless it could be closed down or there was a hugely enhanced Conservative majority packed with people who either failed to understand the simplest propositions or pretended not to out of ambition or cowardice. Impressively, both were soon achieved and here, I think, Cummings comes closest to deserving at least some of the attributions of Machiavellian genius. When parliamentary democracy itself presented an insuperable obstacle to the mythical Brexit Johnson and co. continued to peddle, the solution was simple: torch it all. Parliament was suspended, under a prorogation later ruled unlawful, and shortly after MPs returned to work, Jeremy Corbyn walked straight in to the trap laid by Cummings and agreed to a general election. 'The country deserved better,' the newly contrite Cummings would tell that committee inquiry in 2023, 'than a choice between Boris Johnson and Jeremy Corbyn at the last election.' But that, thanks to him, is exactly what the country got.

It is worth pausing here to reflect on what happened immediately after Johnson and Cummings secured their 80-seat majority. The 'Withdrawal Agreement' was revised and reintroduced to the House of Commons on 19 December 2019. It would pass its second reading the following day. The 'revisions' essentially involved the removal of provisions made in previous versions that were designed to ensure parliamentary scrutiny of what had been negotiated. Iain (Duncan) Smith would even celebrate this, saying, 'If there is anything about this arrangement [the Withdrawal Agreement Bill] that we have not now debated, thrashed to death, I would love to know what it is.' In August 2020, having finally examined the 'fine print', he took to Twitter to complain that the deal 'denies' the UK 'true national independence' and that it 'has to go'. 'They want our money and they want to stop us being a competitor,' he continued. 'The Withdrawal Agreement we signed last year sadly helps them.'[34]

In 2016, then, he, and most other Brexiters, had cheered Brexit because it would somehow restore the British parliament to its proper position as democratic lawmaker. In 2019, they cheered a Brexit bill that would explicitly rob parliament of its democratic right to scrutinise legislation that bore little relation to what Johnson had promised in both 2016 and 2019. And in 2020 they were complaining that the unscrutinised bill had not delivered on the promises that Johnson and his daft chief negotiator, David (now Lord) Frost, had made. These were extraordinary, ridiculous reversals that could only have been undertaken by a prime minister with no conscience leading a party with no integrity in a country with no clue about what was true and what was not because, as we have seen, the majority of the media was either colluding in the deceits and deceptions or failing to call them out.

On 29 January 2020, the UK recorded its first positive results for coronavirus after two Chinese nationals fell ill at a hotel in York. A lethal pandemic had arrived in that country, led by that prime minister, supported by that party and indulged by that media. It is hard to imagine a more catastrophic congregation of circumstances. The official public inquiry into the government's handling of COVID-19 is not expected to conclude until 2026. In the meantime, it is Dominic Cummings who has provided the most detailed account of what was happening behind the Downing Street door. I repeat the caveat that hell hath no fury like a Svengali scorned, but also cite Sir Keir Starmer's words at PMQs on the afternoon of Cummings's appearance. 'Either his former adviser is telling the truth,' he said, 'in which case the prime minister should answer the allegations, or the prime minister has to suggest that his former adviser is not telling the truth, which raises serious questions about the prime minister's judgement in appointing him in the first place.' I was also struck, revisiting the vituperation in his select committee testimony, by an almost perfect irony I missed at the time: Cummings clearly thought that *he* could succeed where all others had failed and bring Johnson down by telling the truth. Of course, by 2020, thanks partly to the machinations of Dominic Cummings, Johnson was almost entirely immune to the truth.

First, we learn that 'The government itself and No. 10 was not operating on a war footing in February on this, in any way, shape or form. Lots of key people were literally skiing in the middle of February.' By 12 March 2020, the necessary sense of urgency was still proving elusive, not least because Donald Trump chose that day to invite the UK to join America in bombing Iraq. 'So, we have this sort of completely insane situation,' said Cummings, 'in which part of the building was saying: "Are we going to bomb Iraq?", part of the building was arguing about whether or not we're going to do quarantine or not do quarantine and the prime minister has his girlfriend going crackers about something completely trivial.' (Ms Symonds was, apparently, upset about a story in *The Times* concerning her pet dog and 'demanding that the press office deal with that'.)

Cummings appeared to confirm suspicions that Johnson had not taken the coronavirus seriously, describing it as 'the new swine flu' and 'just a scare story'. He was even keen to be injected with the virus on live television 'so everyone realises it's nothing to be frightened of'. Of the process which Johnson, colleagues and client journalists would later describe ad nauseam as 'getting all the big calls right', Cummings recalled that he 'made some terrible decisions, got things wrong, and then constantly U-turned on everything'. In another example of reality (or at least the Cummings version of it) being entirely at odds with what the British public were being told, he explained: 'There's this great misunderstanding people have that because it nearly killed him, therefore he must have taken it seriously. But in fact, after the first lockdown, he was cross with me and others with what he regarded as basically pushing him into the first lockdown. His argument after that was: "I should have been the mayor of Jaws and kept the beaches open" ... He essentially thought that he'd been gamed on the numbers of the first lockdown.' On the baffling matter of foreign travellers arriving at UK airports unchecked, he said: 'Fundamentally, there was no proper border policy because the prime minister never wanted a proper border policy.' At risk of irony overload, Johnson had, remember, been propelled to power on a promise to 'control our borders'.

And on he went. Sometimes, it would seem, interminably. There was item after item of evidence that Johnson had approached a lethal pandemic, which would leave almost a quarter of million people dead, with exactly the same insouciance, self-interest and carelessness that he approached everything else in his life. It is hard to feel sorry for Cummings, but his contrition contrasts starkly with his erstwhile boss. 'I apologise for not acting earlier,' he said. 'And if I had acted earlier then lots of people might still be alive.'

It barely touched Johnson, of course. The *Mail* and the *Telegraph* continued to cheer him to the rafters. His running partner, Tony Gallagher, editor of *The Times*, wasn't far behind. Dorries, Rees-Mogg and others continued to insist that Johnson was a man more sinned against than sinning and had weathered yet another storm that would have sunk any other premier. Even when his lies about Downing Street parties unravelled in public, he backed himself to prevail. First, there were no parties. Then, there had been parties but he had been unaware of them. Then, there had been parties and he had been aware of them but he definitely did not attend any. Finally, there had been parties, and he had been aware of them, and he had in fact attended some of them, but he had not realised at the time that they were parties. Indeed, he had been repeatedly assured by underlings that every claim he made in the House of Commons was true.

By June 2023, when the Committee of Privileges found this to be, to coin a phrase, an inverted pyramid of piffle, Johnson was already gone from Downing Street. Finished, as we have seen, by colleagues' refusal to countenance his latest lies about knowingly appointing an alleged sex pest, Chris Pincher, to the Whips' Office. Without in any way minimising the impact of groping – the Standards Committee found in July 2023 that Pincher's conduct was 'profoundly damaging' and an abuse of power – it was, in the context of Johnson's career, a surprising hurdle at which to fall.

Less surprising by far was his response to the publication of the Committee of Privileges report that found that Johnson had committed five serious offences: deliberately misleading the Commons; deliberately misleading the privileges committee; breaching confidence by leaking part of the report in advance; 'impugning' the committee and parliamentary processes; and complicity in a 'campaign of abuse and attempted intimidation of the committee'. Their original recommendation was a 20-day suspension. This would have been increased to 90 after Johnson's letter resigning as an MP revealed parts of the report findings and condemned the investigation as biased. All this seemed to express Johnson's cowardice, calumny and moral corruption with a side order of bogus victimhood and Trumpian bleating about unfair treatment.

The committee also took the unusual step of naming the Johnson allies they considered to have undertaken an 'unprecedented and coordinated' attempt to undermine the inquiry in the media. The list included Jacob Rees-Mogg, by now moonlighting as a GB News presenter, who would be knighted in Johnson's resignation honours. Also there was Nadine Dorries, by now moonlighting as a *Daily Mail* columnist and TalkTV presenter, who would soon be smarting furiously about her failure to land a peerage apparently promised to her by Johnson. Two women later gifted damehoods by Johnson, Priti Patel and Donald Trump fan Andrea Jenkyns, made the cut, as did the Lichfield MP, Michael Fabricant.

It was the final, contemptuous, act of the most disgraceful and disgraced prime minister in British history. Even in resigning, he treated the office as his personal plaything, showering honours not on mere sycophants but on people accused by one of the few remaining checks on executive abuses of treating parliament with contempt. His first appointment upon leaving parliament could have been made with this book in mind: he became a columnist at Paul Dacre's *Daily Mail*. At the end of June 2023, it emerged that even in taking that job he had committed another unambiguous breach of regulations, this time governing the appointments of former ministers. It seems unlikely that Boris Johnson cared one jot about breaking rules designed to combat corruption and uphold integrity in public life. After all, he never had before.

Chapter 10
LIZ TRUSS

Take away the ten days of mourning after the death of
Queen Elizabeth II, and she had seven days in control.
That is roughly the shelf-life of a lettuce.
The Economist, 20 October 2022[1]

ON 6 SEPTEMBER 2022, Liz Truss entered Downing Street as prime minister. It marked, in many ways, an astonishing and quite unexpected alignment of the planets explored in this book. To moderate effect, she had campaigned against Brexit but embraced the new, fact-free political reality it ushered in with often unseemly relish. Having watched Boris Johnson from close quarters for years, she understood perfectly that this new landscape favoured politicians who told voters only what they wanted to hear, however detached those descriptions might be from the observable actuality. As international trade secretary, and later as foreign secretary, she made a speciality of announcing new 'trade deals' to great fanfare. They generally involved either 'cutting and pasting' existing arrangements with EU partners or, as we have seen in the Australian case, negotiating from a position of weakness and compromising the national interest due to a desperate need for speedy announcements. In Truss's telling, however, they were remarkable achievements, indicative both of those elusive 'Brexit benefits' and her own considerable acumen. And when she wasn't being mocked for bizarre outbursts about it being 'a disgrace' that 'we import two thirds of our cheese',[2] she certainly talked a good game. 'We have struck deals so far covering 68 countries plus the EU, worth £744 billion,' she told the Policy Exchange think tank on 14 September 2021.[3] British importers and exporters, robbed by Brexit of friction-less access to their largest international market, might not have shared her enthusiasm, but they would not be selecting the next Tory leader.

Mindful of the thrall in which the Tory party members still held him, Truss uttered not a single syllable of criticism of Johnson, even as her cabinet colleagues had queued up to quit his government. The support of most right-wing newspapers, especially the *Daily Mail* where editor-in-chief Paul Dacre fretted that his longed-for peerage might have disappeared over the horizon with Johnson's premier-ship, had propelled her from a distant third in the first round of voting to an eventual victory over Penny Mordaunt and Rishi Sunak as Conservative leader and prime minister. The *Mail*'s 12 July front page, 'Truss: Back Me or It'll Be Rishi', left little room for doubt about where its loyalties lay. It is also probable that the continuing 'Faragification' of the party saw prejudice toward Sunak's ethni-city work in Truss's favour. After all, according to the National Front-style rhetoric the Brexit debate had ushered back into the mainstream, his foreign-born parents could not be properly 'British'. And finally, more than any other high-profile politician in history, she was completely embedded in the secretly funded 'think-tank' universe. As we have already seen, one prominent Tory commen-tator stated that her arrival in Downing Street rendered Britain an Institute of Economic Affairs 'laboratory', her deputy chief of staff had previously worked for both the IEA and Policy Exchange, while her 'chief economic adviser' hailed, hilariously, from the so-called TaxPayers' Alliance.

It was, in other words, a premiership primed to realise the dreams of almost everybody examined in these pages and she wasted no time in trying to deliver them. For Liz Truss's disastrous tenure in Downing Street was not, as many accounts have already concluded, some sort of *aberration*. It was an absolute and inevitable *culmination* of the forces and manoeuvres detailed here, some conscious and deliberate, some accidental or unwitting, but all, ultimately, calamitous.

On 23 September, her chancellor, Kwasi Kwarteng, announced a 'mini-budget' that would have a staggering impact on the country, the economy and our already diminished international standing. Crucially, and entirely in keeping with the motivations that have broken Britain, he first eschewed the advice of 'experts' and the forecasts of objective organisations. In a violent break with convention, one of his first acts as chancellor had been to refuse to publish the Office for Budget Responsibility's autumn 2022 forecast on the state of the economy. This was of a piece with the disdain for genuine economic institutions displayed by Jacob Rees-Mogg, IEA 'fellows' and sundry *Daily Telegraph* writers, but the ramifications of Kwarteng's decision would resonate far beyond TV studios and comment pages. It spooked financial markets and infuriated members of the Treasury Committee who were responsible for scrutinising the government's plans. 'These forecasts are a vital indicator of the health of the nation's finances, and provide reassurance and confidence to international markets and investors,' said committee chair, the Tory MP Mel Stride. He was stating what was, for most qualified observers, obvious.[4]

Without understanding the extent of the right-wing media/Tory party/think-tank ecosystem, it is, I think, impossible to understand how Kwarteng and Truss could have pressed ahead with their plans for an estimated £45 billion of unfunded tax cuts and a concomitantly massive increase in borrowing *after* seeing the OBR warning. We learned in July 2023, thanks to a freedom of information request, that the OBR stated: 'The economic outlook has worsened significantly since we last produced a forecast in March. Historically high gas prices have already driven inflation to its highest level in 40 years and we expect inflation to rise even further over the next few months.'[5] The worst imaginable circumstances, in other words, for the fiscal policies that the chancellor would announce just five days after receiving the OBR note. But from *within* the ecosystem, it all made perfect sense: look after the rich, wibble vaguely but enthusiastically about 'growth', advance the interests of newspaper owners and the secret funders of 'free-market' pressure groups, and tell people that the wealth will somehow 'trickle down' to the masses. After decades of infiltration, these values were now articles of blind faith, unquestioned in the circles in which these people exclusively move. When Rishi Sunak warned of the havoc Truss's policies would wreak during the leadership campaign, up popped Andrew Neil's *Spectator* to rubbish the claims of the former Goldman Sachs man under the headline 'Who is Sunak kidding with his warnings about sterling?'[6]

Similarly, when Kwarteng announced, inter alia, the abolition of the top rate of income tax, the reversal of a policy to increase the rate of corporation tax, the abandonment of a scheduled increase in National Insurance and the abolition of the planned Health and Social Care Levy, the responses from Brexit-supporting, Johnson-excusing media were completely and horribly predictable. 'This was the dawn of a new age of Trussonomics and the end of 12 years of timid Tory rule,' burbled veteran Murdoch lieutenant Trevor Kavanagh in the

Sun.[7] The *Mail*'s front page on 24 September was almost euphoric, 'At last! A true Tory budget.' Its City editor, Alex Brummer, wrote inside: 'The boldness and courage of Kwasi Kwarteng's debut budget is seismic.'[8] *Sunday Telegraph* editor Allister Heath described it as 'the best budget I have ever heard a British chancellor deliver, by a massive margin'.[9] Nigel Farage tweeted: 'Today was the best Conservative budget since 1986.' IEA 'director-general' Mark Littlewood struggled to contain his excitement. 'This isn't a trickle-down budget, it's a boost-up budget,' he wrote, nonsensically. 'It's refreshing to hear a chancellor talk passionately about the importance of economic growth. The government has announced a radical set of policies to increase Britain's prosperity'.[10] Unfortunately for this assembly of geniuses, and even more so for Truss and Kwarteng, reality was about to intervene. And this time, unlike with Brexit or Johnson or 'austerity' or even immigration, reality could not be distorted by dishonest rhetoric, delusional appeals to British exceptionalism or client journalists plumbing ever new depths of sycophancy and fantasy.

In 2012, when public outcry forced George Osborne to abandon his plans to charge VAT on sausage rolls and Cornish pasties, the budget that contained these proposals was famously described as an 'omnishambles'. A decade later, *The Economist* opined that 'The reaction to Kwasi Kwarteng's fiscal statement on 23 September made the omnishambles budget look like a triumph for the ages.'[11] The chancellor had barely taken his seat in the House of Commons before the consequences of his policies began to become clear. Reuters immediately described how he had 'floored financial markets, sending sterling and British government bonds into freefall'.[12] Larry Summers, a former US treasury secretary, told Bloomberg: 'Britain will be remembered for having pursued the worst macroeconomic policies of any major country in a long time.'[13] It seemed the massed ranks of Murdoch, *Mail* and *Telegraph* media, the type of Tory politicians best placed to prosper in post-Brexit Britain and all their mutual friends in the incestuous network of 'think tanks' were completely wrong about everything they professed to understand better than everyone else.

The two most immediate ramifications of 'the best budget' Allister Heath had 'ever heard a British Chancellor deliver' were a plummeting pound and an attendant increase in what it would cost the UK government to borrow money. This would in turn push up mortgages and the already spiralling cost of living. On Monday 26 September, sterling tanked to its lowest ever level against the dollar and was also significantly down against the euro. British governments borrow money to fund spending by selling bonds or 'gilts' to investors, who get an interest rate in return for buying and holding them. At the beginning of 2022, the government was paying a 1.3 per cent rate on gilts. After the Kwarteng budget, yields on ten-year bonds soon powered past the 4 per cent mark, the highest level since the 2008 financial crisis. The Bank of England was forced to intervene, setting aside £65 billion to stop a run on pension funds. Business secretary Jacob Rees-Mogg would later demonstrate a characteristically acute grasp of the facts by trying to blame the Bank for somehow *causing* the crisis.[14]

On 3 October 2022, ten days after delivering his mini-budget, Kwarteng announced a U-turn on the cut to the top rate of tax. Eleven days later, Truss summoned him back from an IMF meeting in Washington, sacked him and announced another U-turn, this time on the mooted abandonment of a corporation tax increase. Kwarteng's replacement, Jeremy Hunt, promptly abandoned pretty much everything else that had been announced on 23 September. On 20 October, less than a week after the sacking of Kwarteng, Truss announced her resignation. She had been in the job for just forty-five days and inflicted an estimated £30 billion worth of damage on the UK economy.[15]

Boris Johnson would soon be sounding out potential supporters for a return to the leadership of both party and country, and this blind ambition highlights perhaps more than anything else how completely broken Britain has become. In the corrupted ecosystem of British politics, a prime minister hounded out of Downing Street by his own disgusted colleagues could not only conceive of returning to power months later, but do so secure in the backing that he would enjoy from those very colleagues and the majority of the popular press. Literally the same people and organs that had lent their full-throated support to his ludicrous successor and to policies that had, mere days previously, brought the country's economy to its knees. The detachment from reality was complete. The wilful abandonment of scrutiny and accountability by people and institutions historically charged with safeguarding both was by now absolute.

The breaking of Britain was over, not with a bang but a whimper, and most of the people responsible still remain in situ, on the same payrolls and entirely untouched by the consequences of their stupidity, complicity and lies. It's the rest of us who pay.

ACKNOWLEDGEMENTS

First and foremost, Jamie Joseph, my extremely patient and insightful publisher. I still struggle to accept that he has somehow turned me in to an author. Amanda Waters, Howard Watson and David Bamford were also intrinsic to seeing *How They Broke Britain* through to fruition, a particularly tricky task given that so many people in it kept resigning, disgracing themselves or getting fired while I was trying to write about them. Anna Lambert is a brilliant publicist to whom I am enormously grateful. The confidence in me shown by Joel Rickett and his team at Ebury, especially everyone in sales, got me through the moments when I thought this one might never come together. Stavros and his team at Elies in Kardamyli got me through the moments when it finally did. Eleanor Walsh, my producer at LBC, has steered the show to all sorts of new records. Keith helped a bit. Ashley Tabor-King, Stephen Miron, James Rea and Tom Cheal give us the space and support in which to do so. Global is unique in the British media and I am blessed to have a berth there, not least because I have the best listeners – and callers – in the world. They have taught me many of the lessons reflected in these pages and I will never stop being grateful to them. Huge thanks to Richard Lane, Russ Penn, Jim O'Connor, Tom Palmer, Krystian Pearce, Amari Morgan-Smith, Ashley Hemmings, Zak Brown, Ethan Freemantle, Kai Lissimore, Joe Leesley, Caleb Richards, Nat Knight-

Percival, Shane Byrne, Christian Dibble, Alex Penny, Tom Leak, Tom Owen-Evans, Nathan Lowe, Jamie Emery, Keziah Martin, Jack Tolley, Joe Foulkes, Kyle Morrison, Jack Bearne and Reiss McNally for bringing real and unexpected joy into my life. Always and most importantly, Lucy, Elizabeth and Sophia, who put up with a lot at the best of times but never more so than when I'm working on a book. And finally, my dad, to whose memory this one is dedicated. Whenever I told him I was writing a book, usually when my career was stuttering, he would always reply, with apologies to Peter Cook, 'Neither am I, son.' He didn't live to see it finally happen but without his love, influence and example, none of it ever would have done.

NOTES

Introduction

1   Steph Brawn, 'Suella Braverman: It would be my "dream" to see asylum seeker flight to Rwanda', *National*, 4 October 2022.

2   Archie Mitchell, 'Former British army chief dramatically intervenes in government's Rwanda policy', *Independent*, 7 May 2023.

3   Aletha Adu and Rajeev Syal, 'Suella Braverman: small boat arrivals have "values at odds with our country"', *Guardian*, 26 April 2022.

4   Matt Dathan and Valentine Low, 'Prince Charles: Flying migrants to Rwanda is "appalling"', *The Times*, 10 June 2022.

5   Michael Lewis, 'Has Anyone Seen the President?', Bloomberg, 9 February 2018.

6   Andrew Atkinson, 'Brexit Is Costing the UK £100 Billion a Year in Lost Output', Bloomberg, 31 January 2023.

7   *Tonight with Andrew Marr*, LBC, 24 January 2023.

8   Valentina Romei, 'Brexit has cost UK £29bn in business investment, says BoE rate setter', *Financial Times*, 13 February 2023.

9   Adam Forrest, 'Brexit damage as big as Covid, says OBR – predicting five years before incomes recover', *Independent*, 26 March 2023.

10 Matt Frei, 'IMF forecasts "aren't worth the paper they're written on", says Jacob Rees-Mogg', *Channel 4 News*, 31 January 2023.

11 Calum Muirhead, 'UK will be the only major economy except Russia to shrink this year, according to forecasts from OECD', *Daily Mail*, 18 March 2023.

12 *Peston*, ITV, 12 October 2022.

13 Matt Honeycombe-Foster, 'London Influence: IEA way or the highway
    – SpAd advice – Give (time) generously', *Politico*, 8 September 2022.

14 *Peston*, ITV, 12 October 2022.

15 Henry Mance, 'Britain has had enough of experts, says Gove',
    Financial Times, 3 June 2016.

16 Heather Stewart, 'Michael Gove to set out Tory leadership stall after
    forcing out Boris Johnson', *Guardian*, 1 July 2016.

17 Rosamund Urwin and Caroline Wheeler, 'Charles Moore rules himself
    out of running for BBC chairman on "personal" grounds', *Sunday
    Times*, 4 October 2020.

18 Katie Grant, 'Charles Moore rules self out of BBC chairman job for
    "family reasons"', *Independent*, 4 October 2020.

19 Sky News, 11 October 2015.

20 Sean Morrison, 'Jacob Rees-Mogg causes fury by saying Grenfell
    residents should have used "common sense" and fled tower', *Evening
    Standard*, 6 November 2019.

21 Charles Moore, 'Why not marry a dog?', *Spectator*, 6 July 2013.

22 *Daily Telegraph*, 29 October 2021.

23 Robert Peston, 'The truth about me and Dominic Cummings',
    Spectator, 21 November 2020.

24 Jim Pickard, Jasmine Cameron-Chileshe and George Parker,
    'Cummings broadside accuses Johnson of "possibly illegal" acts'
    Financial Times, 23 April 2021.

25 George Greenwood, 'Dowden told officials to back donor's tech festi-
    val', *The Times*, 5 July 2023.

26 Dan Bloom and Mikey Smith, 'Boris Johnson's humiliating "lost" text
    to donor begging for cash to revamp flat', *Daily Mirror*, 7 January
    2022.

27 George Greenwood, 'Dowden told officials to back donor's tech festi-
    val', *The Times*, 5 July 2023.

28 Gavin Cordon, 'Labour demands answers over PM's "Great Exhibition
    2" promise to Tory donor', *Evening Standard*, 7 January 2022.

29 Heather Stewart, Aubrey Allegretti and Rowena Mason, 'Boris
    Johnson's ethics adviser Lord Geidt resigns after Partygate grilling',
    Guardian, 15 June 2022.

30 'Letter from Lord Geidt to the Prime Minister', gov.uk, 17 December 2021.

31 John Arlidge, 'Richard Sharp's vision for the BBC: more guts and no more liberal bias', *The Times*, 3 December 2022.

32 Jim Waterson, 'Richard Sharp resigns as BBC chair after failing to declare link to Boris Johnson loan', *Guardian*, 28 April 2023.

33 Matthew Jamison, 'Brendan Simms and the racist corrupt Henry Jackson Society', LinkedIn.com, 18 February 2018.

34 Allister Heath, 'Britain's declinist Remainer elite is about to be humiliated', *Daily Telegraph*, 7 September 2022.

35 *Daily Telegraph*, 26 April 2023.

36 *Daily Telegraph*, 16 August 2023.

37 David Smith, 'The lady's not for learning: Liz Truss tells US group she was right all along', *Guardian*, 12 April 2023.

38 Hatty Collier, 'David Davis "as thick as mince" and "lazy as a toad", says former Vote Leave chief Dominic Cummings', *Evening Standard*, 17 July 2017.

39 *Today*, BBC Radio 4, 9 July 2018.

40 'Dominic Raab under fire over Dover-Calais comments', bbc.co.uk, 8 November 2018.

41 Joe Owen, Marcus Shepheard and Alex Stojanovic, 'Implementing Brexit Customs', *Institute For Government*, 11 September 2017.

42 Laura Hughes and Jim Pickard, 'Brexit secretary Dominic Raab resigns over EU divorce deal', *Financial Times*, 15 November 2018.

43 Jonathan Bell, 'Raab says Good Friday Agreement not like "cracking novel" but he used it as "reference tool" during Brexit talks', *Belfast Telegraph*, 30 January 2019.

44 Lisa O'Carroll, 'Government admits new Brexit bill "will break international law"', *Guardian*, 8 September 2020.

45 Celine Wadhera, 'Crete hotelier puzzled by Raab's claim sea was "closed" during Kabul crisis', *Independent*, 26 August 2021.

46 Ibid.

47 *Daily Telegraph*, 21 April 2023.

48 *Daily Mail*, 22 April 2023.

49 Ibid.

50 Oliver Milne, 'Tory cronies rally round Priti Patel on her "testing day" despite bullying probe', *Daily Mirror*, 20 November 2020.

51 Laura Parnaby, 'Suella Braverman tells Holocaust survivor she "won't apologise" for "invasion" comments', *Independent*, 15 January 2023.

52 Ibid.

53 Aubrey Allegretti, 'Suella Braverman resignation letter: what she said and totally meant', *Guardian*, 19 October 2022.

54 Ibid.

55 *Question Time*, BBC 1, 23 March 2017.

56 Greg Barradale, 'Suella Braverman claims to have contributed to a legal textbook. The author says she didn't', *Big Issue*, 3 October 2022.

Chapter 1: Rupert Murdoch

1 Estelle Shirbon and Maria Golovnina, 'Murdoch's UK chief told Cameron "we're in this together"', Reuters, 14 June 2012.

2 Sentencing Remarks of Mr Justice Saunders, judiciary.uk, 4 July 2014.

3 Roy Greenslade, 'Andy Coulson hired as Telegraph PR adviser', *Guardian*, 29 March 2017.

4 *Daily Mail*, 18 January 2017.

5 Commons Hansard, Volume 531, 13 July 2011.

6 Lance Price, *The Spin Doctor's Diary*, London: Hodder & Stoughton, 2005.

7 Leveson Inquiry, 14 June 2022.

8 Ibid.

9 House of Commons Culture, Media and Sport Committee, 19 July 2011.

10 House of Commons Culture, Media and Sport Committee report, 'News International and Phone-hacking', 1 May 2012.

11 Oliver Darcy and Jon Passantino, 'Rupert Murdoch acknowledged that Fox News hosts endorsed false stolen election claims', edition.cnn.com, 3 March 2023.

12 Anna Ringstrom and Jeff Mason, 'Trump baffles Sweden with crime comment, says it was based on TV report', Reuters, 19 February 2017.

13 Ibid.

14   Intelligencer Staff, 'All the Texts Fox News Didn't Want You to Read', *New York Magazine*, 9 May 2023.

15   Ibid.

16   Tim Stanley, 'Why liberals are so obsessed with Tucker Carlson', *Daily Telegraph*, 25 April 2023.

17   'Reagan to networks: try airing good news', *Boston Herald*, 4 March 1983.

18   James Bartholomew, 'I invented "virtue signalling". Now it's taking over the world', *Spectator*, 10 October 2015.

19   Robert Booth and Jane Martinson, 'Rupert Murdoch: "I've never asked any prime minister for anything"', *Guardian*, 19 December 2016.

20   BBC Radio 5 Live, 16 February 2020.

21   LBC, 19 December 2022.

22   'Statement on Survation's Poll of Muslims for The Sun', Survation, 24 November 2015.

23   Katie Hopkins, 'Rescue boats? I'd use gunships to stop migrants', *Sun*, 17 April 2015.

24   'Ipso ruling is upheld', *Sun*, 26 March 2016.

25   David Bartlett, 'Sir Bernard Ingham 1996 letter: Liverpool should "shut up" about Hillsborough', *Liverpool Echo*, 16 January 2013.

26   Kelvin MacKenzie, *Sun*, 23 October 2015.

27   Harold Evans, 'How Thatcher and Murdoch made their secret deal', *Guardian*, 28 April 2015.

28   John Biffen, *Semi-Detached*, London: Biteback, 2013.

Chapter 2: Paul Dacre

1   Freddy Mayhew, 'Ex-Daily Mail editor Paul Dacre's Society of Editors' Conference 2018 speech in full', *Press Gazette*, 6 November 2018.

2   Jim Waterson, 'Paul Dacre will get second chance to apply for Ofcom chair, ministers confirm', *Guardian*, 27 October 2021.

3   Paul Dacre, 'The BBC's cultural Marxism will trigger an American-style backlash', *Guardian*, 24 January 2007.

4   Ibid.

5   Olivier Esteves, 'Stigmatising the BBC in letters of support to Enoch Powell (1968)', *OpenEdition Journals*, volume 27, 2022.

6   *Alexei Sayle's Imaginary Sandwich Bar*, BBC Radio 4, 12 September 2019.

7   Freddy Mayhew, 'Ex-Daily Mail editor Paul Dacre's Society of Editors' Conference 2018 speech in full', *Press Gazette*, 6 November 2018.

8   Jon Sharman, 'Wikipedia bans the Daily Mail as a source for being "unreliable"', *Independent*, 9 February 2017.

9   Arjun Kharpal, 'The Daily Mail has "mastered the art of running stories that aren't true", Wikipedia founder Jimmy Wales says', *CNBC*, 19 May 2017.

10 Colin Drury, 'Paul Dacre rips into Daily Mail successor Geordie Greig in astonishing letter to the FT', *Independent*, 12 October 2019.

11 Freddy Mayhew, 'Ex-Daily Mail editor Paul Dacre's Society of Editors' Conference 2018 speech in full', *Press Gazette*, 6 November 2018.

12 Ibid.

13 'What is the #MeToo movement?', *MailOnline*, 4 April 2018.

14 'Media criticised over transgender teacher Lucy Meadows' death', bbc. co.uk, 28 May 2013.

15 Freddy Mayhew, 'Ex-Daily Mail editor Paul Dacre's Society of Editors' Conference 2018 speech in full', *Press Gazette*, 6 November 2018.

16 Helen Pidd and Saskia Murphy, 'Trans teacher believed to have killed herself "had told of press harassment"', *Guardian*, 22 March 2013.

17 *Desert Island Discs*, BBC Radio 4, 25 January 2004.

18 Adrian Addison, *Mail Men: The Unauthorized Story of the* Daily Mail *– The Paper that Divided and Conquered Britain*', London: Atlantic Books, 2017.

19 Miriam González Durántez, 'Paul Dacre should be held to account', *The Article*, 30 September 2020.

20 Anita Singh, 'Prince Harry: "Piers Morgan subjected Meghan and I to horrific personal attacks"', *Daily Telegraph*, 7 June 2023.

21 Robert Philpot, 'How Britain's Nazi-loving press baron made the case for Hitler', *Times of Israel*, 5 August 2018.

22 Richard Norton-Taylor, 'Months before war, Rothermere said Hitler's work was superhuman', *Guardian*, 1 April 2005.

23 Robert Philpot, 'How Britain's Nazi-loving press baron made the case for Hitler', *Times of Israel*, 5 August 2018.

24 Ibid.

25 Estelle Shirbon, 'Branded "enemies of the people" over Brexit case, senior UK judges hit back', Reuters, 29 March 2017.

26 *Sunday*, BBC Radio 4, 6 November 2016.

27 Will Worley, 'Liz Truss breaks silence on judiciary but fails to mention Brexit ruling backlash', *Independent*, 5 November 2016.

28 *Daily Mail*, 24 September 2022.

29 Craig Meighan, 'Liz Truss mocks BBC to sidestep GB News question on controversial report she co-wrote', *The National*, 20 August 2022.

30 *Today*, BBC Radio 4, 19 April 2017.

31 Gavin Cordon, 'Osborne: I'm leaving – for now', *Daily Mail*, 20 April 2017.

32 Patrick Cowling, 'How universities replied to that Brexit letter', bbc.co.uk, 9 January 2018.

33 Jasmin Gray, 'Daily Mail's Attack On "Remainer Universities" And "Anti-Brexit" Academics Sparks Backlash', HuffPost UK, 26 October 2017.

34 Ian Cobain and Matthew Taylor, 'Far-right terrorist Thomas Mair jailed for life for Jo Cox murder', *Guardian*, 23 November 2016.

35 Chris Greenwood and Emine Sinmaz, 'Did Neo-Nazi murder Jo over fear he'd lose council house he grew up in?', *Daily Mail*, 24 November 2016.

36 Jason Groves, 'Fury at Tory "collaborators"', *Daily Mail*, 15 November 2017.

37 Adam Lusher, 'Jo Cox death: Thomas Mair, accused of murdering MP, gives name to court as "death to traitors, freedom for Britain"', *Independent*, 18 June 2016.

38 Alex Amend, 'Here Are the Letters Thomas Mair Published in a Pro-apartheid Magazine', splcenter.org, 20 June 2016.

39 Ibid.

40 Kevin Rawlinson and Jasper Jackson, 'Daily Mail editor received £88,000 in EU subsidies in 2014', *Guardian*, 30 March 2016.

Chapter 3: Andrew Neil

1 Andrew Neil, *Full Disclosure*, London: Macmillan, 1996.
2 Commons Hansard, Volume 731, 19 April 2023.
3 Neil, *Full Disclosure*.
4 Charles Murray, 'Keep it in the Family', *Sunday Times*, 14 November 1993.
5 Martin Walker, 'Why Andy's backing Bambi', *Guardian*, 19 September 1994.
6 Emily Maitlis, James MacTaggart Memorial Lecture, Edinburgh TV Festival, August 2022.
7 'Irish Sea trade border "over my dead body", says Johnson', *Belfast Telegraph*, 13 August 2020.
8 Elizabeth Day, *Observer*, 19 October 2014.
9 Emily Maitlis, James MacTaggart Memorial Lecture, Edinburgh TV Festival, August 2022.
10 Arron Banks, *The Bad Boys of Brexit: Tales of Mischief, Mayhem & Guerrilla Warfare in the EU Referendum Campaign*, London: Biteback, 2016.
11 Jim Waterson, 'Andrew Neil launches 24-hour news channel to rival BBC and Sky', *Guardian*, 25 September 2020.
12 *The Moggcast*, episode 62, ConservativeHome, 13 July 2021.
13 Xander Elliards, 'Who is Robbie Gibb? The "Tory agent" Emily Maitlis says influences the BBC', *The National*, 22 August 2022.
14 Alex Andreou, 'Golden Dawn Definitely Not Nazis, Photos Confirm', *Byline Times*, 10 August 2015.
15 'Greek Tragedy', *60 Minutes* (Australia), 13 April 2014.
16 *Spectator*, 29 September 2012.
17 @sunny_hundal, Twitter, 16 September 2018.
18 Rod Liddle, 'Is it possible to draw Serena Williams without being racist?', *Spectator*, 15 September 2018.
19 James Brandon, 'Reining in the preachers of hate', *Guardian*, 13 January 2009.
20 Matthew Jamison, LinkedIn.com, 18 February 2017.
21 'Census That Revealed a Troubling Future', *Standpoint*, 25 February 2013.

22 Paul Goodman, 'Why the Conservative Front Bench Broke Off Relations with Douglas Murray – and what happened afterwards', ConservativeHome, 17 October 2011.

23 Speech at the One Law For All 'Enemies Not Allies' seminar, Conway Hall, London, 26 January 2011.

24 Mehdi Hasan, 'Douglas Murray, the EDL, Dodgy Videos and Me', HuffPost, 30 July 2013.

25 Gaby Hinsliff, 'The Strange Death of Europe by Douglas Murray review – gentrified xenophobia', *Guardian*, 6 June 2017.

26 *Daily Politics*, BBC 1, 10 July 2016.

Chapter 4: Matthew Elliott

1 Robert Booth, 'A very British Tea Party: US anti-tax activists advise UK counterparts', *Guardian*, 9 September 2010.

2 Laura Kuenssberg, 'Vote Leave broke electoral law, Electoral Commission expected to say', *BBC News*, 4 July 2018.

3 Jason Farrell, 'Vote Leave broke campaign spending rules says Electoral Commission', Sky News, 3 May 2019.

4 *Today*, BBC Radio 4, 17 July 2018.

5 Carole Cadwalladr, 'The Vote Leave scandal, one year on: "the whole thing was traumatic"', *Observer*, 17 March 2019.

6 'Police still not investigating Leave campaigns, citing "political sensitivities"', openDemocracy, 11 October 2018.

7 Robert Booth, 'Who is behind the Taxpayers' Alliance?', *Guardian*, 9 October 2009.

8 Ibid.

9 Ibid.

10 Luke Harding, 'How Kremlin got diplomats to woo Tories', *Guardian*, 30 November 2012.

11 Helen Catt and Sean Seddon, 'Liz Truss resignation honours list criticised by ex-aides', *BBC News*, 25 March 2023.

12 Antony Fisher, *Must History Repeat Itself?*, Churchill Press, 1974.

13 Adam Curtis, 'The Curse of Tina', The Medium and the Message, BBC blog, 13 September 2011.

14 Ibid.

15 Russell Lewis, 'Lord Harris of High Cross', *Independent*, 21 October 2006.

16 John Blundell, 'Lady Thatcher and the IEA', iea.org.uk, 9 April 2013.

17 Ibid.

18 Alan Rusbridger, 'Adam Smith Institute's sense and nonsense, *Guardian*, 22 December 1987.

19 Ibid.

20 Robert Booth, 'Rightwing UK thinktank "offered ministerial access" to potential US donors', *Guardian*, 30 July 2018.

21 'Deep concerns over public health as The BMJ reveals MPs' links to organisation backed by tobacco industry', *British Medical Journal*, 16 May 2019.

22 @Balconyshirts, Twitter, et al.

23 Peter Walker, 'Laurence Fox's political party received almost same donations as Lib Dems', *Guardian*, 3 June 2021.

24 Josiah Mortimer, 'BBC Chairman Donated Tens of Thousands of Pounds to Right-Wing Group Funding Criticism of BBC', *Byline Times*, 24 February 2023.

25 Ibid.

26 *Daily Mail*, 24 November 2021.

27 Mississippi Center for Public Policy Wikipedia page.

28 'What Are Freeports?', gov.uk, 27 October 2021.

29 Liz Truss, 'Allies in fair trade, we share historic bond of friendship', *The Australian*.

30 Commons Hansard, Volume 722, 14 November 2022.

31 Graham Lanktree, 'How Boris Johnson sold out Britain's farmers over dinner with the Australian PM', *Politico*, 1 June 2023.

32 Ibid.

33 Carole Cadwalladr et al., 'Revealed: Brexit insider claims Vote Leave team may have breached spending limits', *Observer*, 24 March 2018.

34 'The Brexit whistleblower: "Did Vote Leave use me? Was I naive?"', *Observer*, 24 March 2018.

35 Heather Stewart, 'Theresa May stands by adviser who outed Brexit whistleblower', *Guardian*, 26 March 2018.

NOTES

36   Carole Cadwalladr, 'Shahmir Sanni: "Nobody was called to account. But I lost almost everything"', *Observer*, 21 July 2018.

37   Ibid.

38   Shahmir Sanni, 'Behind Closed Doors Johnson and his Cabinet Do Not Applaud the NHS – They Ideologically Oppose It', *Byline Times*, 31 March 2020.

39   Dominic Casciani, 'Lobby group admits unlawful whistleblower dismissal', *BBC News*, 12 November 2018.

40   Carole Cadwalladr, 'TaxPayers' Alliance concedes it launched smears against Brexit whistleblower', *Observer*, 11 November 2018.

41   Arj Singh, 'Minister ordered Home Office staff to paint over art for children at asylum centre, charity boss says', *i* newspaper, 4 July 2023.

Chapter 5: Nigel Farage

1   Stuart Jeffries, 'Ukip founder Alan Sked: "The party has become a Frankenstein's monster"', *Guardian*, 26 May 2014.

2   Tom Baldwin and Fiona Hamilton, 'Times interview with Nick Griffin: "the BBC is stupid to let me appear"', *The Times*, 22 October 2009

3   Steve Rose, 'A deadly ideology: how the "great replacement theory" went mainstream', *Guardian*, 8 June 2022.

4   Lionel Shriver, 'Would you want London to be overrun with Americans like me?', *Spectator*, 28 August 2021.

5   C. Wood and W.M.L. Finlay, 'British National Party Representations of Muslims in the Month after the London Bombings: Homogeneity, Threat, and the Conspiracy Tradition, *British Journal of Social Psychology*, 47: 4 (2008), p. 720.

6   Ibid, p. 708.

7   'Respected British magazine publishes defense of Nazi German troops', *Times of Israel*, 18 May 2018.

8   Kashmira Gander, 'Nigel Farage on the NHS: Half of voters agrees that HIV patients cost UK too much money', *Independent*, 7 April 2015.

9   Sky News, 5 April 2019.

10   Glen Owen, 'Nigel Farage's car wheels "were sabotaged in an assassination attempt"', *Mail on Sunday*, 2 January 2016.

11 LBC, 8 January 2016.

12 Gerri Peev, 'Nigel Farage's claim his car wheels "were sabotaged in an assassination attempt" in France are denied by prosecutors and the mechanic who checked his Volvo', *Daily Mail*, 6 January 2016.

13 Adam Sage, 'Farage death plot claims rubbished', *The Times*, 7 January 2016.

14 Ted Jeory, 'Farage's fascist past? Nigel boasted about his NF initials and sang "gas them all", claims schoolfriend', *Independent*, 14 May 2019.

15 Peter Walker, 'Nigel Farage under fire over "antisemitic tropes" on far-right US talkshow', *Guardian*, 6 May 2019.

16 Ibid.

17 Fox News, 20 June 2018.

18 'Nigel Farage Slammed for Saying "Jewish Lobby" Has Disproportionate Influence Over U.S. Politics', *Haaretz*, 1 November 2017.

19 Adele M. Stan, 'Commentary: How Trump mainstreamed hate', Reuters, 13 August 2017.

20 'Watch deleted video of Nigel Farage thanking Steve Bannon and Breitbart for Brexit', *New European*, 6 April 2018.

21 Boris Johnson, 'Keep calm, everyone – now is not the time to do a Nicolas Cage', *Daily Telegraph*, 28 April 2013.

22 Mark Townsend, 'Aaron Banks "writes off £7m loan" as Leave.EU goes into liquidation', *Observer*, 3 September 2022.

Chapter 6: David Cameron

1 David Cameron, *For the Record*, London: HarperCollins, 2019.

2 Ibid.

3 Francis Elliott and James Hanning, *Cameron: Practically a Conservative*, London: Fourth Estate, 2012.

4 Cameron, *For the Record*.

5 'A Primer on the '30s', *Esquire*, June 1960, pp. 85–93.

6 Elliott and Hanning, *Cameron*.

7 James O'Brien, *How Not to Be Wrong: The Art of Changing Your Mind*, London: WH Allen, 2020.

NOTES

8   J. Schwartz, *Cassandra's Daughter: A History of Psychoanalysis*, London and New York: Viking/Allen Lane, 1999.

9   Cameron, *For the Record*.

10 Musa Okwonga, *One of Them: An Eton College Memoir*, London: Unbound, 2021.

11 Nick Fraser, *The Importance of Being Eton*, London: Short Books, 2008.

12 BBC, 7 April 2020.

13 *When Boris Met Dave*, Channel 4, 7 October 2009.

14 Heathcote Williams, *Brexit Boris: From Mayor to Nightmare*, London: Public Reading Rooms, 2016.

15 Barney Ronay, 'Young, rich and drunk', *Guardian*, 9 May 2008.

16 Cameron, *For The Record*.

17 Ben Fenton, 'Cameron: the consummate spin doctor', *Financial Times*, 25 October 2010.

18 James Robinson and David Teather, 'Cameron – the PR years', *Guardian*, 20 February 2010.

19 Daniel Finkelstein, 'Why Purnell mattered', 'Comment Central' blog, *The Times*, 19 February 2010.

20 *Desert Island Discs*, BBC Radio 4, 28 May 2006.

21 Daniel Finkelstein, 'A David Davis guide to fiscal strategy: two and two make … um, er …', *The Times*, 2 November 2005.

22 David Willetts, 'Denis Thatcher was right. "Get back to basic Conservative principles – but don't ask me what they are"', ConservativeHome, 10 May 2022.

23 Peter Mandelson, *The Third Man*, London: HarperCollins, 2010.

24 Nicholas Watt, 'Cameron decision to quit EU group is "dotty", says Tory MEP', *Guardian*, 5 May 2009.

25 James Chapman, 'Ken Clarke exposes Tories' Europe divide with claim leaders are "less Eurosceptic than in the past"', *Daily Mail*, 4 May 2009.

26 Hélène Mulholland, 'Tories unveil group of controversial new allies in European parliament', *Guardian*, 22 June 2009.

27 Ibid.

28 *Desert Island Discs*.

29 Richard Vinen, 'Kind of Blue', *Literary Review*, October 2019.

30 John Cassidy, 'Murdoch's Game', *New Yorker*, 8 October 2016.

31 Andrew Rawnsley, 'The weekend Gordon Brown saved the banks from the abyss', *Observer*, 21 February 2010.

32 Chris Mullin, 'Cameron at 10 by Anthony Seldon and Peter Snowdon review – the great Tory deception', *Observer*, 11 October 2015.

33 John Burn-Murdoch, 'Britain's winter of discontent is the inevitable result of austerity', *Financial Times*, 23 December 2022.

34 John Appleby, 'NHS spending: squeezed as never before', King's Fund report, 20 October 2015.

35 Burn-Murdoch, 'Britain's winter of discontent'.

36 Federica Liberini et al., 'Was Brexit Caused by the Unhappy and the Old?', IZA Discussion Paper Series, September 2017.

37 Thiemo Fetzer, 'Did Austerity in the UK Lead to the Brexit Crisis?', *Harvard Business Review*, 23 August 2019.

38 'NHS continues to be top issue for British voters', Ipsos, 20 April 2015.

39 Andrew Gray, 'Article 50 author Lord Kerr: I didn't have UK in mind', *Politico*, 28 March 2017.

40 Nicholas Watt, 'Exit stage right: pledge to quit big party alliance that haunts David Cameron', *Guardian*, 29 May 2009.

41 *Tonight*, ITV, 10 June 2021.

42 Tim Bale, 'Why David Cameron called the 2016 referendum – and why he lost it', *UK in a Changing Europe*, 4 October 2022.

43 Cameron, *For the Record*.

Chapter 7: Jeremy Corbyn

1 Martin Amis, 'Amis on Corbyn: Undereducated, humourless, third rate', *Sunday Times*, 25 October 2015.

2 David Kogan, *Protest and Power: The Battle for the Labour Party*, London: Bloomsbury Reader, 2019.

3 Simon Walters, '"He just went for me and head-butted me on the nose": Tory MP speaks out over Commons "fracas" with Labour backbencher', *Mail on Sunday*, 26 February 2012.

4 Alex Hunt, Brian Wheeler and Chris Davies, 'Election countdown: 96 weeks to go', *BBC News*, 6 July 2013.

5   Angus Howarth, 'Falkirk: Labour call in police over rigging claim', *Scotsman*, 7 July 2013.

6   Ibid.

7   Andrew Sparrow, 'Miliband wins vote on Labour party reforms with overwhelming majority: Politics live blog', *Guardian*, 1 March 2014.

8   Tony Benn, *The End of an Era: Diaries, 1980–1990*, London: Hutchinson, 1992.

9   Tony Benn, *Free at Last! Diaries, 1991–2001*, London: Arrow Books, 2003.

10 Kogan, *Protest and Power*.

11 Ibid.

12 Ibid.

13 Declan McHugh, 'Why did Labour use this system to elect its leader?', *New Statesman*, 8 October 2015.

14 *Newsnight*, BBC, 21 July 2015.

15 Mobeen Azhar, 'Where is Labour's "Jeremy Corbyn mania" coming from?', *BBC News*, 13 August 2015.

16 Ibid.

17 JC Reporter, 'The key questions Jeremy Corbyn must answer', *Jewish Chronicle*, 12 August 2015.

18 '"Blood libel cleric praised by Corbyn is jailed in Israel for inciting violence', *Jewish Chronicle*, 10 February 2020.

19 Daniel Sugarman, 'Corbyn blamed "Zionist lobby" for blood libel cleric's expulsion from the UK', *Jewish Chronicle*, 2 April 2019.

20 Jake Wallis Simons, 'Jeremy Corbyn DEFENDS a controversial vicar who was banned from social media for sharing "clearly anti-Semitic" material blaming Israel for 9/11 attacks', *Mail on Sunday*, 9 August 2015.

21 Ibid.

22 *Full Disclosure*, 5 March 2019.

23 Matt Seaton, 'Behind the Anti-Semitism Crisis of Jeremy Corbyn's Labour Party', *New York Review of Books*, 17 August 2018.

24 Stuart McGurk, 'Jeremy Corbyn interview: "As far as I know, my team voted Remain. I haven't asked them"', *GQ*, 28 February 2018.

25 Rowena Mason, 'Jeremy Corbyn "not on same side" as David Cameron in EU debate', *Guardian*, 29 February 2016.

26 Tim Shipman, *All Out War*, London: William Collins, 2016.

27 *The News Agents*, 15 February 2023.

28 'Brexit: Hilary Benn sacked as Corbyn faces "no confidence" pressure', *BBC News*, 26 June 2016.

29 *The Axe Files*, CNN podcast, 26 December 2016.

30 John Curtice, 'UK election: Six key lessons from a surprise result', *BBC News*, 9 June 2016.

31 McGurk, 'Jeremy Corbyn interview: "As far as I know, my team voted Remain. I haven't asked them"'.

32 Lucy Fisher and Billy Kenber, 'Jeremy Corbyn: Labour is 'ready to serve' in minority government after election gains', *Financial Times*, 9 June 2017.

33 Ashley Cowburn, 'General election result: Nearly twice as many Labour voters defected over Jeremy Corbyn's leadership than party's Brexit stance, poll finds', *Independent*, 13 December 2019.

34 Rob Merrick, 'Dislike of Corbyn to blame for Labour's election disaster not Brexit, major survey finds', *Independent*, 10 February 2020.

35 Ashley Cowburn, 'Internal Labour report excuses Corbyn and claims Brexit played "decisive role" in election defeat', *Independent*, 29 January 2020.

36 Jeremy Corbyn, 'We won the argument, but I regret we didn't convert that into a majority for change', *Observer*, 14 December 2019.

8. Dominic Cummings

1   Dominic Cummings, 'On the referendum #20: the campaign, physics and data science – Vote Leave's "Voter Intention Collection System" (VICS) now availale for all', dominiccummings.com, 29 October 2016.

2   Tom Harper and Caroline Wheeler, 'Labour asks about Dominic Cummings' years working in Russia', *Sunday Times*, 2 November 2019.

3   Ibid.

4   Richard Morris and Emma Harrison, 'UK "took eye off ball" over Russia threat', bbc.co.uk, 21 July 2020.

5   George Parker, 'Dominic Cummings has "done" Brexit. Now he plans to reinvent politics', *Financial Times*, 26 May 2020.

6   Bagehot, 'An optimistic Eurosceptic', *The Economist*, 21 January 2016.

7   Iain Martin, 'Lord Salisbury: May's conduct of Brexit has humiliated a once proud nation', *Reaction*, 15 April 2019.

8   Brian Wheeler, 'How to win a referendum', *BBC News*, 10 May 2016.

9   Johnny McDevitt, 'Dominic Cummings honed strategy in 2004 vote, video reveals', *Guardian*, 12 November 2019.

10 Ibid.

11 Ibid.

12 Dominic Cummings, 'On the referendum #24N: Actions have consequences', dominiccummings.com, 27 March 2019.

13 Andrew Gimson, 'A profile of Dominic Cummings, friend of Gove and enemy of Clegg', ConservativeHome, 15 May 2015.

14 Chris Tryhorn, 'Spectator makes cartoon U-turn', *Guardian*, 2 February 2006.

15 Gimson, 'A profile of Dominic Cummings'.

16 Dominic Cummings, 'Some thoughts on education and political priorities', *Guardian*, 11 October 2013.

17 James Frayne, 'The power of emotion in political campaigns', ConservativeHome, 27 January 2013.

18 Crace, '"Accuracy is for snake-oil pussies"'.

19 Dominic Cummings, 'Dominic Cummings: how the Brexit referendum was won', *Spectator*, 9 January 2017.

20 Nate Raymond, 'Facebook parent Meta to settle Cambridge Analytica scandal case for $725 million', Reuters, 23 December 2022.

21 Carole Cadwalladr, 'The great British Brexit robbery: how our democracy was hijacked', *Observer*, 7 May 2017.

22 Ibid.

23 BBC, 20 July 2021.

Chapter 9: Boris Johnson

1   Damian Furniss, 'Malton Moan', Facebook, 10 December 2019.

2   Tim Shipman, 'Cameron was a "girly swot" at university, says Boris: London Mayor dismisses PM because he got a first from Oxford', *Daily Mail*, 12 June 2013.

3   Peter Walker, 'Boris Johnson calls David Cameron "girly swot" in leaked note', *Guardian*, 6 August 2019.

4   Clare Dwyer Hogg, 'My greatest mistake: Boris Johnson, MP for Henley and editor of "The Spectator"', *Independent*, 21 May 2002.

5   Sonia Purnell, 'Boris Johnson and David Cameron: How a rivalry that began at Eton spilled out on to the main stage of British politics', *Independent*, 23 February 2016.

6   Jennifer Rankin and Jim Waterson, 'How Boris Johnson's Brussels-bashing stories shaped British politics', *Observer*, 14 July 2019.

7   *Desert Island Discs*, BBC Radio 4, 30 October 2005.

8   Martin Fletcher, 'Inverted pyramid of piffle', *Tortoise*, 15 July 2019.

9   *Daily Telegraph*, 10 May 1991.

10   Jennifer Rankin and Jim Waterson, 'How Boris Johnson's Brussels-bashing stories shaped British politics', *Observer*, 14 July 2019.

11   *Daily Telegraph*, 18 March 1992.

12   *Sunday Telegraph*, 3 May 1992.

13   Rankin and Waterson, 'How Boris Johnson's Brussels-bashing stories shaped British politics'.

14   *Daily Telegraph*, 14 October 1992.

15   *Daily Telegraph*, 19 February 1993.

16   'Euro headquarters to be blown up', *Daily Telegraph*, 31 May 1991.

17   Max Hastings, 'I was Boris Johnson's boss: he is utterly unfit to be prime minister', *Guardian*, 24 June 2019.

18   'Review of Big Caesars and Little Caesars by Ferdinand Mount', *Oldie*, August 2023.

19   Jon Henley, 'Is the EU really dictating the shape of your bananas?', *Guardian*, 11 May 2016.

20   Simon Murphy, '"A couple of black eyes": Johnson and the plot to attack a reporter', *Observer*, 14 July 2019.

21   Dylan Jones, 'It was a wizard idea to hire Boris to write about cars. Then came the tickets …', *Sunday Times*, 24 April 2022.

22   Michael Heseltine, 'Boris Johnson's legacy? He has ruined Britain's place in the world', *Observer*, 11 June 2023.

23   Claire Cozens, 'Heffer admits role in notorious Spectator article', *Guardian*, 28 October 2004.

24 Gaby Hinsliff, 'Boris Johnson sacked by Tories over private life', *Observer*, 14 November 2004.

25 Sean O'Grady, 'Boris Johnson can't even lie competently about the Chris Pincher scandal', *Independent*, 5 July 2022.

26 Hinsliff, 'Boris Johnson sacked by Tories'.

27 Alan Selby, 'BBC receives nearly 600 complaints over Boris Johnson interview', *Press Gazette*, 26 March 2013.

28 'Mayor rules out Commons return and is "sick" of being asked', LBC, 3 March 2014.

29 'Michael Gove: Boris Johnson wasn't up to the job', *BBC News*, 30 June 2016.

30 Sam Blewitt, 'No apology from Boris Johnson after Nazanin Zaghari-Ratcliffe tells him she lived in "shadow of his words"', *Evening Standard*, 13 May 2022.

31 *The Rest is Politics*, March 2022.

32 Nick Hopkins, 'Morning after: Boris Johnson recovers from Lebedev's exotic Italian party', *Guardian*, 26 July 2019.

33 Carole Cadwalladr, 'Boris Johnson and the Lebedevs: how I exposed the prime minister's defining scandal', *Observer*, 16 July 2022.

34 Adrian Zorzut, 'Video resurfaces of Iain Duncan Smith trying to stop MPs scrutinising Brexit agreement he now wants rewritten', *New European*, 5 August 2020.

Chapter 10: Liz Truss

1 'Liz Truss has made Britain a riskier bet for bond investors', *The Economist*, 20 October 2022.

2 Joel Day, 'Liz Truss humiliation after bizarre and impassioned "cheese speech"', *Daily Express*, 9 December 2021.

3 'Policy Exchange speech: Liz Truss sets out Britain's new trade policy', gov.uk, 14 September 2021.

4 'UK lawmakers insist forecasts should accompany mini-budget', Reuters, 20 September 2022.

5 Larry Elliott, 'Kwarteng went ahead with mini-budget despite OBR warning, FOI reveals', *Guardian*, 26 July 2023.

6   Matthew Lynn, 'Who is Sunak kidding with his warnings about sterling?', *Spectator*, 31 August 2022.

7   Trevor Kavanagh, 'Mini Budget was the dawn of a new age of Trussonomics – signalling the end of 12 years of timid Tory rule', *Sun*, 23 September 2022.

8   Alex Brummer, 'Kwasi Kwarteng delivers a genuine Tory Budget that spells the end of Treasury doomsters', *Daily Mail*, 23 September 2022.

9   Allister Heath, 'Kwasi Kwarteng's Budget is a moment in history that will radically transform Britain', *Daily Telegraph*, 23 September 2022.

10   Mark Littlewood, 'IEA responds to mini budget statement', iea.org. uk, 23 September 2022.

11   'Pounded land', *The Economist*, 27 September 2022.

12   David Milliken et al., 'Britain sends investors fleeing with historic tax cuts and borrowing', Reuters, 23 September 2022.

13   Chris Anstey, 'Larry Summers Warns Pound May Tumble Below $1 on "Naive" UK Policies', Bloomberg, 23 September 2022.

14   Alexandra Rogers, 'Experts Rubbish Jacob Rees-Mogg Over Claims Mini-Budget Didn't Cause Economic Chaos', HuffPost, 12 October 2022.

15   Toby Helm and Phillip Inman, 'Revealed: the £30bn cost of Liz Truss's disastrous mini-budget', *Observer*, 12 November 2022.

ABOUT THE AUTHOR

JAMES O'BRIEN is an award-winning writer and broadcaster whose journalism has appeared everywhere from the *TLS* to the *Daily Mirror*. His daily current affairs programme on LBC is the most popular talk show on commercial radio with over 1.4 million weekly listeners and his first book, *How To Be Right*, was a *Sunday Times* bestseller, which won the Parliamentary Book Award for Best Political Book by a non-politician. He is often to be found on Twitter trying not to get into arguments unless absolutely necessary.